Twilight Policing

Twilight Policing

*Private Security and Violence
in Urban South Africa*

Tessa G. Diphoorn

UNIVERSITY OF CALIFORNIA PRESS

University of California Press, one of the most
distinguished university presses in the United States,
enriches lives around the world by advancing
scholarship in the humanities, social sciences, and
natural sciences. Its activities are supported by
the UC Press Foundation and by philanthropic
contributions from individuals and institutions.
For more information, visit www.ucpress.edu.

University of California Press
Oakland, California

Library of Congress Cataloging-in-Publication Data

Diphoorn, Tessa G., 1984– author.
 Twilight policing : private security and violence in
urban South Africa / Tessa G. Diphoorn.
    pages cm.
 Includes bibliographical references and index.
 ISBN 978-0-520-28733-4 (cloth : alk. paper)
 ISBN 978-0-520-28734-1 (pbk. : alk. paper)
    1. Police, Private—Social aspects—South Africa—
Durban. 2. Private security services—Social
aspects—South Africa—Durban. I. Title.
 HV8291.S6D57 2016
 363.28'90968—dc23
                                2015014686

Manufactured in the United States of America

24 23 22 21 20 19 18 17 16 15
10 9 8 7 6 5 4 3 2 1

The paper used in this publication meets the minimum
requirements of ANSI/NISO Z39.48-1992 (R 2002)
(*Permanence of Paper*).

Contents

Illustrations

Acknowledgments

This book project has taken me back and forth between Utrecht and Durban, included a brief intermission in Khartoum and an academic writing endeavor in Istanbul, and brought me back to Utrecht. It has been a worldly adventure that would not have been possible without the guidance and kindness of many people along the way.

I first want to thank the Ministry of Foreign Affairs for funding this research through a program called the Academy of International Cooperation, which was a collaboration between the Directorate for Effectiveness and Quality of International Development Cooperation (DEK) and the Department of Cultural Anthropology at Utrecht University. I also received financial support through the Marie Curie Sustainable Peacebuilding (SPBuild) fellowship awarded within the Initial Training Network under the Marie Curie Actions of the Seventh Framework Programme (F7).

I really want to thank my former supervisors, Dirk Kruijt and Wil Pansters, for their essential and continuous guidance throughout the entire process, and other colleagues in the Department of Cultural Anthropology at Utrecht University for their unremitting support: Kootje Willemse-van Spanje, Katrien Klep, Eva van Roekel, Ariel Sanchez Meertens, Nandu Menon, Floortje Toll, Miriam Geerse, Martijn Oosterbaan, Yvon van der Pijl, Monique Sonnevelt, Ralph Rozema, and Marc Simon Thomas. I particularly want to thank Nikkie Wiegink: you are a dear friend, my greatest listener, and most critical reader. I am also grateful to Ayşe Betül Çelik, Özge Sahin, and Emre Haitpoglu at Sabancı University for their hospitality during my stay in Istanbul.

In addition, I am very appreciative of Steffen Jensen, Antonius Robben, Dennis Rodgers, Helene Maria Kyed, and Finn Stepputat for their valuable advice on various parts of this book. A special thanks goes out to Rivke Jaffe and Erella Grassiani for being excellent and stimulating colleagues and giving me the opportunity to continue working on private security. I also owe much gratitude to David Jobanputra for his great editing work, to Margot Stoete from Kaartbeeld for making the illustrations, and to Suzanne Hoeksema for arranging and correcting the bibliography. I also want to thank Maura Roessner, Jack Young, and the entire team from the University of California Press for their tremendous help and patience.

Now let us turn to South Africa, the place at the heart of this book. Today Durban feels like a home away from home, and this is entirely due to the warmth and hospitality of the many people who helped me navigate through the world of private security. I want to thank Julian Carter and Margaret Kruger for acting as my compasses in the field. I also want to thank Rob Pattman, Monique Marks, and Julie Berg for their friendship and advice. On a personal note, I want to thank the Pillays (Selvi, Santhuri, Leshantha, Venesen, and Divina) and the Govenders for opening their homes to me; indeed the Pillays have become my second family. I would therefore like to dedicate this book to Barry Pillay—a great and kind man who will always be remembered.

I am also very grateful to my dear friends around the globe who have kept me going over the years. I also want to thank my family for their continuous support and faith in my abilities: my dearest brothers, Luuk and Tim, and my parents, Dip and Wilma: Thank you for introducing me to the African continent with my first breath of air and showing me the world. And then there is my beloved Aksel: You have become the sunshine of my life who encourages me when I need that extra push, slows me down when I am in overdrive, and always puts a smile on my face whenever I need it.

Most importantly, I want to thank all my informants who took the time and energy to share their thoughts and experiences with me. Because I have decided to uphold their anonymity, I will not name names here, but I am sure that you know who you are. My appreciation particularly goes out to the armed response officers who are at the heart of this study. I want to thank you for accepting me into your vehicles—and into your lives—and for putting up with my incessant questioning.

I continue to be astounded by your immense generosity and openness. Without all of this, this book would simply not exist.

A great writer, Harry Mathews, once wrote, "Experience itself, past or present: as we represent it in words, it is assuredly modified, it's reduced, it's stripped of what is virtually an infinite ambiguity of interpretation and given only one version of itself—it becomes that other object which is the set of words of our description" (1988: 12). This book is my (own) version of events, and I can only hope that the words I have chosen are an adequate reflection of your perceptions and experiences and that they truly convey how very grateful I am.

Abbreviations and Acronyms

ANC   African National Congress
BAC   Business Against Crime
BEE   Black Empowerment Equity
CID   City Improvement District
CPF   Community Policing Forum
ESCCF   Extended Station Crime Combating Forum
DMA   Durban Metropolitan Area
GOCOC   Ground Operational Coordinating Committee
ICD   Independent Complaints Directorate
IFP   Inkatha Freedom Party
ISS   Institute for Security Studies
KZN   KwaZulu-Natal
NCPS   National Crime Prevention Strategy
NKP   National Key Point
NKPA   National Key Points Act
NP   National Party
PAC   Pan-Africanist Congress
PSIRA   Private Security Industry Regulatory Authority
SADF   South African Defence Force
SAIDSA South African Intruder Detection Services Association

SAP	South African Police
SAPS	South African Police Service
SASA	South Africa Security Association
SASFED	South African Security Federation
SASSETA	South Africa Safety and Security Sector Education and Training Authority
SIA	Security Industry Alliance
SOA	Security Officers Act
SOB	Security Officers Board
SSA	Statistics South Africa
TRC	Truth and Reconciliation Commission
UIP	Urban Improvement Precinct
UNODC	United Nations Office on Drugs and Crime
VOCS	Victims of Crime Survey

A Note on Writing

Before one starts to read this book, I would like to clarify four decisions I made about how to write about policing and violence in South Africa. The first point concerns race. As highlighted by other scholars working on South Africa, race is an inescapable part of South African life, and every ethnographer will have to deal with this issue. Throughout the research process, and particularly during the writing phase, I thought at length about how to approach, define, and discuss issues of race. The diversity of paths taken by other scholars working on and in South Africa did not make this process any easier.

Apartheid legally classified South African society into four racial groups: White/European, Colored, Asian, and African/Native. The term "Black" referred to all "non-Whites." For this book, I employ these same racial categories, because my informants still used them to define themselves and others. However, when I use the term "Black," I am referring to individuals who were previously labeled as "Native" or "African." Another word that I use regularly is "non-White," again because my informants regularly did so. In fact, many informants preferred the label "non-White" to the earlier category of "Black," which encompassed Blacks, Indians, and Coloreds. Like Ashforth (2005), I use capital letters, such as in "White" and "Black," in reference to groups of individuals, particularly as a means of identification. For example, when armed response officers talk of criminals as Blacks, I capitalize the term, because they are making reference to a group of individuals they define according to race.

When I use these terms as adjectives, such as for "a black armed response officer," I do not capitalize them.

The second point concerns anonymity. Although several informants did not object to their identity being made public, and some even encouraged it, the majority of my interlocutors expressed a desire for anonymity. For the sake of consistency, I have decided to extend anonymity to all parties, including the companies and community organizations that I studied; hence, the use of letters to identify them in Chapters 3 and 6. Furthermore, the industry is highly competitive, and many of those who worked in it, particularly company owners, regularly asked me which company I thought was the "best." I refrained from taking part in this debate, which is another reason for not revealing the names of the companies. Moreover, when discussing particular incidents that occurred during my fieldwork, I refer only to months instead of specific dates. This is intended not only to protect the identities of the armed response officers but also, and in particular, to prevent companies from identifying each other.

However, to be able to follow certain informants throughout this book, I provided particular armed response officers with pseudonyms from a range of names that actually exist to make the names realistic. For example, in Chapter 1, I refer to "Bongani;" although this is not the real name of the person being discussed, there is another informant called Bongani. Furthermore, I often use pseudonyms that reflect the racial identity of the informants, such as Sanjeev, a common Indian name that is the pseudonym of one Indian armed response officer. Because I argue that issues of race continue to shape contemporary policing and perceptions of violence, I believe it is important to indicate the racial identities of my informants.

The third point I want to make here is that many of the narratives and quotes in this book have been shortened. However, they have not been altered or corrected in terms of grammar or speech. At a conference, I was once criticized for not removing grammatical errors or swear words, such as "fuck," from my quotes. The person in question argued that my method made my informants look "uneducated" or even "aggressive." Although I understand this point, I do not believe that it is my role to correct or alter the language used by my informants. Rather, I want to give an accurate impression of how they actually speak. I have therefore opted not to remove swear words, slang, or grammatical errors from my quotations.

The fourth point is a temporal one and concerns the time period in which I conducted the research and that in which this book was written. I conducted my fieldwork between 2007–10, and when writing my dissertation (that I defended in 2013), I used data, such as crime statistics, from that time period. In this book, which I completed in early 2015, the majority of the "numbers" are from the period 2010-12, as I believe that it is confusing, and perhaps even unreliable and invalid, to compare data from different time periods. For example, an interview from May 2010 about one's perceptions of crime should not be supported with, or equated to, a survey conducted in 2014. This book is therefore about security and violence in Durban, South Africa, from 2007–12. However, although certain figures may have changed, the processes and mechanisms that I identify in my book have not.

MAP 1. South Africa. Copyright 2013–Kaartbeeld.

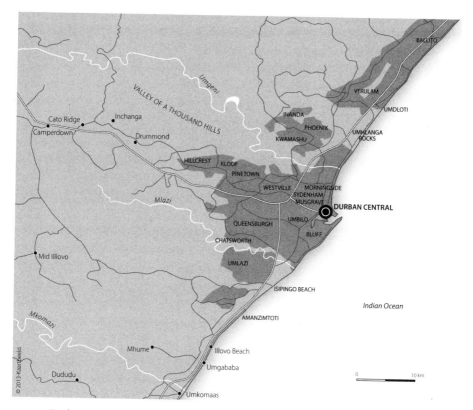

MAP 2. Durban. Copyright 2013–Kaartbeeld.

Prologue

Entering the Twilight

In the summer of 2010, I was living in one of Durban's former Indian townships and studying a community-based private security company (hereafter referred to as the company). Through friends of mine, I found accommodation with a hospitable Indian family. However, a few days into my stay, I noticed that a substantial amount of my money was missing. I tell Sylvia, the mother of the family, about the missing money, and she immediately suspects Thuli, the black maid, for numerous reasons, such as the way she had rushed out of the door the day before and had not come to work today. Sylvia immediately phones Thuli, but she can't reach her, so she proceeds to call anyone who might be able to put us in touch with Thuli. Shortly afterward, Sylvia realizes that a young boy who often assists her with her gardening can probably tell us where Thuli is. He's most likely at school, so Sylvia suggests visiting him there to get more information.

My first reaction is to go to the police station. Although I realize that it is very unlikely that I will get my money back, I want to report the incident for two reasons. The first is for insurance purposes. The second is as a matter of principle—a lot of crime goes unreported in South Africa, and after frequently urging my social acquaintances to report crime, I feel I should follow suit. Just as I'm gathering my things to go to the police station, Sylvia pulls me aside and says, "We need to find Thuli quickly, so we can get the money before she spends it. If we go to the police, we'll be sitting there all morning before anything happens and then Thuli will be long gone. We need to act now, so phone the company." I'm torn about what to do. I know the company will help me, since they probably want to make a good impression. A part of me is also curious about how they will react, given that I am a nonclient looking to make use of their services. Yet I am also a researcher who is studying the firm. Do I want to make my role even more ambiguous by becoming a client as well? All these questions race through my mind, and I feel pressured to make a decision quickly. With Sylvia encouraging me, I decide to phone Paul, the Indian owner of the company, to explain the situation. His voice is stern and serious; he says that someone will come to the house right away.

As soon as I hang up, I know I made the wrong decision. I feel that I'm taking advantage of my privileged role as researcher, that I am consolidating the uneven relationship between the company and myself, and that I am exacerbating the situation. As a researcher, one is always at the receiving end; one has to be grateful that one's informants allow you to be there to conduct one's study. But now, by asking them to assist me by providing a "security service," I am placing myself in a tricky position. Will I have to return the favor? Will they now be expecting certain things from me? Will this impede my ability to be critical? I share my doubts and worries with Sylvia, but she is unmoved and says, "Tessa, this needs to be done now. So let's just see what happens."

Within about three minutes, Kevin, an Indian armed response officer in his early forties, is standing in front of the house; when he comes in and says "Hello Tessa," I immediately feel that this is a personal matter. Sylvia takes the lead in explaining the story to him, reiterating that we need to go to the school as soon as possible to find out where Thuli is. And she stresses that both of us need to accompany him. Kevin returns to the office and comes back with Michael, an Indian armed response officer in his late twenties. Sylvia and I jump into the back of their vehicle to head out into one of the townships that sits among the sugarcane fields. In the car, the armed response officers explain that we need to be cautious, because we're entering a very dangerous area where they are not well liked.

The entire drive is uncomfortable and tense. I remain silent, simply because I do not know what to say. I feel guilty, ashamed, like we are doing something wrong. I keep thinking about what will happen when we find Thuli—what will they, or *we*, do to her? And during the fleeting moments when I'm able escape my own thoughts, I hear the two armed response officers proudly recollecting past glories while Sylvia tries to convince them that they need counseling to cope with the traumatic nature of their occupation. Everything tells me that this entire situation is unethical, but I somehow can't find the courage and moral fortitude to intervene.

When we enter the township, Kevin and Michael start asking people where the school is, but people seem unwilling to help us. I can tell that Kevin and Michael are more on guard here. When we eventually find the school, my feelings of guilt worsen and I become nervous. Here we are, in an armed response vehicle, with two armed guys who look like soldiers, sitting outside a semi-rural, impoverished school. Kevin and Sylvia head over to the school to find the woman in charge while Michael and I wait in the car. They return awhile later and explain that the woman could not find the boy. Sylvia thinks she's lying to protect him. I'm simply relieved that the situation is over and glad we can leave, but then Sylvia encourages the officers to ask people where Thuli lives. And within a matter of minutes, we find a man standing outside a half-empty convenience store who tells Kevin where Thuli's house is.

When we get to the house, an elderly lady approaches us. She tells us that Thuli lives in a house down the hill, but that they can only reach the house by foot. As Kevin and Michael walk down the hill, Sylvia and I stay and chat with the lady. She's very curious as to what has brought us here, and Sylvia tells her everything; hearing of the theft, the lady gets upset and advises us to come at night, when Thuli won't expect us. Kevin and Michael soon return, saying that they only found Thuli's sister, who said that Thuli hadn't been staying there for the last few weeks. Sylvia is certain that this is a lie to protect Thuli. It seems that we've come to a dead end; everybody agrees that it's time to go back, that there's nothing more we can do. I'm incredibly relieved. "Let's get (the hell) out of here," I say.

Feeling slightly more at ease now that this episode has passed, my role as researcher resurfaces during the ride back and I start to ask questions:

Me: So is this normal stuff?

Michael: Yes. Very normal. But this situation was a bit tricky; it could have backlashed on us.

Me: What do you mean? How come?

Michael: You see, if something would have happened, they could have charged us for intimidation or anything like that. We didn't have a warrant or anything like that.

Me: So then why did we go?

Michael: Because . . . yeah . . . we needed to get your money back. But if you went to the police first, opened a case, then we could have acted on that case. We could have arrested someone on that open case. Now it was just an investigation or something like that.

Me: Why didn't you say anything? I would have happily gone to the police station first. I had no idea.

Michael: Because we wanted to help you and show you what we do.

When he says this, I want the ground to open up and swallow me, to forget this incident ever happened. I keep silent for the rest of the ride home. I feel ashamed, stupid, and obligated to them. As soon as I get home, I go to the police station to lay a charge of theft. When I explain the entire situation to the police officer in question, I feel ashamed, like I've been cheating on him by going to the company first. Yet to my surprise, the police officer shows no sign of disapproval, but says, "That's what happens here, and well, you saved us a lot of time."

Later that afternoon, I go to the company office and apologize to the owner for the entire ordeal. He seems insulted by my apologies and says stoically, "If anything happens, no matter what, I want you to phone me first and then the police. So I'm happy you did what you did. It is our responsibility to take care of you. So promise me that you'll do the same in the future." I nod awkwardly and hope that a situation like this never arises again.

. . .

In this episode, we see how various individuals play a role in the manifestation and performance of private security. There is Sylvia, the citizen who has a rather negative view of the state police and prefers assistance from the company; Kevin and Michael, two security officers who provide a policing service with a combined sensation of confidence and hesitation; the police officer who expresses relief and a sense of normalcy about the company's involvement; Paul, the company owner who feels responsible for taking care of me and is eager to show me how they operate; and, of course, Thuli, who although physically absent, is a dominant character who symbolizes the threat—the criminal—reminding us that security is always intended against an "Other." And lastly, there is me: a foreign, white female researcher who is, in fact, the instigator of this entire incident and is faced with a range of methodological obstacles by which I must make both personal and professional decisions.

What we therefore see is a joint performance of security—an enactment of various policing practices that is shaped by the actions and perceptions of various parties. And that is precisely what this ethnography—*Twilight Policing*—is about. Throughout this book, you will read more of such narratives that occurred during my ethnographic fieldwork in which I delved deeply into the lives of the people working in private security. Yet this book describes merely a small segment of their world, a wonky slice of cake cut by a dull knife that provides a glimpse into a very complex world of security and violence in urban South Africa.

CHAPTER I

Twilight Policing

The Performance of Sovereign Power

November 2008

I'm on day shift duty with William, an Indian senior armed response officer in his early fifties, and we're driving through one of Durban's residential neighborhoods. After a quiet morning mostly taken up by a range of administrative tasks, we hear over the radio that there has just been a "robbery on a domestic of a client." The suspect is described as a "Bravo Mike wearing a white jacket and dark pants" and is apparently heading toward a nearby gas station.[1]

By chance, we are driving through that very area, and without any obvious sign of hesitation, William takes action: He slams on the gas pedal, commands me to "keep my eyes open," informs the radio controller that we are "going to check it out," and instructs Bongani, a black armed response officer in his late twenties, to provide backup. Just a few minutes later, we drive by a park and spot a young, black male casually walking by who fits the description. William hits the brakes and jumps out of the vehicle, quickly followed by Bongani, who has pulled up right behind us.

While I remain in the vehicle, I observe how William and Bongani apprehend the suspect: They yell at him to stop where he is, firmly grab ahold of him, and conduct a body search. Bongani stands behind the suspect and clasps his hands behind his back as if he is about to make an arrest, while William stands in front of him and carries out the search. With a commanding tone of voice and intimidating demeanor, William demands that the suspect explain his previous whereabouts and what "he is doing in the area." The suspect initially seems worried and objects to what is happening, but eventually he cooperates, chuckling sporadically as he answers their questions. William and Bongani do not find any money on him or other cause for suspicion, so they let him go. But before they do so, William gives the suspect a sharp shove in the chest and yells, "We know your face now and we're watching you. Don't go doing anything stupid or we'll fuck you up."

William and Bongani get back into their vehicles, and we head toward the client's premises to speak to the domestic worker (maid). She describes how she was robbed of R 100, and after William and Bongani tell her about the man they just searched, she says that he was probably the guy who robbed her.[2] Bongani is angry that they "let the criminal go," but William is convinced that the man they stopped wasn't the criminal because he had a "normal heart rate" and showed no signs of "guilt or fear." When William offers to inform the police so that the domestic worker can report the case, she adamantly declines. "There's no need; please don't," she says. William nods and tells her to phone the security company if she sees the suspect again or if anything else out of the ordinary happens. When we leave the premises, William explains to me how domestic workers never want to report crimes to the police out of fear of revenge attacks on them and their family. We bid farewell to Bongani, get back into the vehicle, and resume our patrol of the area.

. . .

In this incident, we see how a victim of crime sought assistance from private actors, who dealt with the incident in a public space without ever involving the state police. Such occurrences are common across the world and highlight the prominence of "nonstate policing bodies"—actors engaged in the provision of security who are not (directly) aligned with the state. The global growth of nonstate policing has unleashed across academic disciplines an array of questions concerned with violence, (in)security, sovereignty, and (dis)order. What do such incidents tell us about the authority and legitimacy of the state police? How should they be analyzed, and what do they reveal about policing, security, and violence in post-apartheid urban South Africa and elsewhere?

This book analyzes the complex relationships between policing, security, and violence, thereby contributing to conceptual debates about legitimacy and sovereignty. It does so through an ethnographic exploration of the everyday policing practices of armed response officers, such as William and Bongani, and their daily encounters with other actors, such as police officers and citizens.[3] I argue that any analysis of contemporary policing must focus on the entanglements between "nonstate" and "state" policing practices and thereby move beyond the public-private policing divide. I introduce the concept of *twilight policing*, which refers not only to the type of policing practices that I encountered in the field but also to a conceptual framework that enables an analysis of the interconnections between public and private policing beyond the South African context.

SOUTH AFRICA: "A COUNTRY AT WAR WITH ITSELF"

South Africa is known for its high rates of criminal violence, which are so high that South African criminologist, Anthony Altbeker (2007), has labeled South Africa as "a country at war with itself." South Africa is ranked ninth on the global list of homicide rates and has the third highest murder rate in the African continent (UNODC 2013).

Two of the corollaries of this "culture of violence" (Altbeker 2007; Kynoch 2005; Scheper-Hughes 1997) are the prominence and ubiquity of nonstate policing. Neighborhood watches, private security companies, citizen patrols, vigilante groups, gangs, street committees, business associations, and other (collective) initiatives make up South Africa's policing plethora. Since the political transition of 1994 that ended apartheid rule, crime has played a distinctive role in the formation of citizenship in South Africa, where active involvement in crime control constitutes a criterion for being seen as a "good citizen" (Bénit-Gbaffou 2008; Samara 2010; Singh 2008). Crime is *the* deliberated topic, and one does not have to look far to behold the spread and depth of securitization in South Africa: Crime stories occupy the front pages of newspapers, each radio station has its own crime monitor, anti-carjacking presentations and training sessions are readily available and well attended, newspapers and newsletters are filled with "tips on how to be vigilant," tear-gas-like sprays are sold at outdoor markets, and car alarms are the penetrating sound in the nighttime urban realm. It is not only the high crime rates that are important but also, and perhaps more pervasively, the social consequences of crime and violence—fear and securitization—and the numerous measures employed to survive amidst such circumstances.

Among the wide array of policing bodies, the private security industry is unquestionably the leading player.[4] The industry originated in the mining sector, entered the urban centers in the 1970s, and exploded during the height of the political resistance of the late 1980s and into the political transition around 1994. South Africa is globally regarded as the "absolute 'champion' in the security industry" (De Waard 1999: 169). With 8,144 registered private security providers and 487,058 active registered security officers (PSIRA 2013–14),[5] South Africa has the largest private security sector in the world, valued at approximately 2 percent of the country's total GDP (Abrahamsen and Williams 2011; Singh 2008).[6] The industry is also highly diverse, being categorized into twenty types of security services by the Private Security Industry Regulatory Authority (PSIRA), the quasi-state body that regulates the industry.

Approximately half of all South African households used physical measures to protect their homes in 2010, and 11.4 percent employed some form of private security (VOCS 2011: 15). Walk down any road in (urban) South Africa, and security measures are inescapable: The streets abound with high walls, barbed wire, electric fences, closed-circuit television (CCTV) cameras, mobile security guards, armed response vehicles, and the emblems of private security firms. South Africa is a country where the ratio of security officers to police officials is estimated to be high as 7:1 (Clarno and Murray 2013: 214), where private security companies guard police stations, where private security personnel usually respond to crime scenes before the police arrive, where private security company vehicles look like—and are regularly mistaken for—police vans, and where (privileged) citizens increasingly refer to private security firms as "their police." It is a country where many citizens, such as the domestic worker I introduced earlier, choose to call on armed response officers such as William and Bongani for assistance, rather than the state police.

This book is an ethnographic study of the daily policing practices of armed response officers, such as William and Bongani, who are armed private security officers who patrol communities in vehicles and react and respond to triggers such as alarms and panic buttons that are installed on clients' premises. Most of the scholarly work (primarily from the field of criminology) on private security officers, such as Button (2007), Manzo (2006, 2009), Rigakos (2002), van Steden (2007), and Wakefield (2003), is based on European and North American countries, while the daily policing practices of private security officers in countries such as Brazil, India, and Kenya (i.e., the postcolonial world) remain largely uncharted territory. This book fills this gap by focusing on the everyday policing practices of armed response officers in South Africa.

More specifically, this research takes place in the Durban Metropolitan Area (DMA),[7] which, in comparison to Cape Town and Johannesburg, has received less scholarly attention on crime and policing.[8]

As shown in the maps at the beginning of this book, Durban is located along the eastern coast of South Africa in the province of KwaZulu-Natal and covers an area of approximately 2,300 square kilometers. The city has an estimated population of 3,027,974, making it the second biggest in South Africa after the Greater Johannesburg metropolitan area (Marx and Charlton 2003). First known as Port Natal, Durban was founded in the 1820s as a British settlement. The city originally functioned as a minor trading post for internal commerce, but it soon established itself as a colonial port and trading center for the overseas contacts of the Boer Republic of Natalia and the Colony of Natal (Beinart 2001; Brookfield and Tatham 1957). Durban's economy also relied on the sugar industry, which itself depended largely on capital and labor imported from India, resulting in a large influx of Indians, especially between 1860 and 1911. Although they arrived as indentured laborers, the majority of Indians settled down and remained in the area (Davies 1981). This has had a marked impact on Durban's demographics: The Black/African community accounts for 63 percent, the Asian for 22 percent, the White for 11 percent, and the Colored for 3 per cent of its population (Marx and Charlton 2003).

In addition to its demographic composition, Durban was also chosen for its top position in South Africa's crime rates, particularly in terms of murder and aggravated robbery. In 2007, Durban was identified as the violent crime capital of South Africa (Masango 2007, cited in Marks and Wood 2007: 150). In 2009, KwaMashu—one of Durban's largest townships[9]—was labeled the murder capital of South Africa, with more than three hundred murders that year.[10] These prevailing crime rates made it a suitable location in which to analyze the relationships between crime, (in)security, and policing in the urban domain.

THE PLURALIZATION OF POLICING

In the fields of criminology and anthropology, it has been recognized that the public-private policing divide is blurry, weak, nonexistent, or frequently trespassed as state and nonstate policing have become increasingly alike and interconnected. Yet despite this acknowledgment, studies of nonstate policing continue to voice both political and conceptual concerns about the position of "the state." Abrahamsen and Williams (2011) term this the "mercenary misconception," which refers to the reigning perspective that associates nonstate policing, such as vigilantism and private security, with militarization and with illegal behavior that defy and seek to overthrow state legitimacy and authority, particularly in the African continent.

This "misconception" is primarily based on Hobbesian and Weberian understandings of the state and its possession of a monopoly on violence, with security provision as its core function. In this line of thinking, "policing" is inherently associated with the "police" and acts as a public good that is solely supplied by the state. The provision of security by nonstate actors is thus automatically associated with state failure and regarded as "a true Hobbesian nightmare" (Kosmatopoulos 2011: 219). Armed men, such as William and Bongani, are regarded as "power-challengers" (Osaghae 2004) who threaten the authority of the state. The general rationale is that, when the state fails to uphold its end of the social contract, "governance voids" (Kruijt and Koonings 1999) and "brown areas" (O'Donnell 1999) emerge that are readily occupied by nonstate actors.[11] And because the use of violence (or the threat of such) is ingrained in the provision of nonstate policing, the state loses its presumed monopoly on violence.

This "state-failure" perspective is commonly used for postconflict societies or those experiencing political transitions. Studies from the "transition literature"[12] highlight the numerous pitfalls in democratization processes, particularly regarding the redesign of state institutions. Although security is often prioritized to protect citizens during the democratization process, violence often persists, leading to "peacetime crimes" (Scheper-Hughes 1997) and "undeclared civil wars" (Rotker 2002: 19). Political transitions are often described as "dangerous hours" (Scheper-Hughes 1997: 491) that are susceptible to power struggles. Violence and insecurity in such newly created democracies are regarded as signs of a democratic failure (Arias and Goldstein 2010). Many hailed South Africa's political transition as a "miracle," yet high crime rates, inequality, unemployment, the use of violence by numerous nonstate actors, and the increasing demands for more coercive policing practices have darkened this perspective. Like many states in Latin America (Arias and Goldstein 2010), South Africa can perhaps be described as a violent democracy.

Despite its popularity, the state-failure hypothesis does not adequately account for the global proliferation of nonstate policing and has therefore been met with criticism. For example, Abrahamsen and Williams compare private security in Cape Town and Nairobi to show that "there is no automatic relationship between the growth of security privatisation and state weakness or straightforward delegitimization" (2011: 216). The rise of the "penal state," which is characterized by increased funding for the state's law enforcement institutions, further highlights the limitations of the state-failure approach (Wacquant 2008). Such a perspective also ignores how states are increasingly cultivating a political, social, and cultural climate that encourages the increased use of nonstate security solutions (Goldstein 2012; Goold, Loader, and Thumula 2010; Jaffe 2013). Therefore, the premise that the state is absent or incapable of providing security is flawed when attempting to explain the growth and diversification of nonstate policing, particularly for the African continent (Abrahamsen and Williams 2011; Albrecht and Moe 2015; Baker 2008; Bertelsen 2009; Lund 2006; Meagher 2012; Owen and Cooper-Knock 2014).

Yet perhaps the main source of criticism regarding the state-failure hypothesis—one that also lies at the heart of this book—concerns the interconnections between state and nonstate policing, which disintegrate the public-private policing divide. Public policing is traditionally defined as policing carried out by the state in public spaces that (ideally) serves all citizens and is impartial. In contrast, private policing is carried out by private actors who operate in private spaces, and it is therefore not available to all.[13] However, numerous studies have emphasized that public policing is increasingly privatized, "commodified" (Loader 1999), and incorporating a "business-like ethos" (Garland 1996: 455), while private policing is increasingly punitive and executed in public spaces (Berg 2010; Rigakos 2002; Singh and Kempa 2007). Furthermore, various policing bodies contain both public and private characteristics; these "hybrid" bodies (Button 2002; Johnston 1992) are "neither the public police, private security or some form of voluntary initiative" (Button 2002: 12). Public spaces are also becoming more restricted and guarded or are simply disappearing altogether. "Communal spaces" (i.e., spaces that are neither public nor private) are becoming the norm, rather than the exception (Kempa, Stenning, and Wood 2004; Shearing and Wood 2003).[14]

Therefore, rather than thinking in terms of public versus private policing, policing is best analyzed within "a pluralized security landscape" (Loader and Walker 2007: 3), a "kaleidoscope of overlapping policing agencies" (Baker 2008: 5), a "policing web" (Brodeur 2010), or a "security quilt" (Ericson 1994) that consists of "extended policing families" (Johnston 2003) and structures of "multilateralization" (Bayley and

Shearing 2001). For the African continent, Baker (2008) has coined the term "multi-choice policing" to portray how citizens can choose among different security providers, of which the state is just one possibility. Similarly, various frameworks have emerged that serve as interpretive concepts to understand the governance of pluralized policing, such as the nodal framework (Shearing and Wood 2003) and security assemblages (Abrahamsen and Williams 2011; Schouten 2014). Although these frameworks and concepts have different points of departure, they all stress the pluralized nature of policing.

POLICING AS THE PERFORMANCE OF SOVEREIGNTY

This book employs the pluralized perspective on policing, defining it as a social process that is executed by a range of actors to maintain a particular social order (Baker 2010; Button 2002).[15] It analyzes policing as an organized, purposive, and communal social activity that is defined in relation to crime (Baker 2010; Button 2002).[16] But more specifically, I follow other anthropological research on policing in South Africa and conceptualize policing as the performance of sovereign power (Buur 2005, 2006; Comaroff and Comaroff 2006a; Hansen 2006; Jensen 2005, 2007).

Just as the state has traditionally been regarded as the sole provider of policing and security, it has also been regarded as the sole sovereign power: the Leviathan. Like the recognition that policing has never been solely the prerogative of the state, anthropological studies have argued that the state is not the sole sovereign body and that there are in fact "multiple sovereignties" (Bertelsen 2009) found within and across states. This is particularly true of the postcolonial world, which is characterized by fragmented forms of sovereignty (Comaroff and Comaroff 2006a; Hansen and Stepputat 2005a).

Primarily based on the ideas of Agamben (1998, 2005), Derrida (1992), and Schmitt (1985), anthropological studies of sovereignty have proliferated over the past decade. Such studies represent a move away from a focus on *legal sovereignty*, which refers to "sovereignty grounded in formal ideologies of rules and legality," toward the analysis of *de facto sovereignty*, which refers to "the ability to kill, punish, and discipline with impunity wherever it is found and practiced" (Hansen and Stepputat 2006: 296). Although based on different contexts and approaches, these anthropological works view sovereignty as a socially constructed source of power that is reproduced through daily practices and repetitious public performances.[17]

I use Hansen and Stepputat's definition of (de facto) sovereignty as a "tentative and always emergent form of authority grounded in violence that is performed and designed to generate loyalty, fear, and legitimacy from the neighborhood to the summit of the state" (2006: 297). It entails that claims to sovereignty are based on the ability to enforce punishment and to do so through violence. Violence is thus both the source of sovereign power and the quality that differentiates sovereignty from other types of authority. Agamben (1998) defines sovereignty as the ability of a power to define the category of "homo sacer;" that is, those excluded and reduced to "bare life," the life "that is subjected to the violence of law without enjoying its protection" (Rigi 2012: 61). Sovereign power is therefore not inherently linked to control over a particular territory, but concerns claiming sovereignty over the *body* (Das and Poole 2004; Hansen and Stepputat 2005b, 2006). For example, William and Bongani did not use (severe) physical violence while searching the suspect, but the way they held him, spoke to him, and threatened him with the statement "we'll fuck you up" highlights the importance of the *ability* to use violence. Throughout this book, I analyze incidents where both the ability to use violence and violence itself were used to claim sovereignty.

I want to further emphasize that sovereignty is not a fixed form of power, but rather is "an unstable and precarious form of power" (Hansen 2005: 171) that must be habitually revoked. Sovereign power is not something that simply exists out there that one can possess or execute; it is a form of authority that must be repeatedly claimed and reclaimed through "exercises of sovereignty" (Sieder 2011: 163). I therefore regard claims to sovereignty as performances: They are not single acts or deeds, but consist of numerous practices that are part of a larger social process (Turner 1982: 91). Performances are always conducted "for someone, some audience that recognizes and validates it as performance" (Carlson 2004: 73). Although they involve a set of preestablished sequences, they are also flexible, changeable, and very often shaped by improvisation. For example, when an armed response officer responds to an incident of crime, he is guided by a particular protocol, a set of procedures.[18] Yet this response is affected by other variables that are not known beforehand and that often emerge from the performance itself.

Furthermore, claims to sovereignty are essentially about creating communities and constructing social borders. Violence is the means by which these borders, and thus comminutes, are enforced and created: Violence constructs order out of (perceived) disorder (Benda-Beckmann and Pirie 2007). Violence is not only defined in reference to its relationship to power (Robben and Nordstrom 1995) and cannot be analyzed solely as an instrument; rather, it is deeply rooted in social structures and maintained through social practices (Besteman 2002; Bourdieu 2002; Das et al. 2000; Foucault 1977; Galtung 1969; Scheper-Hughes and Bourgois 2004). Violence constructs moral communities, distinguishes between right and wrong, and differentiates "insiders" from "outsiders" (Buur 2005, 2006; Jensen 2005; Pratten and Sen 2007). For example, William and Bongani asked the suspect "what he was doing in the area" and whether he "belonged there." The social process of defining criminals as "bare beings" (Agamben 1998) and as "matter out of place" (Douglas 2002) and then of protecting oneself from these socially constructed threats is suffused with power relations that draw socially imagined boundaries between "insiders" and "outsiders" within and across communities. Such exclusionary policing practices make sovereign power visible (Buur, Jensen, and Stepputat 2007: 15–16).

This visibility of power is particularly evident in urban areas: Cities are characterized by exclusion and divisions, in which "divided cities" (Beall, Crankshaw, and Parnell 2002; Caldeira 2000; Walton 1978) and "fractured cities" (Koonings and Kruijt 2007) are becoming the norm. We are witnessing a process whereby the most affluent members of society seal themselves off in "communities of security," such as gated communities (Caldeira 2000; Lemanski 2004; Low 2004) guarded by private security companies against the "Other"—often the "dangerous poor." Poorer citizens are forced to resort to more informal or illegal methods of security, such as gangs. This division creates "pockets of safety" (Shaw 2002: 112–13) whereby security and policing increasingly operate as "club goods"—"'quasi-public' goods that are available to members of a club but restricted in some form or other to non-members" (Crawford 2006: 120). As a club good, policing is inherently exclusive when membership of the "club" is defined. Various forms of nonstate policing are expressions of social ruptures and class differences, which are further consolidated by distinct policing practices.

During apartheid, violence was framed in terms of political resistance, whereas now it is generally framed as criminal (Samara 2003, 2010; Scheper-Hughes 1997). The South African state has repeatedly invoked this discourse on crime and security to unify the country, with statements such as "crime affects us all" and "crime sees no color" suggesting a national problem that is experienced by all citizens, regardless of race or class. Crime is not framed as an exclusive experience, but as one common to all South Africans. Yet the responses to crime are exclusionary and unequal, as the dissimilar forms of nonstate policing attest.

In South Africa, social borders are defined along axes of race and class. In 1994, the country had one of the highest levels of income inequality in the world, and little has changed since then (Seekings and Nattrass 2005: 3–4). Approximately 14 percent of the total population can afford private security services, with the rest being forced to resort to other means of personal protection (Whitfield 2008: 16). Race also continues to be a salient factor in defining social relations in South Africa (Chipkin 2007; Habib and Bentley 2008; Hansen 2012; MacDonald 2006; Samara 2010), where "pockets of safety" are highly racialized. The criminal is often equated with the "young, black male," referred to as a "Bravo Mike" by armed response officers. Policing strategies aimed at eliminating crime reinforce such imaginaries. Although the post-apartheid state intended to eradicate repressive policing practices that were primarily enforcing racial segregation, current policing practices, both state and nonstate, are reinforcing apartheid-based social divisions.

SOVEREIGNTIES AND THE STATE

Conceptualizing policing bodies as sovereign bodies allows me to examine how different state and nonstate actors claim authority to produce a particular social order. Yet I also want to problematize how sovereignties continue to be defined according to their relationship with the state. I argue that such categorizations are not clear-cut because of the blurred boundaries between legal and illegal domains. This is evident when analyzing the distinction, in both emic and etic terms, between vigilantism and private security. Furthermore, I want to demonstrate that the relationships between sovereignties and the state are not linear, but are diverse and complex, as several authors have also shown (Humphrey 2007; Rigi 2007, 2012; Rodgers 2006b; Sieder 2011).

Vigilantism is a generic term to describe acts of violence or organized forms of security.[19] Johnston has provided what many regard as the classic definition of the term:

> Vigilantism is a social movement giving rise to premeditated acts of force—or threatened force—by autonomous citizens. It arises as a reaction to the transgression of institutionalized norms by individuals or groups—or to their potential or imputed transgression. Such acts are focused upon crime control and/or social control and aim to offer assurance (or "guarantees") of security both to participants and to other members of a given established order. (1996: 232)

Although Johnston (1996) emphasizes that vigilantism is not always illegal, it is routinely defined as such. For example, Landman (2010: 230) categorizes vigilantism as a form of "illegal nonstate violence;" Martin (2013: 154) describes it as an informal security node whose "methods of control must be predominantly carried out in ways deemed illegal by the state;" and Baker (2008) defines vigilantes as "informal organized security groups." Vigilantes are therefore conceptualized as actors who operate illegally and/or informally and assert power. In South Africa, vigilantism is also associated with illegal behavior and is differentiated from other forms of policing, such as community policing and private security, on the basis of its "illegal" use of violence.

Private security companies, in contrast, are described as "formal security nodes" (Martin 2013) and "formal commercial security groups" (Baker 2008). They are defined as actors that operate within the legal ambit of the state, primarily due to state regulation systems. In South Africa, for example, the PSIRA is a state-led regulatory system that stipulates how the private security industry must operate and determines forms of (judicial) punishment in the event of misconduct. The use of coercion by private security officers is thereby regarded as an extension or outsourcing of state coercion that operates within the legal parameters of the state. Private security officers are engaged in "institutional violence," which is violence emanating from the state and its "formal allies" (Pansters 2012: 24). Private security companies are therefore seen as "permissible sovereign bodies" and vigilantes as "nonpermissible sovereign bodies."

This conceptual and perceptual difference between vigilantism and private security illustrates how state law defines particular sovereignties as illegal or legal. Yet such a categorization overlooks the complexities of the practices of such sovereignties. The use of violence by a vigilante organization may be defined as illegal, but citizens may view it as legitimate and legal, and the same holds for the use of violence by private security officers. For example, the apprehension of the suspect by William and Bongani may not have been tolerated in other contexts. As is also evident in the growth of "pockets of safety," there are contesting ideas about the legitimate use of violence and the (necessary) means to create social order, issues discussed at length in the field of legal pluralism (Comaroff and Comaroff 2006a; Merry 1988). In this ethnography, I demonstrate that condoning or supporting the use of violence by armed response officers is not uniform, but varies according to the company, armed response officer, client, police officer, and so on. Defining sovereign bodies as illegal or informal as opposed to legal or formal ignores this variability. In fact, the presence of numerous conflicting social discourses about the legitimate use of violence points toward a disintegration of illegal versus legal binaries.

This disintegration is augmented by the fact that state representatives, such as police officers, may themselves not abide by the law, either by participating in crime and violence or by "upholding zones of exception where illegal groups operate with impunity" (Hansen and Stepputat 2006: 305).[20] State representatives very often operate in nonstate zones—zones of illegality, while nonstate bodies operate in state zones—zones of legality—often in a type of "dirty togetherness" (Podgórecki 1987). More recently, Owen and Cooper-Knock (2014) discuss the idea of "police vigilantism" to capture how the state police is engaged in the illegal exercise of force and, in doing so, mimics the behavior of actors who are referred to as vigilantes. Just as particular policing bodies cannot be defined as wholly public or private, they cannot always be defined as exclusively legal or illegal. Referring again to the distinction between vigilantism and private security, I argue that, despite state regulation, private security companies do not always operate within the legal ambit of the state. Similarly, vigilante groups do not always operate outside this domain. Like Gordon (2006: 238), I question the extent to which vigilantism and private security are in fact distinct phenomena, an issue that resurfaces throughout the rest of this book.

Furthermore, such a distinction implies a linear relationship between state and nonstate sovereignties. Like the idea of "pockets of safety," it presupposes a situation in which sovereignties operate distinctly. Several studies, such as Leeds's (1996) analysis of the emergence of "parallel power systems" in Brazil, reinforce the notion of distinct claims to sovereignty that operate in discrete domains. However, numerous authors have shown that these relationships are much more diverse and complex. Rodgers (2004), for example, talks of "competing sovereigns" in his study of gangs in Nicaragua, while Sieder (2011) refers to "contesting sovereignties" in her research on indigenous authorities in Guatemala. Both studies reveal a struggle between different claims to sovereignty. In her study on the *marshrut* system in Russia, Humphrey refers to a "localized form of sovereignty" that is "nested within higher sovereignties" (2007: 420). In a similar vein, Rigi (2007, 2012) develops the concept of a "chaotic mode of domination" to analyze the shifting balances of power and the means by which the coercive apparatus of the state transcends "the boundaries between the legal and illegal, the formal and informal, the legitimate and illegitimate, public and private" (2007: 41). Taken together, these studies highlight the multiplicity of relationships between sovereignties that cut across the state versus nonstate and the legal versus illegal divides.

STATE AND NONSTATE ENTANGLEMENTS

I draw on the earlier mentioned studies to develop my fourth step of argumentation, in which I analyze the multidimensional relationships between state and nonstate sovereign bodies, which are continuously in flux due to shifting temporal and spatial circumstances. Building on existing anthropological insights into the state (Kapferer and Bertelsen 2012; Krohn-Hansen and Nustad 2005; Sharma and Gupta 2006; Trouillot 2001), I argue that sovereignty is a form of power that is relative to the performance, assertion, and infringement of other sovereign bodies (Hansen and Stepputat 2006; Humphrey 2007; Latham 2000; Rigi 2007, 2012).

In developing my argument, I employ the ideas of Abrams (2006) and Mitchell (2006), for whom the state comprises two features. The first is the state system, which refers to the various institutions and practices of the state. The second is what Mitchell (2006) calls the "state effect," which refers to particular representations and understandings of the state; that is, the way in which the state is "discursively produced as an entity that is distinct from and sits above the non-state realm" (Sharma and Gupta 2006: 16). These two features are connected, co-dependent, and mutually reinforcing: Together they create "the state."

The state is thus not simply the sum of the institutions and bodies that execute "state functions;" rather, it is imagined and socially constructed through everyday practices (Das and Poole 2004). The state is not something that can be separated from society, but is "constituted *through* society" (Sieder 2011: 170, emphasis in original). Thus, when William and Bongani were patrolling the streets and searching the suspect, they were not only contesting state sovereignty and undermining the power and legitimacy of the state police; they were also reinforcing ideas of what the state is by acting like the state.

Nonstate policing actors operate like state actors (Davis 2010; Jaffe 2013; Rodgers 2006a) by performing statist functions and appropriating "languages of stateness" (Hansen and Stepputat 2001: 5). As noted by Baker (2008: 19), "such policing groups do everything that the public police does and do it as the police do it." Although nonstate policing actors may view themselves as separate from the state apparatus, they are simultaneously acknowledging the state and demarcating their role in relation to the state. For example, armed response companies portray themselves as "service providers" that operate in a market system, but they also mimic the state police by designing vehicles that look like "cop cars" and uniforms that resemble those of the public police. In other words, they are appropriating the state's "marks of sovereignty" (Bodin 1992, cited in Hansen and Stepputat 2005b: 7) and particular "state spectacles" (Hansen and Stepputat 2001) to obtain legitimacy.

Similarly, when citizens resort to nonstate actors for security, they both display a lack of confidence in the state police and define themselves vis-à-vis the state. When citizens demand that private policing agents act like the state—such as by patrolling public spaces and arresting suspects—they are in effect expressing what they envision, demand, or expect from the state. Although particular state bodies—in this case, the public police—may not be the sole actors enforcing these practices, this does not mean that statist practices are not produced. Thus, the performance of "unstately stateliness" (Lund 2006: 677) by nonstate actors also constitutes what the state is: The meaning of the state is reliant on the meaning of the nonstate, and vice versa. Nonstate policing practices are thus mechanisms through which ideas and representations of the state are discursively fabricated.

In his work on security and violence in the barrios of Bolivia, Goldstein describes the state as a phantom, one that is "simultaneously here and not there" (2012: 81); the state is not always physically present through state institutions and representatives, but is nevertheless extant in (re)producing violence and insecurity. In the course of my research, I identified many cases where the state police was not physically present, but where the idea of the "state" was. These ideas and perceptions shape notions of violence, security, and authority and affect how policing agents operate—further highlighting how labeling the state as absent, weak, or malfunctioning elides its role in nonstate policing, violence, and (in) security.

Thus, even as nonstate actors may undermine the authority of the state, they simultaneously seek a degree of recognition from and partnership with the state. They may function as an alternative to the state and thereby challenge its authority, but they also reproduce particular ideas of what the state should be. Like Arias (2006) and Nordstrom (2000), I employ a network approach to explore the multistranded engagements between sovereign bodies. More specifically, I use the "local security network" concept proposed by Dupont (2004, 2006). Dupont defines a security network as "a set of institutional, organizational, communal or individual agents or nodes that are directly or indirectly connected in order to authorize and/or provide security to the benefit of internal or external stakeholders" (2006: 38). Following this logic, local security networks are "initiatives that seek to harness the public and private resources available in local communities" (Dupont 2004: 79).[21] A security network approach analyzes security as a system of agencies that coincide to produce a particular type of social order.[22]

Local security networks consist of "dominant and dominated actors" (Dupont 2004: 84). They are therefore not "egalitarian social structures" (84); some networks are complementary, while others are competitive. Local security networks consist of different types of relationships, making them porous, flexible, dynamic, and context dependent. I use local security networks as an analytical tool with which to examine the ground-level interactions between nonstate and state bodies. Doing so allows me to analyze how state sovereignty is reproduced, contested, and reformulated as nonstate actors claim sovereignty. Thus, this book seeks to provide insights not only into nonstate policing but also into the role of the state police, and perhaps of the state at large.

TWILIGHT POLICING

This brings us to twilight policing, the conceptual framework through which I analyze how different sovereignties overlap, complement, and compete with each other. Twilight policing originates from "twilight institutions." This term was first outlined in a special issue of *Development and Change* from 2006 and refers to the way in which particular institutions in Africa both strengthen and challenge the state's authority. Twilight institutions are defined as institutions that "operate in the twilight between state and society, between public and private" (Lund 2006: 678). Such institutions exercise public authority, actively shape governance, and enforce decisions and rules on a collective level.

Twilight institutions challenge the state by exerting alternative forms of governance and legitimized authority, yet they strengthen the state through "symbolic borrowing" (Thumala, Goold, and Loader 2011: 294) and by mimicking statist practices. This multidimensional relationship creates a particular twilight zone, a zone of "ongoing contestation" (Buur 2006: 741). This zone does not necessarily comprise processes where public actors become more privatized or private actors become more publicized—two processes that are frequently discussed in the policing literature—but it concerns the imbrication of public and private elements, which makes "it difficult to distinguish unequivocally between what is state and what is not" (Buur 2006: 750). It is similar to Auyero's (2007) "gray zones," which are sites "where the deeds and networks of violent entrepreneurs, political actors and law enforcement officials secretly meet and mesh" (quoted in Pansters 2012: 24).

How can we use the concept of twilight institutions to understand the policing practices of private security officers and companies at large? As the majority of the policing literature illustrates, private security companies are corporate actors that are steered by market interests and traditionally operate in privately owned spaces, yet they are also increasingly taking over state police functions such as the provision of security in public spaces to nonpaying citizens. They supplement the state by frequently working alongside state bodies in both formal and informal partnerships, yet they also substitute for and challenge the state by providing particular services that the state does not. In this way, they influence how citizens perceive the state and its ability to act as their custodian.

However, to classify all armed response companies as twilight institutions would be to ignore the diversity among companies, armed response officers, and their interactions with others. Furthermore, this book focuses not on institutions but on policing practices. Thus, rather than speaking of "twilight institutions," I use the core elements of this notion to develop the concept of "twilight policing": Doing so involves three conceptual changes. The first is a focus on policing (i.e., an analysis of everyday practices that are performed by individuals, rather than looking at institutions in which practices are seen as being performed top-down). Twilight policing refers to policing practices that are habitually performed by armed response officers and that emerge from a dual process of collaboration and competition between state and nonstate bodies. It occurs in a twilight zone between state and nonstate, and between illegal and legal spheres. The twilight zone is a collection of spaces where the lines between public and private and legal and illegal are continuously in flux.

The second change is that I use an agency-based perspective by incorporating the emotional experiences of performing such practices and how they shape the actual performance. According to Lund (2006: 673), the term "twilight" in "twilight institutions" implies that the "contours and features of these institutions are hard to distinguish and discern" and does not refer to the temporal aspect of twilight, which would suggest "that these institutions should gradually disappear." In contrast, I use the term "twilight" not only to evoke an in-between period, such as the period between day and night, but also to emphasize a state of uncertainty, unpredictability, and obscurity that is experienced by armed response officers. Third, in relation to my conceptualization of policing as the performance of sovereign power, I regard both the ability to use violence and its actual use as central to the policing practices of armed response officers. Twilight policing thus concerns punitive and disciplinary practices and thereby differs from twilight institutions in which violence is not a prerequisite.

I further argue that twilight policing is a *joint performance*. It consists of policing practices that are shaped by the various interactions between different actors. For example, the suspect, the domestic worker, and the physical absence of the state police influenced how William and Bongani acted. Throughout this book, I discuss other factors that are not directly evident in such episodes, such as company policies and state regulation, but that also influence how a performance unfolds. Analyzing twilight policing as a joint performance further emphasizes the interconnectedness of policing practices.

Yet I also aim to analyze what these entanglements (re)produce—the performative nature of policing practices—whereby their mere enactment reproduces a series of effects (Butler 1997). Twilight policing practices are iterative: They are based on existing understandings of violence and security, and through their habitual enactment, they lead to further actions and meanings. Thus, performances not only signify how meaning is given but also their enactment gives them further meaning. They do not simply make claims to sovereignty but also produce state effects. Therefore, I analyze not only how various actors "meet and mesh," as Auyero (2007, cited in Pansters 2012) does with his "gray zones," but also, with recourse to the performative nature of policing, what is generated *through* this meeting and meshing and how the ontology of the actors changes through such performances. Twilight policing concerns claims to sovereignty that are neither public nor private, but that are the outcome of the imbrication of these two domains, creating something "new"—something "twilight."

"SIERRA FOXTROT GOLF":
DOING THE ETHNOGRAPHIC FIELDWORK

Such an analysis is best approached through ethnographic fieldwork, which allows one to examine everyday practices and uncover local dynamics and perspectives over an extended period of time. In contrast to most of the criminological studies of private security officers, which generally use a quantitative approach to present the "typical security officer" in a particular space and time,[23] this book is an ethnography and is based on twenty months of ethnographic fieldwork conducted between 2007–10.[24] Although ethnographic accounts of the state police are increasing,[25] the only ethnographic exploration of the attitudes and daily endeavors of private security officers is Rigakos's (2002) excellent account of Intelligarde, a private security company in Toronto, Canada. Because the findings of Rigakos's research closely resemble my own, I refer to his work throughout this book. I therefore accept Goldstein's invitation to develop a "critical security anthropology" in which anthropologists "can explore the multiple ways in which security is configured and deployed—not only by states and authorized speakers but by communities, groups, and individuals—in their engagements with other local actors and with arms of the state itself" (2010: 492).

My most imperative research method—that is, the one that I used the most and the one that was most significant in collecting my data—was participation observation: "a method in which a researcher takes part in the daily activities, rituals, interactions, and events of a group of people as one of the means of learning the explicit and tacit aspects of their life routines and their culture" (DeWalt and DeWalt 2002: 1). It was the primary source of my data; it was my key research method to observe firsthand what occurred on the ground and how different actors and interactions shaped the joint performance of twilight policing. As in Chisholm (2014), participant observation allowed me to "engage in a deeper level with the men I was researching" (350). In practical terms it meant accompanying armed response officers in their vehicles during their shifts. This resulted in one company giving me the nickname "Sierra Foxtrot Golf"—Special Female Guest—for the purpose of radio communication.

My second main research method was conducting interviews of various types. Most took place in Durban; where they occurred elsewhere, this is indicated. I conducted semi-structured interviews with company owners and people in positions of authority, such as leaders of organizations and high-ranking police officers, to make full use of the limited time available (to us). Other interviews were less structured and were guided by mental topic guides, often taking place over lunch or while walking around a particular area. In total, I conducted 167 interviews that were prearranged (i.e., where an appointment was made in advance).

However, this figure excludes the open interviews and unplanned conversations I carried out during periods of participant observation. It is this second type—the more informal interviews—that generated the majority of my data. I also conducted several group interviews, particularly among security officers, but in a rather ad hoc way; they were more of a "group talk" than a formal focus group discussion. In addition, to trace the developments of policing in South Africa over the past few decades, I recorded the life histories of several individuals who had been working in the industry for a long time.

During interviews and participant observation, I used both recording and writing devices. When going "on duty," I always carried my recorder with me, but because it was practically impossible to record all twelve hours of each shift, I only recorded conversations that I deemed to be important at the time. I always carried a notebook in which I would jot down keywords related to events, such as *car chase;* themes in conversations, such as *trauma;* and my own emotions, such as *anger.* After each shift, I wrote up field notes that I branded *mosaics of data*, which included jotted-down keywords, fragments of transcribed interviews, and detailed field notes written later. Unlike Murray (2003), I did not distinguish between personal, observational, or methodological notes, because I believe that such a categorization disregards the interconnectedness between emotions, method, and knowledge (Diphoorn 2013). Rather, personal accounts and methodological issues were woven throughout the notes as a key ingredient of the empirical data, resulting in "messy texts" (Denzin 1997) that voiced various facets of the research process.

In addition to participant observation and interviews, I also conducted a small amount of data analysis, such as of employee contracts, contracts between companies and clients, minutes of meetings, and reports created by companies and community organizations. I initially planned to carry out a large-scale survey of several companies to complement the qualitative data. However, this was not possible due to time constraints. As an alternative, I sent a form to eleven companies to acquire basic information about them, such as the number of people they employed, their overhead costs, and their salary expenses. All of the companies completed the form, but they all omitted particular sections, and I am also certain that many did not provide accurate information, particularly regarding sensitive issues. One example was the amount of salaries paid to armed response officers: For almost all of the companies, the amount stated on the form was higher than what the armed response officers showed me on their pay slips. Therefore, although these forms provided some baseline data (see Chapter 3), the validity of this data is questionable, and I therefore did not rely heavily on this information.

Although I frequented several companies and interviewed the owners of more than twenty firms, I focused on four companies for in-depth analysis. I selected these firms to reflect the diversity of the industry. The first is an internationally owned company that operates globally. The second is a Durban-based company that operates solely in the DMA. The third and fourth are community-based companies: One operates in an affluent, predominantly white area, whereas the other operates in a former Indian township on the outskirts of the city.

In total, I spent approximately 750 hours with armed response officers in their vehicles; this amount included only the actual time spent in their vehicles during their shifts. My days "on duty" alternated between the four companies; I would do a Monday night shift with company A, followed by a Wednesday day shift with company B, and so on. For example, in July 2010, I went on shifts with each of the four companies. Furthermore, my 750 hours on duty and the additional time I spent in the field were not spread evenly across the four companies. I spent less time with two of the four companies for practical reasons: One of the companies was less forthcoming when providing information and access, while the other was smaller and thus required less consideration. Eventually, personal relationships also played a role in how I spent my time: I established better rapport with certain employees of particular companies and thus spent more time with them. In addition to the 750 hours spent on the road, I regularly hung out at the company offices, conducted participant observation in the control room, and accompanied technicians and sales reps on their rounds.

In the early stages of my fieldwork, I accompanied numerous armed response offices in their vehicles, finding myself with a different officer for each shift, and sometimes even in several vehicles during the same shift. As time passed, however, I increasingly accompanied the same few individuals. Of the dozens of armed response officers whom I spoke to, I developed close relationships with several individuals, especially with Gayle, Brian, Michael, David, and Nick. I spent a great deal of my time with these five men, visiting them at their homes and meeting their families. This allowed me to get a better sense of the person behind the uniform and to analyze the impact of their work on their personal lives. They are my key informants, and their stories and our experiences together form the core of this book.

In addition to the armed response officers, I also spent approximately one hundred hours with citizens on their patrols in different parts of Durban to understand the community aspects of policing, as well as approximately eighty hours with state police officers during their shifts. These patrols were not systematically chosen, but were selected using a snowball method and occurred quite sporadically and across the city. I also completed the private security training courses of levels E, D, C, and armed response training at one training school;[26] worked as a car guard at several sites (a shopping mall and residential areas) for a few days; tagged along with private investigators and bodyguards; took a polygraph test; and interviewed numerous people who were somehow related to "security." All of these additional efforts allowed me to gain a richer understanding of private security, policing, and crime in South Africa.

While conducting this research, a range of ethical, practical, and moral concerns surfaced, as I discuss in detail elsewhere (Diphoorn 2013). This research was emotionally charged, because, after all, researching violence is emotional—for both the informants and the researcher—and it carries additional responsibilities that exceed those associated with traditional ethnography (Ghassem-Fachandi 2009; Robben and Nordstrom 1995). Yet because I conceptualize policing as a performance, it seemed judicious to understand and elucidate my own participation as an actor, both on and off stage, in the numerous performances discussed throughout this book. It is for this reason that my emotions and perceptions permeate the empirical vignettes.

THE BOOK

In summary, this book is an ethnographic analysis of the daily policing practices of armed response officers and their interactions with other actors in Durban, South Africa. The next chapter, "'Old School' Policing versus 'the New South Africa': Violence and Security in South Africa," provides a historical account of policing and security in South Africa. It presents a twofold argument. The first is that nonstate policing has existed in South Africa for decades and that the current policing panoply is not a recent or post-apartheid development. The second argument is that contemporary policing in South Africa is marked by contesting discourses on the "right" style of policing, particularly concerning the use of violence. Twilight policing is a manifestation of this contestation, a surfacing of uncertainties and various forms of "in betweenness."

The next four chapters examine the different actors and local security networks that set the stage for the performance of twilight policing. Chapter 3, "'The Promising Horse': The Armed Response Sector," analyzes the industry at large. In addition to providing a descriptive account of the sector, this chapter examines three of its defining elements: the disciplinary measures and forms of surveillance implemented by companies, the (re)production of masculinization processes that define the industry as a "man's world," and the racial hierarchies within the industry that put "Whites on top and Blacks at the bottom." Chapter 4, "'Wanna-Be Policemen': Being an Armed Response Officer," provides a descriptive account of the lives, perspectives, and experiences of armed response officers. I examine their motivations, how they distinguish themselves from other private security officers, a typical day "on the road," the different tools they use while on duty, and the occupational hazards they face. Taken together, Chapters 3 and 4 show how the occupational culture of armed response is designed to resemble that of the state police and so fosters an environment for twilight policing practices.

The next two chapters analyze the interactions between armed response officers and other actors through the framework of local security networks. Chapter 5, "'It All Comes Down to Them': Daily Interactions with the 'State,'" examines the relationship between private security agents and the state. The first section focuses on state regulation and the post-apartheid state strategy of "partnership policing," in which the private security industry is given a "junior role." The second and larger section examines on-the-ground interactions between armed response officers and police officers. The first claim made in this chapter is that such encounters—which are often informal and ad hoc—are marked by both cooperation and competition, which constantly redraw the boundaries between state and nonstate policing. The second claim is that police officers, as state representatives, play an active role in drawing armed response officers into the twilight zone.

Chapter 6, "'Getting Connected with the Community': The Beneficiaries of Armed Response," analyzes the relationships between armed response officers and citizens and/or clients. In this chapter, I distinguish between formal and informal local security networks, which I then subcategorize into high-maintenance, collaborative, and competitive local security networks. The first argument I make is that clients are the dominant actors in such networks in that they largely define what armed response officers do. The second concerns the current trend in the industry: the establishment and growth of "collective arrangements," both formal and informal, whereby citizens "club" together to collectively benefit from armed response. Through these arrangements, armed response companies increasingly serve "communities of security," which mandates them to operate in public spaces. The dominant position of clients and the growth of collective arrangements entail that armed response officers engage in an array of policing tasks that take place in the public sphere, thereby providing the backdrop for the performance of twilight policing.

Chapter 7, "Performances of Twilight Policing: Public Authority, Coercion, and Moral Ordering," analyzes performances of twilight policing and their punitive, disciplinary, and exclusionary nature. Drawing on Goffman's (1959) dramaturgical approach, I present three empirical vignettes that show how twilight policing is a joint performance—a manifestation of actions undertaken through the coming together of various local security networks. In the final section of this chapter, I examine twilight policing at the micro level, describing its performance as strenuous and capricious. Twilight policing is analyzed as a liminal experience in which individual armed response officers engage in a twilight sensation of belonging and exclusion.

I end this ethnography with an epilogue, "Expanding the Twilight," which examines three threads that are woven throughout this entire book. I then offer some final thoughts about what these themes mean for "the state." The aims of this epilogue are to tie together the different claims of this book; to emphasize the meaning, significance, and contribution of twilight policing; and to propose how it can serve as an analytical framework within which to examine the imbrication of state and nonstate policing practices beyond South Africa.

CHAPTER 2

"Old School" Policing versus "the New South Africa"

Violence and Security in South Africa

February 2009

During a busy morning shift, Brian and I take a short break to grab a bite to eat on one of Durban's busy streets lined with restaurants, bars, and shops. The company Brian works for has many clients on this street, so he reckons it's a good place to stop and monitor what's going on. While eating our snacks in the vehicle, we see a vagrant walking down the road making a lot of noise; it is obvious that he is intoxicated. Brian grunts and gets out of the vehicle to "deal with the situation." He approaches the vagrant, tells him that he is disturbing the peace, and asks him to leave the area, but the vagrant refuses. Growing impatient, Brian grabs the man by his sweater and forces him into one of the side streets, away from public view. Then, two elderly white women who have apparently been observing the situation come out of nowhere and start yelling at Brian, accusing him of hurting an innocent man and taking unnecessary measures. "You can't just go hitting people anymore," one of them shouts at him. The women proceed to lecture Brian about human rights, equality, and treating people with decency. Brian remains silent, nods, and shows his obedience and subordination. As soon as the women leave, he rolls his eyes, comes over to me, and says, "Can you believe this shit?"

A few hours later, Brian and I receive word from the control room that there has been a break-in at a client's residence and that one of the suspects has been apprehended by one of Brian's colleagues. When we get to the premises, we encounter the white male client screaming at the handcuffed black suspect and demanding that Brian's colleague beat him to punish him for his deeds. Because Brian is of higher rank, he takes over control of the situation. While we wait for the police to arrive, the client repeatedly demands that Brian assault the suspect to "teach him his lesson." When Brian refuses to do so, the client becomes agitated and accuses him of not doing his job properly. "Back in the day, you would have done differently," he says sardonically. "What has happened to this country?" The client threatens to switch to another company, one that will "do as I want" and employs men who are "man enough." Luckily for Brian, the police arrive shortly afterward and take over.

. . .

In this vignette, the first incident shows how two citizens show concern for the welfare of the vagrant, frown on the use of coercion and intimidation, and remind Brian that violence is no longer socially acceptable. The usage of the word "anymore" indicates a change from a previous order. The second incident depicts a different situation: The use of force and punishment is actively demanded; reference is made to "back in the day," presumably a period when a different mandate existed that tolerated coercion; and the client expresses frustration about the current state of affairs. These two incidents, which occurred within a few hours of each other, highlight an ongoing struggle between public demands for a forceful approach to policing reminiscent of the apartheid era and the policing style envisioned by the post-apartheid state, which promotes human rights and democratic policing. Although these episodes occurred in white suburbia, this tension is experienced among all classes and races, with similar views expressed in many of Durban's black and Indian townships.

The "old school" and "new school" modes of policing are widely regarded as opposite ends of a spectrum: The former is seen as authoritative, efficient, and "hard;" the latter as democratic, inefficient, and "soft." Between these two ends lies a field of possibilities marked by friction to which each actor in the policing panoply is exposed. This indeterminate status alludes to an ongoing quest for the "right" style of policing, which as Marks and Wood point out, is "at a crossroads" (2010: 323), and plays a large role in shaping the uncertainty and ambiguity that define twilight policing.

This chapter, which presents the contextual background of twilight policing, has two objectives. The first one is to examine the development of policing and security in South Africa over the last few decades, with a particular focus on the role of the private security industry. This examination reveals that alliances and connections between public and private policing bodies are not new phenomena. The second objective is to analyze the transition currently taking place in South African policing, which exists in a space between eradication of the "old" and implementation of the "new." The dissonance between the old school versus the new South Africa shows that South Africa is home to competing discourses about the "right" style of policing, particularly concerning the use of violence. Twilight policing is a manifestation of this contestation, a surfacing of uncertainties and various forms of "in betweenness."

This chapter has a chronological structure. The first section examines the militarized and repressive policing style of the apartheid state and looks at how race has determined citizens' experiences of state policing. The second section analyzes the emergence of the private security industry, which supplemented apartheid policing through various forms of legislation and social networks. These two sections show that nonstate and state policing in South Africa have operated side by side, and often interchangeably, for decades. The third section focuses on the transition period of the early 1990s, which was marked both by the implementation of new policing strategies that centered on democratic and community policing approaches and by the boom of the private security industry. This section highlights the uncertainty and instability of South Africa's political transition and shows how this ambiguity was the main source of the private security industry's exponential growth. The fourth section presents a brief overview and analysis of contemporary policing and shows that policing strategies are fiercely debated in South Africa. It discusses current predicaments faced by the South African state, particularly its public perception and legitimacy, the debate surrounding the "shoot to kill" policy, and the private security industry's transition from a "club to a business" (Singh 2008). The chapter concludes with a short discussion of how historical and contemporary processes in South Africa shape the context in which twilight policing is performed.

APARTHEID POLICING

Any contemporary analysis of South African policing must incorporate the structural impact of the apartheid regime in order to show how apartheid racially segregated South African society and how policing bodies maintained this segregation.

Racial Segregation

Officially implemented in 1948 when the National Party (NP) came to power, apartheid had the fundamental goal of segregating races in political, economic, cultural, and social spheres. During apartheid, race was the "overriding feature of all facets of life in the society" (Posel 2001b: 65). Various laws, such as the Urban Areas Act (1923), the Population Registration Act (1950), and the Group Areas Act (1950), legally constructed the notion of race, which divided South Africans into four categories: White/European, Colored, Asian, and African/Native.[1] The term "Black" referred to all non-Whites. Although there was a strong biological basis for apartheid's racial classification, Posel argues that race is a sociolegal concept. Before 1948, race was not deemed to be a fixed category, but was a "legal and bureaucratic construct" (2001a: 92) that was largely determined by one's social standing. After 1948, however, state efforts aimed to create fixed and uniform standards of race as an imperative constituent of the nation-building process. Nevertheless, social factors permeated this classificatory process, so that it incorporated education levels, speech, and general appearance.

Although all state bodies played a part in the implementation of apartheid ideology, responsibility for maintaining racial segregation fell chiefly to the state police (Gordon 2006). Established in 1913, the South African Police (SAP) was based on a colonial model that was highly militarized from its inception (Brewer 1994; Brogden and Shearing 1993; Marks 2005). After apartheid was officially implemented in 1948, state policing came to focus increasingly on race relations, race control, and political policing. As segregationist policies were implemented throughout the 1950s, black political resistance against the regime escalated, leading to the notorious Sharpeville massacre of March 1960, when the SAP opened fire and killed sixty-nine protesters. In April 1960, the two main liberation movements—the African National Congress (ANC) and the Pan-Africanist Congress (PAC)—were banned. In the decades that followed, however, underground movements flourished, and exiled communities were instrumental in strengthening international opposition to the apartheid regime. Protests such as the Natal Strikes of 1973 and the Soweto uprising of 1976 tested the power and authority of the nationalists. As resistance increased, however, so did police brutality, and ruthless methods, such as torture, were commonly used (Beinart 2001; Brewer 1994). The militarization of the state police particularly intensified during the 1980s when resistance against the regime spread.

Policing during apartheid therefore focused on maintaining a racist political and social order and not on crime prevention or investigation. State policing served the white minority with Blacks policed in order to protect white privilege. Seventy-five percent of the country's police stations were concentrated in white areas, and those that did exist in black areas were vastly under-resourced (Shaw 2002: 11). As Shaw states, "Black people were policed for control and not crime prevention; the police aimed to prevent crime in white areas not by reducing it in black areas but by preventing the uncontrolled movement of black people" (2002: 1).

Policing in the townships largely revolved around the enforcement of "pass laws," which controlled the movement of Blacks into white areas, and of laws that focused on social behavior, such as liquor and tax laws (Brogden and Shearing 1993: 63). Because the violence in the townships did not threaten Whites, it was largely disregarded (Kynoch 2005). The result was that Whites and non-Whites experienced policing very differently, as highlighted by Steinberg:

> And so blacks and whites lived in parallel worlds. White people assumed that providing security was the role of the state. Black people knew that if they wanted security, they would have to acquire it themselves, whether in exchange for money, or neighbourliness, or ethnic and political solidarity. (2008: 161)

Because of the lack of state police engagement in crime prevention, various forms of nonstate policing flourished in the townships, including self-defense units of the ANC, street committees, gangs, and people's courts (Glaser 2000, 2005; Kynoch 1999; Schärf 1989). Violence went hand in hand with protection and was rife in the townships. Although the violence was not always connected to political resistance, it was labeled as "political" (Kynoch 2005). And because violence maintained disorder in the townships, it did not pose a real threat to the security forces, but was exploited to promote further internal power struggles and divisions (Gordon 2006: 68).

Self-Governance and State Proxies

In addition to the Group Areas Act of 1950, which segregated residential areas according to race, the apartheid state created self-governing homelands, also known as tribal reserves and "Bantustans," some of which some were independent.[2] The police were responsible for the relocation of Africans to their designated residential areas and homelands (Brewer 1994: 225). The Bantustans were governed by tribal structures, and power was exercised through traditional chiefs. In KwaZulu, the Inkatha Freedom Party (IFP), a Zulu cultural-nationalist organization led by Chief Mangosuthu Buthelezi, maintained control through a highly centralized government that operated predominantly through networks of patronage. With the creation of these homelands, policing was decentralized to homeland police forces.

During the 1980s, violence—both resistance and state suppression—reached new heights. With the exiled ANC threatening to make the townships "ungovernable," the apartheid state declared a state of emergency in thirty-six magisterial districts on July 21, 1985. To suppress the burgeoning resistance movement, Prime Minister P. W. Botha implemented a "dual strategy" (Hornberger 2011: 27). The first part, known as the "total strategy," placed the military in charge of security, allowing it to penetrate everyday life in the townships (Cawthra 2003; Cock and Nathan 1989). The second part focused on seeking legitimacy for the state among the non-white population by winning their "hearts and minds." In alignment with the notion of self-governance manifested in the Bantustans, the Black Local Authority Act of 1982 was implemented "to devolve the government of black townships to local authorities without resources, capacity or legitimacy" (Marks 2005: 46).

This act paved the way for the creation of the black municipal police, better known as the "Community Guards" or "Blackjacks." The Blackjacks were employed by local councils to protect black councilors (state officials) and municipal property in the townships. Their main objective was the enforcement of the pass laws (Brogden and Shearing 1993). They received much more rudimentary police training than white police officers and were not allowed to carry firearms. In addition, Special Constables, popularly known as "Kitskonstabels" (instant constables), were introduced in 1986 to further support the black municipal police. Together, the Blackjacks and Kitskonstabels conducted the bulk of the black-on-black policing in the townships, functioning as the prime executors of brutal policing tactics (Brewer 1994: 305; Brogden and Shearing 1993: 83; Fine 1989).

The main explanation given by the state for the creation of these black police forces was a shortage of manpower. However, as Brogden and Shearing have argued, these black police were also "a part of the game plan designed to confuse and conceal the reality of everyday policing in South Africa from both local and international audiences" (1993: 69).

Recruiting black police officers eliminated the negative publicity accruing from international news footage of white police officers attacking blacks; it enabled images of police violence to be framed as "black-on-black violence." The violence exacerbated by the increase in attacks on black policemen at the end of the 1980s forced the government to move them to police barracks outside the townships (Brewer 1994; Hornberger 2011).

In addition to these formally established black policing bodies, which functioned as "satellites of the SAP" (Shaw 2002: 13), the apartheid state also supported vigilante groups that were instigators of violence. Vigilante groups that were directly supported by the SAP and local councils were known as the "third force" (Brewer 1994; Brogden and Shearing 1993: 85; Ellis 1998; Minnaar 1992).[3] The homeland police, vigilante groups, and black policing bodies functioned as allies of the apartheid state police (Hornberger 2011; Marks 2005). The "ungovernability" strategy of the ANC and the militarized brutality of the state police (exerted through its satellites in the townships) not only intensified violence in the townships but also created divisions between those supporting the liberation movements and those aligned with the apartheid state. The most common method of killing in the townships, known as *necklacing*, whereby a tire filled with gasoline was placed around a person's neck and then set on fire, became a notorious and ruthless form of murder.

Thus, although ostensibly designed to promote self-governance, the policing strategies in fact served as a means for the apartheid state to police the townships indirectly and from "a distance" (Hansen 2006: 281). The black experience of state policing in the townships during the apartheid era was predicated on encounters with the state's proxies: the Blackjacks, black homeland police officers, Kitskonstabels, and vigilantes.

THE PRIVATE SUPPLEMENT TO THE STATE

A wide range of actors executed policing in the townships. Some were political figures, while others were criminals; some were aligned to the apartheid state, while others were fighting to overthrow it. Townships were riven by violence, which went largely unnoticed in the white areas protected by white policemen. Furthermore, the private security industry played a large role in supporting the apartheid state; that is, in protecting white privilege.

The growth of the private security industry directly correlated with the widening protests by liberation movements and the increasing repression by the apartheid state (Grant 1989; Irish 1999; Shaw 2002; Singh 2008). Before the 1970s, private security companies operated only in rural areas and on industrial sites. Private security was particularly prominent in the mining industry, a large part of South Africa's economy and a drive of migrant labor of black workers from across the country (Beinart 2001; Brogden and Shearing 1993; Philip 1989). Security in the mining industry was primarily provided through in-house security, with guards employed and trained by the mining companies themselves (Philip 1989: 214). This was in contrast to contract security, which involves contracting a third party, such as a company, to provide security services, the more common form of security provision in contemporary South Africa. By the mid-1970s, approximately ten private security companies were operating in Durban, and by the end of the 1980s, such companies conducted the vast majority of policing in white areas.[4]

The National Key Points Act (NKPA)

With state forces increasingly called on to deal with political unrest throughout the country, supplementary manpower was needed on the ground. After an upsurge in strategic attacks by the ANC, such as the hit on a fuel plant outside Johannesburg (Shearing and Berg 2006: 201), there was a desperate need for additional security that would not deplete state resources. This need was primarily met by extracting resources from the "crime prevention sector" (Cawthra 2003; Shaw 2002). Through various new laws, tasks that had previously fallen under the remit of the state police were handed over to the private sector (Brogden and Shearing 1993; Grant 1989; Irish 1999; Singh 2008).

One of the most important new laws was the establishment of the National Key Points Act (NKPA) 102 of 1980. The NKPA stipulated that responsibility for security provision (predominantly guarding) at strategic sites deemed crucial for national security should be transferred to the management/owners of these sites. The Minister of Defence determined which sites were to be labeled as National Key Points (NKPs). Although the task of providing security was reassigned to private individuals, authority and control remained in the hands of the state.[5] The South African state used the manpower and public funds freed up by this move to strengthen the armed forces, while simultaneously maintaining control over the private agents now overseeing its strategic sites. Private security firms (and the individuals they employed) formed alliances with the state. As Grant (1989: 109) stated a few years after the NKPA's introduction, "The National Key Points Act is clearly part of the security apparatus of the state."

For private security firms, the protection of NKP sites demanded the use of paramilitary skills and tactics. The work was highly lucrative and "propelled the security firms into elite status" (Singh 2008: 44). The National Key Points Act thus played a key role in the emergence of private security in the form of "firms" that were "managed by former policemen or soldiers who maintain[ed] formal and informal contacts with the SAP" (Prior 1989: 198).

The Security Officers Act (SOA)

The collaborative relationship between the private security industry and the apartheid state was further strengthened by the passage of the Security Officers Act (SOA) of 1987 and the accompanying creation of the Security Officers Board (SOB). The SOA was "a framework for the extension of the network of a state-corporate 'partnership' policing further into civil society" (Brogden and Shearing 1993: 72). After a period of exponential growth in the private security industry during the 1980s, there were increasing demands for a formal regulation system. Such a system was particularly needed for the purposes of monitoring and controlling security officers, who were predominantly black males, as shown in the following quote of a white man who owned a guarding company at the time:

> You see, during the 1980s, when the ANC went crazy with planting bombs all over the place, and on strategic places too, things changed, the industry exploded. There was once a bomb explosion on Smith Street outside the White House, you know that building where they used to renew the *dom passes*[6] . . . well . . . yes, I happened to be in the area and I immediately. . . . You see, I have a military background, so my natural instinct is to go to these places, not run away from them. Anyways, I drove to the site and quickly noticed that the watchman[7] that usually worked on that site was missing. Now everyone, including the police, assumed he was dead, but I knew better. He was ANC—a spy. You see, in that time, the ANC was smart, they knew that watchmen were posted at important sites, strategic for the South African government, and they infiltrated this sector. Four out of the 27 bombs that went off in Durban, planted by the ANC, were on my sites, I worked those sites . . . and in all of them, the guard was involved, they were ANC . . . they used many ways to enter the industry to attack the South African government. For ex-

ample, they would go to jail, pay bail for some criminal, and then force him to work as a guard, as a spy for the ANC. . . . This is how it all got started, the SOB; we needed a way to screen the guys coming in. We needed to know that these guys were okay, and not going to bomb the sites where we had our money coming in.[8]

To overcome this "political problem," company owners used their collective contacts within the SAP to set up an informal screening system whereby the SAP would assess potential employees to determine their viability for employment by a private security company. As time passed, this informal system was formalized by the then Minister of Law and Order through the SOA (Grant 1989: 107). The main goal of the SOA was to monitor and regulate the employees in the industry through the oversight of the Security Officers Board (SOB). The act entailed compulsory registration with the SOB and laid down rules regarding disqualification and withdrawal of registration. The SOA was thus the first step toward state regulation of the industry, currently implemented and enforced by the Private Security Industry Regulatory Authority (PSIRA). In this period, however, regulation symbolized a partnership between the public and the private.

Armed Response: "Techies" and "One-Man Shows"

The NKPA primarily affected the guarding sector, but other parts of the industry, such as the armed response sector, also grew because of the increasing political pressure on state law enforcement. The armed response sector emerged in the late 1970s through "techies": companies that installed alarms for commercial businesses. Armed response began as a basic system: Alarms were connected to phones that sent messages to the nearest police station in the event of an activation. Clients were referred to as *key holders*, and although they sometimes received the alarm notifications, the vast majority of those notifications were diverted to police stations, which then sent officers to the sites in question. Because of the high percentage of false alarms and the shortage of manpower in the SAP, particularly in the 1980s, there was a call for change, as a white former owner of an armed response company recalled:

The system in the 70s, early 80s, it was quite rudimentary and simple, and the amount of false alarms were great, and the police being under pressure, as they were at that time . . . attending to alarms wasn't high on their list of priorities, and you could never prove that the police in fact got the call . . . so . . . it left quite a big void in the market.[9]

Recognizing this vacuum, existing companies developed a system that no longer required the assistance of the police, who warmly welcomed this innovation. One company, Chubb, established a system known as the *warden service*, whereby key holders were notified of an alarm activation and then contacted Chubb Security, which instructed a warden to go to the residence along with the key holder. Other companies slowly adopted this system. The wardens, who were often company owners, were the first form of armed response as we know it today. Other companies directly employed individuals specifically for this purpose:

> So we employed these individuals to do an armed response; instead of getting the key holder to meet a warden on the premises, we would send our armed-reaction guy around; he was armed and he would do an investigation. Rather than having two people go to the site, we reckoned it would be easier to just have one, and have him officially linked to us, the company. And we wanted to make it easier for the client. . . . If he could see a positive break-in, he would come back to the control room, this would be put on radio and the control room would then get hold of the key holder and the police. . . . If it was a false alarm or [there was] no visible sign of entry, we would just record it and the customer would get a history of what happened.[10]

Thus, the armed response business was initiated by companies that initially specialized in the technical side of security and only later made the move to providing armed reaction services. This stands in contrast to the second type of entrant into the market: the "one-man shows" that emerged in the mid-1980s. These largely comprised ex-policemen or ex-SADF soldiers who served a handful of clients using their own vehicles and firearms.[11] One of the companies with which I worked closely started as a one-man show. The owner was a police reservist who decided to establish his own business. For ideological reasons, the company began as a free service available to all citizens. But as word spread and more and more people sought the owner's assistance, the company gradually converted citizens into "clients" and expanded into alarm installation.

The armed reaction sector thus started with two types of companies: the techies and the one-man shows. By the end of the 1980s, both forms existed, and several companies were created through a fusion of the two. A handful of established companies—Total Highway Security, Rennies, Chubb, ET, Night Guard, Cobra, and Contact—provided a service that was referred to as "armed reaction." Unlike the guarding sector, the growth of the armed response sector was not directly supported by legislation, but it was promoted by police officers on the same basis: It released police officers from particular tasks, particularly in the crime prevention sector, allowing them to concentrate on the job of maintaining racial segregation.

The "Old Boys' Network"

The political and financial connections between the industry and the apartheid state—at both national and local levels of policing—created and maintained an "old boys' network" (Singh 2008) of social relations among white men operating within the industry and the apartheid armed forces. Singh (2008: 43) describes this network as a "club" where "membership was exclusive and largely restricted at the administrative levels to those with police, intelligence and military backgrounds." The South African Security Association (SASA), established in 1965, was a direct manifestation of the old boys' network. SASA functioned as a type of "gentlemen's club" whose membership was limited to larger firms (Grant 1989).[12]

As in the state armed forces, the representative face of the private security industry was a white man with a military or policing background; the private security sector was a white man's world. At the outset, the industry comprised white expatriates from Kenya, Zimbabwe, and Zambia who had served in colonial police forces and immigrated to South Africa after those states became independent (Shaw 2002: 112; Singh 2008). The industry was therefore initially an English-speaking domain, but this changed significantly during the 1980s because of the state's favoritism displayed toward Afrikaner SADF and SAP personnel. As time passed, soldiers from the SADF and police officers from the SAP entered the private security industry, a process referred to as "poaching," and the sector became increasingly Afrikaans (Shaw 2002: 112; Singh 2008). Brogden and Shearing (1993: 72–73) cite a pamphlet from a private security company operating in Johannesburg in 1989 to illustrate how most companies were made up of former police officers. The pamphlet depicts a tough and sturdy man wearing a police-like uniform with the caption of "super Cop." The owner of the company states, "I employ only ex-policemen-trained professionals. We drive around in black cars with tinted windscreens. Our guys are good-looking, people you can trust."

Because former policemen dominated the industry, there were numerous similarities between the public and private forces. Through a review of newspaper articles and reports, Brogden and Shearing (1993: 72–73) demonstrate how private security companies used comparable equipment to the SAP and SADF and operated similarly, particularly with regard to their racist policies and the use of force. Because they were former colleagues, private and public police officers were quick to cooperate. Although working for different agencies, they shared the same objective: to safeguard white privileges. The old boys' network thus resulted from and further facilitated the entrance of former policemen and soldiers into the industry (Shaw 2002; Singh 2008).

Taken together, the National Key Points Act, the Security Officers Act, the evolution of the armed response sector, and the creation of the old boys' network testify to the history of alliances and connections between the public and private armed forces, which had the common aim of protecting white property and privilege. Private security firms provided logistical, technical, and personnel support to the SAP (Brogden and Shearing 1993: 73), which often relied on the extensive surveillance activities of the private sector (Philip 1989). The private security industry was regarded as the "major 'hidden' supplement to the state police" (Brogden and Shearing 1993: 71). Although profit making was the prime motivation for private security companies, many chose to identify with the discourse of state sovereignty rather than framing themselves in market-based terms (Singh 2008: 44).

THE TRANSITION ERA: CHANGE AND UNCERTAINTY

As should now be apparent, in the late 1980s and early 1990s, policing in white and non-white areas was fundamentally different. In white areas, the state police provided protection and security—primarily by containing the violence in the black townships—and the private security industry supported the maintenance of white privilege. Although rarely on the receiving end, whites were aware of the *"skop, skiet, donder"* (kick, shoot, and thunder) mentality that prevailed among the state police and generally perceived it as an efficient policing style. In the townships, meanwhile, violence was the norm, stirred by actors who were either aligned with the state or striving to overthrow it.

Democratic Policing

The post-apartheid state aimed to transform this divergent experience of policing by eliminating the oppressive practices and reputation of the existing system and creating a state police that served all South Africans. During the first years of transition (1990–94), policing was a top priority, and when the ANC assumed power in 1994, the security sector required large-scale reform. The new state police was formed through the amalgamation of eleven different police forces: the SAP, the police forces of the "independent states," and the agencies that policed the six "self-governing homelands," such as KwaZulu.[13] The amalgamation was a complex and often volatile process. Not only were relations between officers strained by past differences but varying levels of training also complicated the integration of the various members into a unified force, as one Indian police officer recalled:

> It was difficult, then. Many might say now that it wasn't a big deal, but it was. We had to force our mind to think differently; we had to learn how to work with our former enemy, and trust him, for back up. Different cultures, languages, skills, styles, everything was different. And for the first few years, it was rough. And I think we're still dealing with it; it isn't over yet.[14]

Under the South African Police Service Act of 1995, the name of the police force changed from the South African Police (SAP) to the South African Police Service (SAPS). Several watchdog organizations were established to monitor police behavior, such as the Independent Complaints Directorate (ICD), which was set up to investigate police misconduct (Hornberger 2011: 44). The 1996 National Crime Prevention Strategy (NCPS) and the 1998 White Paper on Safety and Security mandated a state focus on law enforcement, social crime prevention, visible policing, service delivery, institutional reform at the national level, and policing at provincial and local levels (Cawthra 2003; Shaw 2002). The NCPS envisioned a "multi-agency approach" (Singh 2008: 14) whereby the government would work alongside other actors, such as the private security industry and businesses, to combat crime. A new paradigm of policing thus emerged, one that "was not merely about transforming the police; it was also about transforming society *through* the police" (Hornberger 2011: 4, italics in original).

The main aim of the police force was to restore relationships with citizens, particularly non-white communities; this goal was encapsulated in the mantra of democratic and community policing. As thoroughly outlined in the government's Community Policing Policy Framework and Guidelines of 1997, community policing forums (CPFs) were created as platforms for direct engagement and communication between police officers and citizens. These forums centered on empowerment, accountability, and solving crime together with communities and were concentrated in areas that were previously neglected by the state (Cawthra 2003; Jensen 2008; Leggett 2005; Shaw 2002; Steinberg 2011; van der

Spuy 2000). Increasing police accountability and legitimacy would be the driving force, based on the premise that once the new police force was under political control and regained its legitimacy in formerly neglected areas, order would be restored (Shaw 2002).

The Boom of Private Security

The transformation of the SAP into the SAPS primarily revolved around improving legitimacy and accountability: Tackling crime was not seen as the core aim (Cawthra 2003; Shaw 2002). Yet as crime rates continued to rise after 1994, antigovernment sentiment intensified, and the government's response primarily focused on denying that crime was a problem. This failure to tackle crime was one of the main reasons for the exponential growth of the private security industry in the late 1980s and early 1990s. As influx controls broke down in the late 1980s and crime started entering the white suburbs, many Whites became fearful for their future; from their point of view, the change in government entailed a loss of economic privilege, a decline in political power, and a reduction in social status. Many feared the consequences of the national elections of 1994 and demanded immediate protection from Blacks, who seemed set to spill over into the suburbs seeking revenge (Shaw 2002). Private security companies readily provided this protection.

Private security was increasingly seen as indispensable for the white minority, who were the main users of such services. Assessing the situation in 1993, Brogden and Shearing stated that "private security companies . . . have assumed much of the day-to-day policing of the white suburbs" (73). Because of the movement of many policemen to the private sector, clients often equated private security with the police. In the eyes of many clients, the change from a public to a private security body entailed little more than a change in uniform (Brogden and Shearing 1993: 73; Shaw 2002). And because the state police had served them well, they held similar confidence in the private security industry. This was especially true for the armed response sector, which experienced a rapid growth during this period, as one white company owner explained:

> Armed reaction really grew then, and it was just on the back of fear. Nelson Mandela had been released, ANC was unbanned, and everybody thought that everybody was going to come through the front doors and get rid of all the whites in the country. And electronic security, armed reaction, realized a growth; I don't think this country will ever see that type of growth again. It was huge, absolutely massive. I remember that we had people phoning us all

the time, asking for alarms. We just couldn't handle it; we had to recruit new guys everyday to keep with the growth. It was unbelievable.[15]

After the boom of the early 1990s, armed reaction companies seemed to be everywhere. A white former owner of an armed response company recalled, "In the mid 1990s, around '96 or so, there was virtually a different armed reaction company on every street corner."[16] The continuous demand for private security was matched by a growing number of suppliers, including both former police officers and ex-combatants who had not been merged into the new armed forces. Several chose to work for private military companies operating abroad, but many entered private security domestically (Cock 2005; Mashike 2008).

CONTEMPORARY SOUTH AFRICAN POLICING

The 1990s thus constituted a decade of transformation and uncertainty. In this section, I examine how the situation has changed since then by reflecting on recent crime trends, the highly debated "shoot to kill" policy, and the transformation of the private security industry from a "club to a business" (Singh 2008: 43).

Crime Statistics: A "Commodified Knowledge"

Crime remains a serious problem in contemporary South Africa, and combating crime is regarded as a national priority by the state and citizens. Perhaps the biggest change over the past decade is that the "crime problem" is no longer denied or masked.[17] The management of crime statistics and their accessibility to the general public remain a sensitive issue. In 2000, the Ministry of Safety and Security imposed a moratorium on the release of crime statistics, stating that they were not valid and reliable. The moratorium was lifted a year later, but the release of crime statistics remains a widely contested issue, and citizens regularly feel that they are being "left in dark" and "lied to."[18] Comaroff and Comaroff highlight how crime statistics have become "commodified knowledge" (2006b: 210) in South Africa, where citizens regard statistics as "information as an inalienable right" (222). This also became apparent during my fieldwork, in which citizens vigorously discussed crime statistics when they were released.

In this section I do not present a comprehensive analysis of South Africa's crime statistics, but instead outline a few relevant trends.[19] In

2010–11, there were 44 murders, 181 sexual offenses, 278 aggravated robberies, and 678 burglaries per day in South Africa (Lebone 2012: 708). These figures seem very high, but in fact, since 1994, the overall rate of serious crime in South Africa has decreased by 20 percent, murder rates have dropped by 52 percent, and attempted murder rates have fallen by 55 percent (Lebone 2012: 708).[20] Recent victimization studies also show signs that the crime situation is improving, with a general overall decline since 2007 (Statistics South Africa 2011: 27). Of South African households polled between 2008–10, more than 40 percent believed that violent and nonviolent crime rates had decreased, while 35 percent believed there had been an increase (2011: 2). Furthermore, the Victims of Crime Survey (VOCS) shows a continuous improvement in feelings of safety. In 2003, 23 percent felt of respondents reported feeling it was safe to walk alone in their area at night, with this figure rising to 37 percent in 2010. Likewise, in 2003, 85 percent felt it was safe to walk alone in their area during the day compared to 88.2 percent in 2010 (VOCS 2011: 8).

The increased sense of safety may suggest a reduction in crime rates, but this is not necessarily the case across the entire spectrum of crime. Some forms of crime, such as commercial crime (i.e., corruption, fraud, money laundering), have actually increased over the last decade. Crime has increased in another category—the so-called trio crimes, which include business robberies, carjackings, and house robberies. Figure 1 depicts trio crime rates in South Africa between 2002–03 and 2011–12. The graph shows an increase in all three types of crime from 2004–05 to 2008–09.[21] Between 2009–10 and 2011–12, there was a decrease in both house robberies (from 18,438 to 16,766) and carjackings (from 14,915 to 9,475), but business robberies continued to rise (from 13,920 to 15,951). Taking the whole period into consideration, we see that business robberies increased by 190 percent and house robberies by 85 percent, while carjackings decreased by 35 percent.

In this discussion, I focus on trio crimes as opposed to other crime categories (e.g., sexual violence) for two reasons. First, these crimes play the most prominent role in shaping people's perceptions of crime and safety, particularly because of their violent nature (Altbeker 2007; Burger, Gould, and Newham 2011; Shaw 2002). Such crimes have a deep impact, both directly, such as through the sudden loss of possessions or cash, and indirectly, such as through enduring emotional trauma. Approximately 53 percent of South African households believe that housebreaking and burglary are the most common types of crime (Sta-

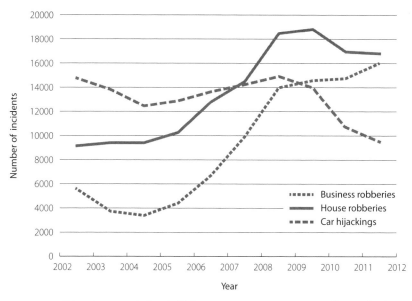

FIGURE 1. Trio crime rates in South Africa, 2002–2003 to 2011–2012. Source: Institute for Security Studies (ISS).

tistics South Africa 2011: 2). In 2011, home robbery was both the most commonly experienced and the most feared form of crime in South Africa (4).

The second reason for my focus on trio crimes is the link between them and the private security industry. Trio crimes are precisely the forms of felony that the private security industry is intended to combat, and they are therefore those that private security officers are confronted with most often. Furthermore, as the incidence of these crimes continues to rise, the demand for private security services also looks set to increase.[22] The continuous growth of the industry is thus closely tied to the rise in rates of trio crimes.

"Shoot to Kill"

On August 16, 2012, the South African state police opened fire on striking platinum miners, killing thirty-four and injuring seventy-eight. The incident, hereafter referred to as the "Marikana Massacre," grabbed news headlines across the globe and raised questions about the nature of public order policing in South Africa. Numerous media reports declared the episode the most lethal use of force by the state police since apartheid.

Debates centered on why the police officers opened fire and whether it was a case of self-defense or an outright attack on the strikers. Concerns about the use of force by police officers became even more pressing in late February 2013, when video footage was released that showed a Mozambican taxi driver being handcuffed to the back of a police vehicle and dragged through the streets. The man in question was later found dead in a police cell.

These incidents, along with many others that have not received international attention, prompt concerns about the use of force by the state police (Jensen 2014). The constant references made by journalists and analysts to the apartheid era signal an identification with the past. Policing in the new South Africa is ostensibly aimed at eliminating the oppressive practices and reputation of the state, yet the Marikana Massacre and other incidents force us to question whether state policing has indeed been transformed over the last two decades. Steinberg (2008, 2011) argues that the South African state police are unable to win consent from citizens, and as a means of gaining legitimacy and displaying authority, they are increasingly resorting to paramilitary methods reminiscent of the apartheid state. Hornberger (2013), in contrast, argues that it is the "proactive part that people play in compelling police officers to enact features of an authoritarian state" (605) that is fundamental to understanding the re-militarization of the South African state police.

Throughout 2010 and 2011, the news media provided extensive coverage of a bill in parliament proposing amendments to Section 49 of the Criminal Procedure Act that would expand police power to permit the use of lethal force when making an arrest. It was popularly known as the "shoot to kill" policy. Like the discordance between old school policing and policing of the new South Africa, there were both public outcry and support for these amendments. Support centered on the need to provide the police with more power (particularly legal power) to arrest criminals and effectively combat crime. The potential amendments were also touted as a means to decrease police fatalities, of which there were one hundred between 2009 and 2010 (Bruce 2011: 40).

There is a dominant perception among citizens and police in South Africa that criminals have more power than the police, that the South African constitution cares more for criminals than police officers, and that the state is generally too liberal and lenient. "Human rights policing" practices are seen as antithetical to the development of a penal state capable of effectively addressing crime (Comaroff and Comaroff 2006b; Hornberger 2011; Jensen 2014). The use of force is regarded as a key factor in empowering police officers and enabling them to acquire legitimacy. In my field-work, every police officer, regardless of race and rank, voiced feelings of inadequacy, fear, and powerlessness in combating crime. More specifically, many expressed reluctance to attend particular crime scenes for safety reasons and fear of potential retaliation from criminals. The following quote from an Indian police officer portrays this fear:

> This whole shoot to kill thing in the media, it's bullshit. Policemen are shit scared to do anything. I can give you so many examples of policemen who will not attend a crime, like an armed robbery, in progress, because they're too scared. They'll wait till it's over, till the suspects are long gone. They know that if they go, and something happens that can be questioned, they'll have to put up with the shit. I've seen so many cases of suspects accusing police officers of theft. If any shooting occurs, there's an investigation; in the meantime, the policeman isn't being paid, or has to wait in jail. How is he supposed to feed his family? So many of us think: I'm gonna avoid the heat, come in later, and save my ass! Criminals are treated better than we are, with all this talk of human rights. It's like our hands are cuffed, not theirs.[23]

In her work on the public order police in Durban, Marks (2005) notes how officers still reminisce fondly about apartheid policing practices, with some claiming that they were more efficient and therefore preferable. Hornberger (2011) analyzes "nostalgic talk" among state police officers as a means to understand how they construct "the past in direct reaction to the present" (104). Such talk, she claims, shows how police officers believe(d) their use of violence in the past meant that they were "respected" and effective.

Yet the "shoot to kill" policy not only evoked support but also unleashed an outcry, with opponents worrying that its more repressive policing would exacerbate the current police abuse of force, corruption, and misconduct. This potential result was particularly worrying because there were 1,092 fatalities due to the use of force by police officers between 2008 and 2010, the highest number since the creation of the Independent Complaints Directorate (ICD) in the late 1990s (Bruce 2011: 3). The increasing militarization of the police also points toward a revival of apartheid ways. In April 2010, the South African Police Service put in place a new ranking structure that resembled the pre-1995 military rank system, in which senior superintendents became colonels, directors became brigadiers, and the commissioner became general once again (Hornberger 2013).

These divergent responses to the "shoot to kill" policy highlight the contrasting public perceptions on how to police South Africa. Similar to my analysis of the old versus the new, Jensen (2014) argues that contemporary South African policing is characterized by two "conflicting logics of exceptionality." A need to reform the police coexists with a need to tackle the crime problem, yet both rely on contrasting logics of exceptionality that demand extraordinary measures.

From "Club to Business"

The militarization of the state police and increasing public demands for more forceful policing have also affected other policing agents, such as the private security industry. Since the political transition in 1994, the industry has experienced continuous growth, as can be seen in Figure 2, which shows the number of private security companies operating in South Africa between 2001 and 2011.[24] The decrease in the number of companies between 2001 and 2004 was due to mergers within the industry (discussed further in Chapter 3) and does not imply a reduction in security provision.

In addition to this growth, the industry has been transformed from a "club to a business" (Singh 2008: 43). During the transition and after 1994, the post-apartheid government viewed the private security sector with suspicion, seeing it as part of the old order, and feared that it would foster the development of private militias bent on overthrowing the ANC government (Shaw 2002; Singh 2008). This was particularly true for the SOA, which was seen as a partnership between the industry and the old state that served to protect "the economic interests of a white-dominated and controlled industry" (Minnaar 2005: 95).

To further tighten control over the industry, the Private Security Industry Regulation Act No. 56 of 2001 expanded regulation over the industry and created the Private Security Industry Regulatory Authority (PSIRA) as that regulatory body. PSIRA introduced numerous changes from the regulatory regime under the Security Officers Act (SOA), such as requiring in-house security forces, locksmiths, and private investigators to register with the state (Berg 2003). Yet a more profound change concerned the relationship between the industry and the state. Whereas the SOA was regarded as a partnership between the two bodies, PSIRA was conceived as an industry watchdog. Numerous employees in the industry—particularly those who experienced the SOA's provisions firsthand—felt that the government had hijacked the SOA and taken away its opportunities for input, which was a cornerstone of the SOA (see Chapter 5).

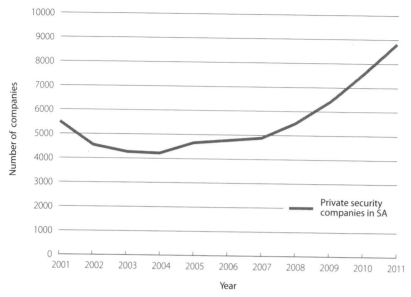

FIGURE 2. Registered private security providers in South Africa, 2001–2011.
Source: PSIRA Annual Reports.

In addition to increasing regulation, the state also aimed to change the racial composition of the industry, in which the majority of owners and managers of companies were white. In 1996, the then-general secretary of the Black Security Companies Owners Association, Steve Dube, declared that Blacks only held approximately 4 percent of the top positions in the industry (Irish 2000: 25). In response, the post-apartheid state implemented various efforts to "de-whiten" the industry by increasing access for non-white workers. The government also promoted partnerships and mergers between small black-owned companies and larger white-owned companies, and there were cases of black-owned companies buying out their white-owned competitors (Irish 1999).

Despite their apparently democratic intentions, many of these buyouts and mergers were (and still are) viewed by many industry personnel as strategic alliances on behalf of white former owners to win government contracts, rather than as dedicated efforts to change the racial imbalances of the security industry. Since 1994, government contracts have proven to be very lucrative, especially for companies with a racially diverse or non-white racial composition (Irish 1999). Companies have often been accused of putting on a "black face" to win such contracts; in these cases, a firm may employ a black chairman, but control remains

in the hands of the previous (white) owners. During my research, many
informants accused several black owners I knew of being "puppets" for
white former owners.

Despite efforts to escape the legacies of apartheid, the industry remains racially imbalanced. The majority of management and high-paid
positions are still occupied by white men who employ a predominantly
non-white force of private security officers, particularly in the guarding
sector (Abrahamsen and Williams 2007). Thus, despite the changes of
the last two decades, the industry, particularly in terms of management,
remains a white-dominated one, as an informant emphasized:

> Private security is still a white man's world. It may function more as a busi-
> ness, but that army mentality is still deep in the minds of many. Former
> policemen are still valued higher than any *oak*,[25] and the black man is still
> seen as the guard, at the low end of it all. And it's gonna take a while before
> that is out, it really is.[26]

To acquire government support today, the discourse of private security
has changed. While state support was previously obtained by framing
security in terms of state sovereignty, it is now obtained by marketing
security as a commodity. However, many in the industry do not appreciate this transformation. For some, the "soul" of the business has disappeared, and the industry has become "cutthroat," steered by fierce
competition and "financial issues" rather than by "crime and passion."
The white owner of a guarding company once told me:

> The industry at the moment, it's cut-throat and vicious. You know, back in
> the day, it was all about fighting crime, helping people, you know, really putting
> your heart and soul into this business. Now it's a dog-eat-dog world; every-
> one wants their slice of the pie, and they want a big piece too. It's all about
> money, money, money. And these regulations—they are good intentions and
> they do help, I must admit that, but with every little thing you do, you have
> to write it down or they'll give you a fine. Back then, I would have encour-
> aged my children to get into the game, but now I say: don't even go there. If
> you want a happy, headache-free life, stay away from private security. Be-
> cause it will eat you up and spit you out! That I can promise you.[27]

The increasingly competitive nature of the industry is evident in the large
number of employers' associations. There are currently thirty-eight such
associations in South Africa (Shearing and Berg 2006: 203). Although
there have been numerous attempts to merge these groups into one
overarching organization, such as the South African Security Federation
(SASFED) in 1986 and the Security Industry Alliance (SIA) in 2003, these

umbrella organizations are widely regarded as inefficient. Rivalry between associations and companies, often initiated and prolonged by personal vendettas, hampers coordination within the industry.

CONCLUDING REMARKS

The year of 1994 heralded great change for South Africa. For the state police, the end of apartheid rule implied the transformation of a militarized police force that protected white privilege and controlled the movement of non-Whites into a force dedicated to democratic policing for all citizens. A similar, albeit less drastic, transformation occurred within the private security industry, which had previously aligned itself with and been endorsed by the apartheid state. Since 1994, the industry has evolved from a club to a business, with private security services now framed as a commodity rather than as a political instrument.

This chapter sought to provide a historical backdrop against which to understand the emergence of twilight policing. It showed that there have always been interconnections between state and nonstate policing in urban South Africa. During apartheid, the state created proxies to police the non-white population from a distance and established alliances with the private security industry as supplementary means to protect white privilege. The post-apartheid state also envisioned a "multi-agency approach" (Singh 2008: 14), yet one that was organized with transparent and democratic intentions. The post-apartheid state was initially suspicious of the private security industry, but today it is increasingly seen as a cooperating party. This shows that the relation between public and private policing cannot be adequately understood with recourse to simple dichotomies.

Furthermore, although South Africa may no longer be referred to as a society in transition, I argue that the public dispute over policing strategies and goals shows that South African policing is at a crossroads due to divergent attitudes about "who the police should be" (Marks and Wood 2010: 312). Tackling the crime problem may be a common objective, but it stands in opposition to other objectives (Jensen 2014). Furthermore, the means to reduce crime provoke contestation, particularly concerning the use of violence. The South African case shows the tribulations endured by transitional societies. It demonstrates how, in attempts to reconfigure the security sector, old structures and practices persevere and shape the "new"—and when the "new" fails to deliver the expected changes and crime statistics remain high, elements of the "old" are often brought back. I am not implying that apartheid state policing is universally venerated, yet its "efficiency" has not been forgotten and is something that is perceived to be lacking in contemporary policing.

Contemporary South African policing is filled with contesting policing practices, elements of the old and new that are marked by and reinforce uncertainty and contestation. And since the fight against crime has become increasingly pluralized, both state and nonstate bodies experience this uncertainty. As I show in the following chapters, twilight policing emerges from these contesting discourses, particularly regarding standpoints on the use of violence.

CHAPTER 3

"The Promising Horse"

The Armed Response Sector

August 2010

A team of four black armed reaction officers in company uniform are standing in a huddle, preparing themselves for the next test of their fitness. They've already completed the shooting competition, in which they had to shoot targets from five different positions, as well as the multiple-choice test on armed response theory. Their white manager is giving them a pep talk; he is telling them that they "must do well" and gives them tips on how to get through the obstacle course as fast as possible. Then, one by one, the officers set off along the course, which is dotted with tires, tracks, and walls, forcing them to run, jump, and climb. Their manager observes each man closely while the others cheer him on. At the end of their turns, each one is panting and catching his breath. Once everyone has completed the course, there's a break before the final test, the driving competition, where they'll have to demonstrate their skills in "precision and skid driving." Ultimately, each of them wants to earn the prestigious title of "Best Armed Reaction Man."

. . .

This vignette describes a scene from the Armed Reaction Man Competition, an annual event held in Johannesburg, in which teams of armed reaction officers from companies from across South Africa compete against each other. In 2010, seventeen four-member teams competed outside Pretoria at Zwartkops Raceway so that one of the winners could earn the prestigious title of "Best Armed Reaction Man." Throughout the day, I observed the different competitions and spoke to reaction officers, the organizers of the event from the South African Intruder Detection Services Association (SAIDSA), and owners and managers of the companies. When I left that evening to catch my flight back to Durban, I realized that this event served as a looking glass through which to examine the most prominent features of the occupational culture of the armed response sector.

The first such feature is the division between management and operations (i.e., the armed reaction officers). Throughout this event, they operated as two distinct entities, and hierarchy defined the minimal amount of interaction they had with each other. On the one hand, the owners expressed pity for the armed reaction officers, citing their poor working conditions and the dangers they faced in the line of duty. On the other hand, they used a rather condescending tone when discussing or talking to the officers, frequently complained about their recklessness, and highlighted the social and economic gap between themselves and their employees. This divide is further defined by race, the second key feature of the armed response sector. The vast majority of the owners in the sector (and perhaps the industry at large) are White, while the vast majority of the armed reaction officers are non-White. A third noticeable feature is the sexual composition of the participants: This was an armed reaction *man* competition, and women were an absolute minority. The male dominance of the sector leads to the (re)production of a macho subculture in which particular masculinities are cultivated and praised. In fact, these masculine attributes are used to measure and define what it means to be a "good" armed reaction officer.

These three building blocks—hierarchy, race, and gender—are the cornerstones of the occupational culture of the armed reaction sector and the performance of twilight policing. Various studies of private security have pointed to the existence of a private security occupational culture.[1] Similar to concepts developed in the field of public police studies (Chan 1997; Punch 1985; Reiner 2000; Westley 1970), this notion implies that particular practices, rules, justifications, and structures determine how policing is performed within and among policing bodies. However, as studies on the state police have also shown (O'Neill, Marks, and Singh 2007), the variation among officers, policing bodies, and contexts makes it problematic to speak of an occupational culture for the entire industry. In South Africa, there are many different types of private security officers, including security guards, national key point protection officers, cash-in-transit officers, private investigators, and bodyguards. Thus, to speak of a private policing occupational culture in South Africa ignores the diversity of the industry. Therefore, following O'Neill et al., I use the term "occupational culture" in a broad sense to refer to "the way things are done around here" (2007: 2).

The aim of this and the next chapter is to describe and analyze the numerous structures, processes, and practices that shape the armed response sector in Durban, South Africa. My first claim is that the armed reaction sector constitutes a specific niche of policing with its own distinct occupational culture, which I describe with reference to the industry at large. My second claim is that the occupational culture in which armed response officers operate is more similar to that of the state police than to that of other types of private security officers. Like Loyens (2009) and Rigakos (2002), I argue that these two policing bodies—the state and the private armed response sector—exhibit more similarities than differences. When reading Andrew Faull's (2010) stories about members of South Africa's state police, I was struck by the similarities with my own informants. The congruence with the public police is a core factor in the performance of twilight policing, because it shows how and why armed response officers are entering the public realm. By incorporating "languages of stateness" (Hansen and Stepputat 2001: 5), armed response officers are increasingly acting like the state police and finding themselves in the twilight zone. However, I do not structure this chapter according to the similarities and differences between the two policing bodies, as Loyens (2009) does, but make reference to the public police throughout.

This chapter thus analyzes how the occupational culture of the armed response sector cultivates particular traits that encourage armed response officers to enter the public sphere. It also looks at the companies and particular structures and practices of the sector that shape this occupational culture. The first section examines the different companies and the various factors that define how they operate. The second section focuses on the forms of discipline, control, and surveillance that companies exert over armed response officers. Such mechanisms divide the sector into distinct hierarchical categories, most notably those of management and operations. The third section analyzes how gender and race shape the armed response sector, arguing that, while the predominance of masculinities has a unifying effect, race accentuates the division between management and operations.

The next chapter delves more deeply into the lives, perspectives, and experiences of the armed response officers: It discusses their motivations, a typical day on the road, the different tools they are allowed to use on duty, and the occupational hazards they face. Although this chapter focuses on the perspectives of the companies and management and Chapter 4 on those of the armed response officers, the perceptions of these groups influence each other and are therefore discussed in both chapters. Taken together, these two chapters aim to provide an encompassing analysis of the occupational culture of armed response, out of which emerges the performance of twilight policing.

THE COMPANIES

Retrieved from PSIRA's Annual Reports, Figure 3 shows the growth in the number of registered security businesses in the three main sectors of the industry—guarding, armed reaction, and cash-in-transit—between 2005 and 2011. A cursory glance reveals that all sectors have experienced continuous annual growth and that guarding is the largest sector, followed by armed response and cash-in-transit.

Although Figure 3 shows more growth in the guarding sector than in either armed response or cash-in-transit between 2010 and 2011, members of the industry predict that the armed response sector will experience the greatest growth rates over the next few years. In fact, it grew 263.5 percent between 2005–10 (Lebone 2012: 802). The armed reaction sector is, as one key informant stated, "the promising horse" of the industry.[2] These expected growth rates are based on continuous technological progress, a steady demand for armed response, and an increase in both formal and informal partnerships with police officers (see Chapter 5) and community initiatives (see Chapter 6).[3]

Unfortunately, PSIRA does not provide provincial and sectorial breakdowns in its annual reports, which would tell us, for example, how many armed response companies are operating in each province or city. Using available data, I have calculated some rough estimates of the number of companies and officers working in the armed response sector in KwaZulu-Natal. In Table 1, the non-italicized figures are from PSIRA's annual reports, and the italicized figures are my own calculations. Although more recent figures are available, I chose to use the 2010 data to aid comparison with Table 2, which also uses data from 2010.

Let me explain how I arrived at these estimates. According to PSIRA, KwaZulu-Natal (KZN) is home to 16 percent of all security businesses (1,199 of 7,459). Applying the same ratio to the armed reaction sector (i.e., 16 percent of 2,701) yields an estimate of 432 armed reaction busi-

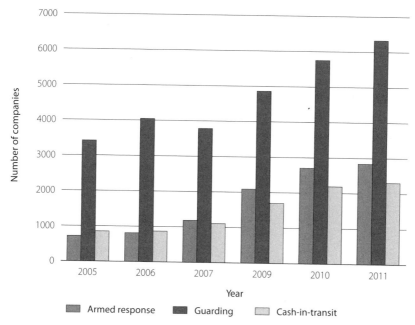

FIGURE 3. Registered security businesses per sector, 2005–2011. Source: PSIRA Annual Reports.

nesses in KwaZulu-Natal. The second calculation allows us to estimate the number of armed reaction officers. According to PSIRA, the armed reaction sector makes up 36.2 percent of the industry. Applying that percentage to the 387,273 registered security officers in South Africa, we come up with 140,193 armed reaction officers in South Africa (i.e., 36.2 percent of 387,273). If we apply the same ratio to the 65,323 registered active security officers in KwaZulu-Natal, then we can estimate that there are 23,646 armed reaction officers registered in the province.

When I discussed these results with my informants from different parts of the industry, all of them claimed that the figures were much too low. They estimated that there were between 600 and 900 companies providing armed response in KwaZulu-Natal. This disparity in our estimates, they argued, was due to the existence of unregistered companies. In the industry at large, such companies are referred to as "fly-by-nights" because these unregistered companies appear and disappear quickly. In 2010–11, 176 security service providers were labeled "untraceable" by PSIRA, and in the following year (2011–12), 122 providers were identified as such.

TABLE I THE ARMED REACTION SECTOR IN 2010

	Registered security providers	Armed reaction providers	Registered active security officers	Armed reaction officers
South Africa	7,459	2,701	387,273	140,193
KwaZulu-Natal	1,199	432	65,323	23,646

SOURCE: PSIRA reports and author's calculations.

Though prominent in the guarding sector, fly-by-nights are relatively rare in the armed response sector, primarily because of the large amount of startup capital needed for this kind of company. More common, however, are "bush companies" (i.e., companies that are not registered and that therefore operate in the "bush" to evade detection by PSIRA). Bush companies are similar to the "one-man shows" of the 1980s (i.e., companies operated by a single individual using his own vehicle and firearm); they operate in confined areas, often defined by a few street corners, and engage in violent turf wars with competing companies. For the purpose of this analysis, I ignore the bush companies and focus instead on the 400 known companies that we can assume exist.

Many in the industry—particularly members of the South African Intruder Detection Services Association (SAIDSA), the leading employers' association in the armed reaction sector—regard the continued existence of bush companies as a nuisance. SAIDSA serves as the watchdog of the armed reaction sector; it regulates the section through various bylaws and regulations. Although SAIDSA is not legally mandated to impose these regulations, members who do not comply with them are kicked out of the association and any form of misconduct is reported to PSIRA.[4] In fact, many employees in the sector ascribe more authority to SAIDSA than to PSIRA, as one white company owner explained:

> SAIDSA really looks after our sector. Together, all of us, we create the rules and regulations and determine what is needed for this sector to work efficiently and by the law. The inspections are thorough, so if you're not being inspected by them, then your company is probably not meeting all the standards that it should. SAIDSA membership is actually the way to see if a company is really legit or not. PSIRA is not focused; it's a mess.[5]

Table 2 presents basic information about eleven armed reaction companies from data collected in 2010. The previous chapter discussed how

TABLE 2   ARMED REACTION DETAILS FOR 11 COMPANIES IN DURBAN IN 2010

Company	Number of clients	Number of vehicles	Vehicle/ client ratio	Monthly premium
A	33,000	60	550	250
B	25,000	48	520	260
C	20,000	35	571	220
D	5,000	7	714	209
E	4,000	7	571	205
F	2,200	7	314	280
G	2,100	6	350	178
H	1,600	5	320	250
I	1,500	4	375	200
J	500	4	125	300
K	390	2	195	285

SOURCE: Questionnaire completed by company owners/managers and compiled by the author.

the armed response sector emerged in the late 1980s through the work of "techies" and one-man shows. In the intervening years, these two components gradually merged, so that current armed response companies generally provide both technical installation and armed reaction. Although there are still some "pure" techies, this book is primarily concerned with the provision of security through armed response.

The data from Table 2 are derived from a questionnaire that I gave to eleven armed reaction companies in the Durban area. Although much of the information provided to me appeared to be inaccurate, the data in Table 2 have been crosschecked several times and appear to be valid. Table 2 is arranged according to company size, with each company referred to by a letter to preserve their anonymity. The largest company, company A, has 33,000 clients, while the smallest company, company K, has just 390 clients. I distinguish between large companies (20,000 or more clients), medium-sized companies (2,000 or more clients), and small companies (less than 2,000 clients). Table 2 includes three large companies, four medium-sized companies, and four small companies.

A Standard "Call-Out"

Although each company has its own unique operating procedure, all companies undertake three main tasks: alarm installation and maintenance (involving technicians and sales agents); the reception and coding of signals received from these devices (the entire operations of the control room); and the provision of armed response (the armed reaction officers). So how does this process actually work? Client A pays company A to install an alarm monitoring system in his/her house; it may range from a single alarm to an elaborate system of multiple alarms, beams, and panic buttons. When this system is triggered, a signal is sent to the control room of company A, which is the hub of armed reaction—the place where signals are received and coordinated. For large companies, a control room generally consists of twenty or more computers that are monitored by controllers, who in turn are managed by a control room manager. Smaller companies usually have between one and three controllers in the control room.

When an alarm or panic button is activated, a controller receives notifications concerning the specifics of the signal (such as the location and time) on his or her computer. Because of the prevalence of false alarms, the controller first contacts the client to inquire why a notification was received. If the client answers the phone and informs the control room that everything is fine and that the alarm or panic button was activated by accident, the notification is recorded and no further action is taken. However, if the client cannot be reached or there is any cause for concern, the controller will radio the armed response officer who is patrolling the area near the client's premises. The controller will provide the officer with all relevant available details, such as the address of the client and the type of alarm notification. All communication is based on the NATO phonetic alphabet code, with each company using different codes to refer to different alarms and signals. The armed reaction officer then proceeds to the residence of the client to provide armed response.

The course of action that an armed reaction officer takes on arrival at a client's premises depends on various factors, such as the rules of the company, the wishes of the client, the type of alarm, and the specifics of the crime scene. Generally, the officer enters the premises either by using a remote control or a key or by climbing over a gate/fence. He then conducts a perimeter check and examines the windows, doors, and fences for signs of forced entry. Armed response officers are never allowed to enter a property without the property's owner (i.e., the client) permission. If the armed reaction officer believes that there has been a "positive" (i.e., some form of criminal activity, such as a break-in), the client is informed immediately. In such cases, a higher ranking officer will often go to the site to oversee the situation. If the armed response officer arrives to find a crime in progress, he is (officially) supposed to stand back and call for backup from the nearest armed reaction officer. In reality, however, this does not always happen.

If the armed reaction officer does not observe any form of activity, he will provide the client with a call slip to notify him or her that an officer was on site and conducted a check. Call slips are also used to note down all observations, such as an open window or unlocked door. The armed reaction officer then leaves the site and is ready to respond to the next alarm notification. Throughout this entire process, which is referred to as a "call-out," the control room is continuously updated via radio communication. Some companies, particularly the larges ones, also use telephonic communication.

This brief overview describes a standard call-out in which the notification is a false alarm (i.e., there is no evidence of any criminal activity) and the client is not on site. However, when clients are on site or when a crime has been committed, the call-out can assume a number of different forms, as becomes clear throughout the rest of this book.

"The Big Players Make the Rules"

If we look at Table 2, it is interesting to note that there are no operating security companies that have between 5,000 to 20,000 clients in Durban. This is primarily the result of the numerous takeovers and mergers that have taken place since 1994.

Around the turn of the millennium, also known as the "takeover period," foreign investment began to transform the industry. During this period, international security companies started to buy out or merge with various South African companies. A considerable amount of foreign investment flowed into the country's private security industry, primarily through the local subsidiaries of foreign companies such as ADT and Group 4 Securicor (Irish 1999). The prevalence of mergers and takeovers during this period is evident in industry statistics showing a decline in the number of armed reaction companies from 673 in 1999 to 450 in 2000 (Irish 2000). The contraction of the industry also brought together different sectors, such as guarding and armed reaction, under the same owners. As a consequence, companies began to provide both guarding and armed reaction services.

Because of these takeovers and mergers, the entire private security industry has become a type of oligopoly, in which a few large companies dominate the market. In 2006, approximately 20 of the 4,721 companies employed more than 1,000 security officers each, while roughly

2,000 companies employed 5 or fewer (Shearing and Berg 2006: 203). The armed response sector has similarly become an oligopoly. In Durban, there are three so-called big players: ADT, Chubb, and BLUE.[6] They "make the rules" for the sector, particularly with regard to wages, security training, and service delivery.

The "Infrastructure Base"

As discussed in Chapter 2, the private security industry is currently described as "cutthroat" because of its fiercely competitive nature, itself a product of market saturation. Like the rest of the services provided by the industry, armed response is no longer seen as a luxury good reserved for the elite, but is instead widely regarded as a necessity and is found across all strata of society, except the lowest socioeconomic domain. This expansion of armed response occurred not only because of an increase in both supply and demand but also because companies specifically targeted lower income sectors of society to acquire new clients during the 1990s. The white marketing manager of a large company explained this marketing strategy to me as follows:

> Around this time, we specifically addressed lower-income areas—not townships, but areas with a middle class, a growing one, that could afford the monthly premium. In this industry, there are two main costs for the clients: the alarm installation fee—somewhere between 1,000 to 2,000 rand, depending on the client—and the monthly premium. Now, many people can afford the 200–300 rand a month, but don't have the disposable income for that once-off fee. So what we did, we took that away and offered them a "free alarm," and we specifically went to these areas, like the Bluff and Chatsworth, to get new clients. And it worked; we got in thousands of them through this system.[7]

Furthermore, within the structure of an oligopoly, the price of armed response (i.e., the monthly premium paid by clients) is fairly similar across the sector, as can be seen in Table 2. The monthly premiums range from R 178 to R 300, with an average of R 240. Although clients complained about this monthly expense, their issue was not so much with the amount as with the very fact that they had to *pay* for security in the first place. Security is widely regarded as a "grudge purchase" (Goold et al. 2010), an unwelcome yet necessary acquisition. Most clients expressed agitation about the annual 10 percent increase implemented by companies. This form of recurring and increasing payment, in which a monthly premium of R 250 could rise to R 366 between 2011 and 2015, is the core profit generator of the armed reaction sector.

According to my informants, the profit margins of the armed reaction sector range between 5 and 15 percent. Although the monthly premiums from clients play an important role in determining the profit margins, it is the "infrastructure base" (i.e. the ability of a company to serve all of its clients with its vehicles) that is the decisive factor. Table 2 shows that companies' vehicle-to-client ratios range between 1:125 and 1:714, with an average of 418.6. In other words, one vehicle (and thus one armed response officer) serves an average of more than four hundred clients. This vehicle-to-client ratio determines the financial success of a company. For example, the owner of company H informed me that each armed reaction vehicle costs approximately R 13,400 to operate per month, regardless of the amount of clients. With clients paying a minimum monthly premium of 250 rand per month, this means that at least 53.6 clients are needed to cover the costs of one vehicle. However, company H has 320 clients per vehicle, which means that the company receives R 80,000 per month for that vehicle, resulting in a net profit of R 66,600 for one vehicle and R 333,000 for five vehicles. Although this profit estimate excludes other large overhead costs, such as office rent and equipment, the main point here is that the more clients served per vehicle, the greater the profit. However, the vehicle-to-client ratio must not become too high: If one vehicle serves too many clients, its reaction time will be slow, resulting in poor service delivery and a potential loss of clients. Maintaining the right infrastructure base is key to a company's success.

Given the importance of balancing the vehicle-to-client ratio, when a company expands into another geographical area, it needs a guarantee that it will attract a certain amount of clients for this expansion to be feasible. This also explains why companies need both startup capital and a handful of clients when they enter the sector. In fact, starting an armed response company from scratch is rare; the majority grew out of guarding companies that branched out into providing armed response for their existing clients. In 2009, I interviewed a businessman who had owned a guarding company for eight years and had recently expanded his business to provide armed reaction with two operating vehicles. When I met him again in 2010, however, he told me that he had had to shut down his armed response section because of the financial difficulties of maintaining the infrastructure base.

The infrastructure base also explains why community-based companies are able to flourish: They are confined to a smaller geographical area and thus need fewer clients per vehicle to meet their costs. It is for this reason, combined with their local appeal, that community-based companies continue to operate despite the ever-present threat of takeovers. As the manager of one large company explained, "They're like white ants: you don't see them or maybe feel them right away, but they're there, slowly eating away [at] your clients."[8]

"Strongholds" and "Way out There"

When I first came to Durban in October 2007, I was particularly fascinated by the fragmented nature of the security industry: Every street displays the logos of numerous different companies, and it is normal for several firms to operate in the same area.

However, large companies do have geographic strongholds where they seek to create clusters of clients to support their infrastructure base. For example, ENFORCE security has a stronghold in Ballito, a coastal town just outside Durban, and BLUE Security has many clients in the Umbilo and Musgrave areas. Company employees often talk quite possessively about certain areas, using phrases such as "My Umhlanga Rocks" or "Our part of Kloof." Community-based companies also dominate particular areas. For example, Securelink only operates in a confined part of the Upper Highway Area, Park Patrol primarily operates in the Bluff and Yellowwood Park, and Marshall Security operates solely in Durban North. Moreover, it is likely that geographical monopolies will increase in the future. Recent years have seen a growth in collective clients (see Chapter 6), whereby citizens "club" together to arrange armed security provision for a specific area, such as a street or neighborhood. Although "turf war" is perhaps too strong a word to describe the level of competition, the increasing aggressiveness of companies in pursuit of lucrative deals with collective clients will likely lead to more geographical strongholds.

There is, however, one geographical area of neglect, namely the black townships. When I first asked informants about companies working in the townships, my question was often brushed aside or ridiculed: One simply did not work "way out there." Many companies feel that these areas pose too many dangers for their armed reaction officers. Their refusal to serve the townships does not reflect a lack of prospective clients, therefore, but rather a security concern. Some companies use the subcontracting system to work around this challenge; they install the alarms for clients in the townships and then subcontract with another company to provide the armed reaction service, thereby avoiding the risk to their own officers.[9]

Not all companies shun the townships, however. In March 2009, I visited a friend who lives in a black township in the north of Durban. On arriving at his house, I noticed that he had installed an alarm system since my last visit in 2007 and that the provider was a large internationally owned company. He was surprised by my startled reaction and explained that it was quite normal for him to have such a system; many of his neighbors were also installing alarms. Toward the end of my fieldwork, I was able to interview the owners of three companies that solely or primarily work in townships, such as Umlazi and KwaMashu. Two of the owners felt that other companies exaggerated the risk in the townships, whereas the third claimed that the townships were indeed far more dangerous than other areas, but that they were worth the risk. It became clear that these companies' operational style and financial models, such as their pricing structures, meet the standards of the armed response sector. It is not necessarily the case, therefore, that clients in the townships pay lower monthly premiums than those in other areas. Furthermore, all three owners highlighted how the townships were "untapped markets" and gloated about the growth their companies had experienced by working there.

"The Foreigners" and "the Locals"

During my first interviews with company managers in 2007, several of them posed the same question: "Are you going to focus on the foreigners or also include the locals?" Although I was aware of this foreign-local distinction, I did not yet realize how great a role it played in the way that companies define and differentiate themselves, which largely stemmed from the "takeover" period. In this crude binary, the term "the foreigners" refers to any internationally owned company, while "the locals" denotes nationally owned companies of any size. The former, which include global brands such as Chubb and ADT, purposely profile themselves as companies that adhere to international standards. The latter, meanwhile, highlight their local connection—*local is lekker*[10]—and emphasize their accessibility and being "one of us"—a part of the community.

This difference in ownership results in different operational styles. Local companies have a reputation for being more active and policing oriented, while international companies are perceived to focus more on customer service, something that I observed firsthand while out on patrol with officers from one such company. Although all companies engage in customer-based practices, this company employed a high-ranking armed reaction officer specifically to visit new clients or those who had recently experienced some form of crime. Furthermore, international companies are known to adhere to rules more strictly than their local counterparts. An example that was often given by my interlocutors concerned the rules about entering the premises of a client. Armed reaction officers from international companies are instructed not to attempt to climb over a fence if it is more than one meter taller than them. In contrast, owners of local companies are known for employing a bolder rule of thumb: "If I can get over that gate, so can you!" Local companies are thereby seen as "go-getters" that encourage their armed reaction officers to chase suspects, while international companies instruct their officers to focus on the client and avoid risky situations.

The background of the managers and/or owners also shapes these differences in operational styles. Those with a policing background who have "been in the trenches"[11] tend to implement operational styles that encourage their armed reaction officers to be proactive, to vigorously look out for suspicious vehicles and persons, and to chase suspects when the opportunity arises. Managers with a financial background, meanwhile, focus more on "numbers," and international companies are often associated with this approach. In fact, many local company owners complained that both the sector and the industry as a whole were becoming too "financial" and that the "heart of it" was being lost, which resonates with the description of the industry as "cutthroat." According to a white company owner who had been working in security since the 1980s, there has been a transformation from a "personalized, hands-on sheriff living in the suburb to an industry where accountants make the decisions."[12] Like several other interviewees, he claimed that this shift started during the takeover period, when international companies entered the market and recruited managers with financial backgrounds rather than former police officers.

Although I do not mean to suggest that *all* international companies employ managers with financial expertise and discourage their armed reaction officers from taking risks, or that *all* local companies recruit individuals with a policing background and encourage their officers to chase suspects, this division is clearly apparent in both reputation and practice. The distinction is an important one, because it influences the way an armed reaction officer operates on the ground. Although the expansion of armed response into the public domain—a core element of twilight policing—has occurred across the entire sector, it is more common among local companies that not only are more likely to have established social networks in the community but also generally employ a more proactive approach to policing the streets. This does not mean that an armed reaction officer working for an internationally owned company will never chase a suspect or approach one in a public space, but only that this he is less likely to do so.

Branding the Policing Style

The cultivation of different policing styles by companies is also reflected in their marketing strategies and the design of the company's image. Figure 4 shows three armed response officers from BLUE Security standing in front of a vehicle.

Marketing employees from BLUE Security told me how they had invested a lot of time in choosing imagery and symbols from American cop shows to represent their company. Rather than associating themselves with the South African state police, the company employed popular images of state policing elsewhere to obtain a sense of authority and professionalism. The look of both the vehicle and the uniforms was intended to resemble those of American police officers. In fact, when a colleague came to visit me in 2008 and saw one of their vehicles drive by, she initially thought that it was a state police car. Furthermore, BLUE wanted to portray itself as a "community-policing" company, with the "boys from BLUE" seen as part of that community.[13] Its uniforms are thus designed to project "professionalism" and "assistance."

Figure 5 shows three armed response officers from Reaction Unit South Africa (RUSA), a community-based company. In choosing the aesthetics for their company, the owners sought to project a militaristic image of a "tough force" of men. As can be seen from the photo, the armed reaction officers are dressed head to toe in black. In addition to the standard equipment (radio, firearm, and bulletproof vest), they are required to wear army chains, kneepads, bandanas, and black sunglasses.

Figures 4 and 5 show two examples of how companies brand themselves in specific ways to project a particular policing style. Although this branding is clearly a marketing strategy, it is also an important means of ensuring public compliance and exerting authority. Companies take the physical appearance and attire of their armed response officers very

FIGURE 4. Three armed response officers from BLUE Security. Photo taken by the author.

seriously. In fact, armed response officers are penalized when they do not adhere to the brand image.

Managers across the industry repeatedly highlighted how important it was for security officers to "look professional" or "tough," since their officers are the public face of their companies: They are what clients and other citizens see on the streets. In addition, according to Singh, companies started to profile security officers "as individuals rather than as an undifferentiated mass" (Singh 2005: 163) in the late 1990s. Since then, security officers have increasingly been at the forefront of advertising campaigns, and today they are publicly commended for their good performance in newspaper and magazine advertisements and press releases. The white owner of a guarding company referred to private security officers as "ambassadors of the industry," offering the following explanation of this term:

> The guards are the first thing a customer sees, so he has to look professional, neat, and smart. We have to invest in that, because it's what clients see first. Of course we want to help him economically, but it's in our own interest to invest in his wellbeing for marketing purposes.[14]

FIGURE 5. Three armed response officers from Reaction Unit South Africa (RUSA). Photo taken by the author.

DISCIPLINE, CONTROL, AND SURVEILLANCE

Company owners regard strict compliance with regard to uniforms and physical attire to be important in maintaining their companies' reputation and client approval, but it also serves to instill a strong sense of bodily discipline, authority, and hierarchy. Singh (2005) argues that such mechanisms of control and supervision function to keep the officers on a tight leash and to ensure that they display maximum performance. Rigakos describes the surveillance techniques exerted over officers as "an obsession for security firms" (2002: 101).

The instilling of discipline through control and surveillance is a recurrent feature of the private security industry, occurring during training,

FIGURE 6. Start of the parade. Photo taken by the author.

registration, and recruitment, as well as "on the road." The process begins at the training facilities, where students are molded into docile, obedient, and utilizable employees who do not "exercise independent judgement" (Singh 2005: 167). When I participated in the security training, I witnessed how students who arrived late to class were punished by being assigned various strenuous tasks, such as doing pushups or running laps. Another example of the routine inculcation of respect for authority was the parade that was conducted daily at 11:00 a.m. sharp, which required the students to stand in three evenly spaced lines and follow commands issued by the training instructor (see Figure 6).

Employing the "Good" Ones

The recruitment procedure is the next phase of surveillance and control. In addition to satisfying the formal requirements of the job, all security officers undergo some form of psychological testing, for which companies use a range of techniques, including panel interviews, aptitude tests, integrity checks, polygraph tests, and psychometric evaluation. These techniques are used to assess officers' capabilities, to understand their distinctiveness, to compare them to "the norm," and to focus on their "moral habits" (Singh 2008: 54). The importance of screening potential employees is emphasized in the following quote from the manager of a large company:

We gotta make sure the guys coming in are good guys, that they know what they're doing. We check the training, run it by the SAPS, you know, the standard, the usual stuff. But besides all that, I want to speak to the guy—make sure he's really qualified. I wanna know I'm not dealing with an alcoholic who's gonna be late for work everyday and has to support five girlfriends. I don't need to know everything, but I want to get a sense of the caliber of these men. I always trust my own instinct; if it doesn't feel good, no matter what it says on paper, he's out. Now you see, this is just with the guards. But with armed reaction, it's very important you know what you're hiring. You have to know that these guys are not messing around and meet the standards. So that's why we have these long interviews, make them fill in extra forms, do a few written tests, stuff like that. The more the job requires, the more important it is that we trust the guy. I mean, people's lives are on the line.[15]

Recruiting armed reaction officers is seen as difficult for operational managers. This is in stark contrast to the situation in the guarding sector, where, as one Indian guarding supervisor said to me, "If you fire one, you know you have dozens of guys waiting in line to get the job. There's always more where that came from. In reaction, it's different."[16] The recruitment pool for the armed response sector is relatively small, which means that finding high-caliber officers can be an arduous process, as a white armed reaction manager of a medium-sized company explained:

Companies working in armed reaction are always in need of more officers. If you have the expertise, training, and skills as an armed reaction officer, it's easy for you to find a job, because there is always a company who will need you. We don't have a lot of choice in the matter; there are a few good guys and that's it.[17]

The recruitment of armed reaction officers sometimes occurs through traditional means, such as advertisements in newspapers, but the most common method is "poaching," whereby officers are recruited directly from other companies. Although poaching occurs at all levels, managers often instruct their higher ranking officers to act as "scouts" and "snoop around" for good reaction officers from other companies.[18] The main targets are small security companies, which often spend many months training officers only for them to be poached by a larger company that can offer higher wages. The white owner of a small company offered the following account of this process:

I train the guys, make them understand the trade, the ins and outs, and then here comes [name of company], offers them more money, and they're gone. I'd like to pay them more, but I just can't. And people even make jokes about it at meetings, other owners, you know—I'll just go and steal some of [name of owner]'s guys.[19]

The result of this poaching is a high turnover of staff, a trait observed throughout the security industry worldwide.[20] In South Africa, the guarding sector experiences the highest labor turnover of approximately 15–20 percent per month (Clarno and Murray 2013: 214). In the armed reaction sector, too, there is a high turnover of employees, but most remain within the same circles, switching between companies like in a game of musical chairs. I knew of a handful of reaction officers who worked for several different companies during my three years in Durban; I would meet them working for one company one day and then, months later, would meet them again working for another company. Therefore, although various forms of testing and control are used during the recruitment process, the limited number of available armed response officers constrains these procedures.

A crucial part of the recruitment process is the criminal record check. Although PSIRA's approval of a candidate's registration implies that the officer does not have a criminal background, numerous companies perform additional police checks, often through their own contacts within the SAPS. In the armed reaction sector, pre-employment polygraph testing is common among companies that have the financial capacity. During these tests, recruits are questioned about their past behavior to determine their credentials and suitability for the job. Similarly, some company owners check applicants' financial backgrounds for evidence of previous irregularities, which might suggest corrupt practices.

Disciplinary Codes and Surveillance

On joining a company, security officers are informed of their employer's disciplinary codes, which outline professional offenses and corresponding penalties. Penalties include a hearing, a written warning, a final written warning, and dismissal and are categorized according to first-, second-, and third-time offenses. There is some variation between the companies in this regard; for example, sleeping on duty as a first offense was punished with dismissal by one company and with a written warning by another. However, certain forms of misconduct, such as engagement in criminal activity while on duty, assault (physical and verbal) against another reaction officer or a client, desertion of one's post, and being under the influence of intoxicating substances while on duty, result in immediate dismissal in every company I studied.

During my fieldwork, I attended numerous disciplinary hearings for reaction officers who had committed offenses. Minor matters, such as arriving late on duty, were often dealt with by higher ranking security officers, but more serious forms of misconduct, such as failing to perform a call-out, were brought directly to management. However, much of the misconduct that I witnessed went unreported, including numerous incidents of alcohol consumption and sleeping while on duty, visits to prostitutes, and use of reaction vehicle as taxis.

One of the most common measures used to prevent or detect misconduct is electronic surveillance. In addition to cameras, various types of equipment are used to monitor the productivity of a security officer. During one of my strolls around the Securex annual private security convention in Johannesburg in June 2008, I arrived at the stand of a company specializing in the sale of surveillance devices. Its main product was an electronic appliance that obliged guards to "check in" at certain spots along their patrol route to ensure that they were working efficiently. I struck up a conversation with the two white salesmen and politely inquired about their product. The first, younger man told me how the product was designed to counteract "the bad and lazy nature" of the guards, to ensure that "you keep control, that you're getting your money's worth." The second salesman corroborated his colleague's claims and elaborated:

> You see, these guards, these black guys, they need 20 hours sleep in a 24-hour day. They're lazy. They don't want to work, they just want to earn money so they can go home and drink. But the companies pay them to stay awake. What's the point of paying someone to sleep? Now this system helps you with that. You know exactly what the guard is doing. You can check his patrols, how long he takes, anything. So you can catch him. If you need to fire him, you have proof, on paper, that he isn't doing his job properly. It gives managers more power, more power to fire those lazy ones.

In her discussion of Performer Guard Patrol Systems, a similar electronic surveillance system, Singh (2005, 2008) argues that such mechanisms aim to control the guards' behavior, eliminate any form of "creative or independent decision making," and "exercise a constant pressure to conform" (Singh 2005: 169).

Armed reaction officers are also exposed to numerous forms of surveillance while on duty. For example, they are required to use an occurrence book (OB) to record their activities, such as their mileage details, the exact times they receive call-outs and arrive at the sites, and the number of call slips they leave. Companies with the financial capacity have installed satellite-tracking systems in their vehicles, and a few now boast that they have "live tracking" facilities, which allow them to monitor the location and movement of vehicles in real time. Managers and owners claim that such surveillance methods are intended to help the officers, particularly when clients accuse them of misconduct. For example, if a client asserts that the armed reaction officer was late reaching the premises, the data from the tracking systems can be used to verify or refute this claim. One company owner demands that its reaction officers take photos of the premises they attend to prove that they have conducted a perimeter check, should accusations be made to the contrary. Managers thus contend that surveillance processes exist to ensure accountability and transparency, to deliver maximum performance to customers, and to protect the reaction officers from clients who make unreasonable claims.

For most private security officers, however, these various forms of surveillance instill a sense that they are untrustworthy and in need of constant monitoring. A black security guard working at a shopping center described this feeling as follows:

> When we start this job, we know that we have to do our best. We know that we are being watched, that the managers are controlling us. Everything we do, we have to write down. There are cameras all around us. I feel that they are watching me all the time, like a dog, like they cannot trust me.[21]

In March 2011, I heard rumors that a few companies were considering installing small cameras inside their vehicles to monitor the armed reaction officers. Several armed reaction officers expressed outrage about this possibility. One of them said to me,

> They [the companies] doing this because they don't trust us. They want control over us. We already have to keep track of every flippin' thing we do, and now this? So now I can't eat in privacy, talk to my wife on the phone in privacy? I don't think it's even legal, something like this. If they do this, I'm out, gone!

Hierarchy and Ranking

Hierarchical structures and ranking are also used to cultivate obedience and discipline (Button 2007; Singh 2008; van Steden 2007; Wakefield 2003). According to Rigakos, a hierarchical structure in a company establishes "a role model system" and a "distribution system in which officers are ranked by skills, aptitudes, and experience" (2002: 104).

Creating a hierarchy displays to those on the "lower levels" what is needed to reach the "higher levels," providing the former with goals and incentives. Although each armed reaction company has a different hierarchical system, these systems are generally based on a division into the geographical areas patrolled by armed reaction officers and managed by area supervisors, who are also referred to as sergeants, lieutenants, or area managers. Managers claim that hierarchy is a normal part of policing and that it determines the quality of the officers' performance.

Giving awards to officers also instills discipline. Singh and Kempa argue that having a system of rewards embedded in a company's modus operandi "helps solidify the self identity/image of the guards as both skilled and compliant" (2007: 308). In most companies, particular actions such as making an arrest are rewarded with prizes, pay increases, and possible promotions, while good performances are also recognized in company newsletters. In one of the companies that I encountered during my fieldwork, the armed reaction officers are evaluated annually to determine their appraisals (additional bonus money). Every year, the "best" armed reaction officers receive an award for their performance at the annual Christmas party. The white armed reaction manager of a large company referred to these rewards as "morale-boosting" mechanisms:

> [The aim is] to motivate the guys to keep them here and ensure that they do the job well. You need Christmas parties, awards, and bonuses to ensure high performance, keep them at your company, and boost morale. You've got guys that go the extra mile, that have real passion, but you also have those that just do what the job requires and that's it. I can't punish them for it, but it is my job to motivate them to go that extra mile, keep them on their feet.[22]

The white manager of a medium-sized company told me how his armed reaction officers were financially rewarded for their "hard work." The value of these rewards depends on the act:

> If the guy goes and arrests a shoplifter, it's not quite the same as a guy that goes out there and saves a woman from being raped. If he does that, he'll probably get a bonus of anything between 800 to 1000 rand. . . . It's to make sure that they see it is a privilege, that hard work pays off.[23]

By being rewarded for these types of activities, officers are encouraged to perform in a particular way. Rewarding the making of arrests encourages a proactive operational style, while not doing so serves to discourage officers from taking certain risks, such as chasing a suspect. Methods of instilling discipline and obedience thus favor certain policing styles over others. But more importantly, disciplinary measures create and consolidate a division between management and operations that influences the occupational culture of the sector, particularly on the ground.

RACE AND GENDER

In the course of my research, the two aspects of my identity that appeared most prominent were race and gender. I was repeatedly reminded that I was a *wit stekkie*—slang for white woman—which was further affirmed by the ascribed nickname, "Sierra Foxtrot Golf" (Special Female Guest). Although gender plays a role in any ethnographic fieldwork, it weighs heavier for a female studying police institutions because of the inherent masculinity of such an environment (Huggins and Glebbeek 2009; Marks 2004; Westmarland 2001b). My gender not only clearly shaped my role as researcher (Diphoorn 2013) but also highlighted how I differed from my informants and how race and gender play a crucial role in this industry. In this section, I discuss how gender and race shape the private security industry, particularly by influencing the divide between management and operations. I argue that the entire armed response sector (re)produces particular masculinities, which unites those working within it. In contrast, issues of race exacerbate the divide.

"A Man's World"

Studies on the occupational culture of the state police have identified a "cult of masculinity" (Brown 2007: 206) as one of its most prominent characteristics. Notions of masculinity and masculine attributes are generally equated with police work and largely influence the identity construction of police officers. Activities associated with policing and security imply a sense of protection and a need to provide safety. This contains a gendered bias, because particular characteristics required to do the job, such as physical strength, courage, and aggression, are widely regarded as masculine (Brown 2007; Higate 2012; Monaghan 2002; Reiner 2000; Westmarland 2001a).

This predominance of males and masculinities also plays a large role in shaping the occupational culture of private security. Although masculinity is a socially constructed concept (Joachim and Schneiker 2012), it greatly influences how the industry portrays itself both to the public and among its constituents. Women are a minority in the private security industry around the world, and attributes perceived to be feminine are restrained, discouraged, or even penalized.[24] In South Africa as well, the security industry is regarded as a "man's world": Females are a minority and are completely absent in certain sectors. As was the case at the Armed Reaction Man Competition, I was surrounded by men for most of my fieldwork, and only a few women were included in my research. Whenever I attended events involving management, such as company meetings and gatherings of employers' associations, there were rarely any women present. Women who do work in the industry primarily do so in areas regarded as "safe," such as sales, marketing, training, and the control room.

Females are also a minority of private security officers. In 2010, there were 67,517 active female registered security officers compared to 319,756 active registered male security officers (i.e., 17.43 percent).[25] Female security officers predominantly work in low-risk divisions, such as retail, special events, and the hotel industry, and they rarely work night shifts. This gender distinction starts at the training schools, where girls are persuaded to select "suitable" courses. During a focus group discussion with training instructors, one of the males said to me,

> We don't encourage girls to take armed reaction or cash-in-transit, because they won't find a job. Nobody will hire them. So it's a waste of their time and money. It's too dangerous. Even doing night shift guarding on industrial sites is too risky. Do you think that girls can handle that type of pressure and danger? So we tell them to do retail or control room.[26]

During my research, I did not encounter a single female armed reaction officer. Managers repeatedly stated that they have a strict policy of not employing women for such positions. One white company owner informed me that he had employed a female armed reaction officer in the past, but had to let her go because he felt that he could not guarantee her safety.[27] Because armed reaction officers operate alone in a vehicle, female officers are particularly vulnerable to sexual violence. This practice of driving solo distinguishes private from public policing: Although females are also a minority in the state police, they routinely operate with a male partner and are therefore less at risk.

When I asked my informants about female armed reaction officers, they laughed and joked about the prospect of women doing their line of work. The informants in Rigakos's (2002: 83) research shared these sentiments and expressed a lack of confidence in the ability of women to do the job, especially when providing backup during dangerous situations. Several of my informants recalled two women who had worked as armed reaction officers in the past, but this pair of officers were not regarded as "real women" because they were "butch," lesbian, and possessed certain male characteristics. Thus, for many informants, the mere notion of "female" armed reaction officers upset gender categories, because they felt women should not perform security-related duties, such as climbing over fences, handling firearms, and chasing suspects. These jobs are firmly established in the domain of men. My male informants' perception of women as unfit for security work was also extended to me. Gayle, an Indian armed response officer in his early forties, once asked me, "Tessa, you have the heart of a man—how can you do this and still be a real woman?" For many of my informants, I confounded gender categories and represented an unsolvable mystery: I possessed female characteristics and fulfilled their idea of what it entails to be a woman, yet I also displayed male characteristics simply by doing this research.

The armed reaction sector, and perhaps the industry as a whole, is characterized by a dominant macho subculture that glorifies and rewards masculine attributes. There is an ongoing process of "masculinization"—a "strategy to affirm superiority . . . by drawing on what are considered accepted and desirable male attributes" (Joachim and Schneiker 2012: 498). If armed response officers possess and display particular masculine attributes, they are praised and rewarded, as was evident during the Armed Reaction Man Competition.

Furthermore, for many of my informants it seemed that armed response work provided a space in which to exert and emphasize masculine attributes that they might need to minimize or conceal in their private lives. When I asked them what they enjoyed about this line of work, common responses included "here I can be a man" and "here there are no women telling me what to do." On duty, armed reaction officers continuously competed among each other to demonstrate their "strength" and "toughness." Cars, guns, and women were the main topics of social conversation. Discussions about sexual performance, sexual encounters, and girlfriends were also very common, with many officers boasting about their performance and capability to "get so many women." Although some may have initially restrained themselves, many informants openly discussed their sexual experiences either directly with me or in my presence. My female presence may have triggered and perhaps heightened the performance of this macho culture and the exhibition of their masculinity (Diphoorn 2013).

Therefore the armed response sector is one that applauds masculine attributes. Although women work in this sector, they are a minority and operate in areas that are perceived as "soft" and "feminine." The dominance of males and the glorification of male qualities strongly shape the occupational culture of the entire armed response world. Companies often operate as "masculinity multipliers" (Joachim and Schneiker 2012: 507), in which both managers and operations reproduce masculinities.

"Whites on Top and Blacks at the Bottom"

Although management and operations are both dominated by males, they are starkly divided by race. This was palpable at the Armed Reaction Man Competition, where the management was predominantly white and operations was predominantly non-white. As discussed in Chapter 2, efforts were made to address the racial imbalances in the private security industry and increase the amount of non-Whites in management, particularly around the time of the political transition. Despite the changes of the past two decades, however, Whites continue to occupy the majority of the higher ranking positions, and security officers are still predominantly non-White (Abrahamsen and Williams 2007; Singh 2008; Singh and Kempa 2007). As one white company owner explained, the hierarchy in the industry can be summed up with a simple phrase: "Whites on top and Blacks at the bottom."[28]

This division also became clear regarding my own role in the field and how my being white was interpreted. Primarily because of my skin color, most of my informants initially assumed that I worked for "management" and believed that I was granted access to study them on account of my whiteness, as illustrated by the following transcript of a conversation I had with Nick, a high-ranking Indian armed response officer in his thirties:

Me: Well, I'm white. Do you think that played a role in me being here with you now?

Nick: [He thinks for a while and smiles.] Yes, I do.

Me: So if I was black or Indian, the managers at . . . wouldn't have helped me out or allowed me to conduct my research?

Nick: Yes. Of course, you being a foreigner helped. And I think that they just interested in what you do. . . . But yes, you being white definitely made it easier.

Me: And do the other guys think this as well?

Nick: Of course!! When you first came, the first few days, I was nervous! I mean, all of a sudden there's this wit chick in my car, I felt that you were like evaluating me or whatever.

Me: And that's because I'm white?

Nick: Yes, no. I mean, if they would have put anyone in my car, it would have made me nervous, but you being white definitely made it more serious. And when the other guys met you, everybody was asking each other: What's this *witto* doing here? Is she here to spy on us for the big boss? Because you're white and the managers are white, many people saw a connection. You can understand that, can't you?

Me: Of course. And how is it now?

Nick: It's different now. . . . I mean, you're different, and I tell you everything. The guys like you being here, they enjoy your company, but in the beginning, we were nervous, we didn't understand it.

Me: And do you think that I would have been accepted quicker if I was an Indian or a black female?

Nick: Yes. It would have made the guys less nervous. But at the end of the day, you've been accepted, because we trust you, because of the way you are. But your colour is always there, and any new guy coming in will think the same.

Many informants echoed Nick's sentiments, and understanding their perceptions clarified the nature of countless other interactions I had. For example, when we encountered clients, they always started speaking to me first, seemingly under the assumption that I held a managerial position, even though I informed them that I was a researcher and not a company employee. It seemed that my whiteness exuded a degree of authority, which unquestionably also occurs within the company itself, where Whites are assumed to be in high-ranked positions.

In the private security industry, this assumption is still accurate: Although many armed response officers aim to reach management level, they rarely do so. The highest positions that most of them can attain are those of guarding supervisor or high-ranking armed reaction officers, such as area managers. In fact, some owners were open about how race affected their decisions to promote certain individuals to certain ranks, as the following quote from one white owner reveals:

Only black guys are supervisors, because only they can understand the cultural things. For example, a guard needs time off to go back to his village to slaughter a goat for a ritual, or something like that. See, I don't agree with all that and I don't understand it. But a black guy will understand the importance and work with it. That's why they're in charge for stuff like that. So I think when there's black guards, you need a black supervisor, and another company with Indian guards will need an Indian supervisor, 'cos they understand each other's ways.[29]

Within the private security industry, armed reaction is the most racially diverse sector. Although the majority of armed reaction officers are non-white, one is more likely to encounter a white armed reaction officer than a white security guard. This is primarily because there were very few non-white armed actions officers before 1994. As discussed in Chapter 2, many police officers left the force in the late 1980s and early 1990s to work as reaction officers or to set up one-man shows, and these men were all white. The armed reaction sector was thus initially a completely white domain in terms of both management and operations. This changed in the mid-1990s, when, as one white company owner explained, it became

difficult to find good white guys. Before, they were coming from the police, but now, with armed reaction earning less, this wasn't happening. And we just couldn't find good white guys anymore. So around then, you saw blacks and Indians coming in, particularly blacks. It was a problem, big problem at first, with clients, they didn't want it, but it happened, because we didn't have a choice—it was difficult to find a good white reaction guy. And it still is. They're an absolute minority. It's turned around.[30]

In Durban, where there is a large Indian community, many armed reaction officers are Indian. In 2009, the racial composition of the armed reaction officers of company B, a large company, was 51 percent Indian, 33 percent Black, 8.3 percent Colored, and 7.7 percent White. Most members of the industry would regard this as very racially diverse; the majority of companies have armed response personnel who are 90–95 percent black or Indian.

When I asked my informants about the racial makeup of armed response officers, some argued that it occurred randomly, while others emphasized the importance of word of mouth among certain communities in recruiting officers. However, some companies still adhere to strict racial recruitment policies. In Johannesburg, I met a white owner who only employed white armed reaction officers in accordance with his clients' demands. In Durban, I interviewed Indian owners who specifically recruited Indians. Similarly, the black owner of a company working primarily in the black townships stated that he only recruited black officers for security reasons, claiming that white and Indian officers would be targeted because they did not understand "the township ways."[31] Race-based recruitment for this occupation therefore occurs for all races, and although many managers do not openly admit it, clients' racial preferences also play a role.

Interracial stereotyping by both management and reaction officers is common throughout the industry. It is normal for employees to assume that members of their own race are more suited to the risky nature of the job than their colleagues from different backgrounds. White officers claim they are better because of their toughness and the military training many received during apartheid, while black officers assert that the violence in the townships and their role in the struggle against apartheid make them more capable. Stereotypical comments from white officers, such as "Indian guys can't get the job done—they're too scared," contrast with those of their Indian counterparts, such as "Only Indians can handle this type of pressure; Whites are too weak." This interracial stereotyping raises two interesting points: Most officers assume that certain skills and attributes are directly related to race, and reaction officers, regardless of race, value the same characteristics and are unified in their understandings of what it means to be a "good" armed reaction officer, namely the link to violence, danger, toughness, and other masculine attributes.

In the armed reaction sector, race plays a key role in distinguishing management from operations staff. When an armed reaction officer is promoted to a higher rank, such as that of supervisor or area manager, the "race card" is readily played. If a white officer is promoted, for example, others interpret that promotion as evidence of racism, as an attempt to maintain white dominance; if a black officer is promoted, it is interpreted as a sign of affirmative action. However, these forms of racial stereotyping do not necessarily influence how the officers conduct their work alongside each other on the ground. Race does play a large role in their profiling of criminals and how they police the public (see Chapter 7), but it does not necessarily affect how they police the streets *together*, as a policing body. Although armed response officers may be socially stratified along racial lines—Indians socialize with Indians, Blacks with Blacks, and so on—the security they provide is steered by crime, danger, and the need to police efficiently, not by race.

CONCLUDING REMARKS

The aim of this chapter was to analyze the occupational culture of the armed response sector, one of the largest sectors in the private security industry, which is widely regarded as "the promising horse." Like the rest of the industry, the armed response sector operates as an oligopoly in which the big players determine rules and standards, particularly with regard to salaries and bonuses and service delivery. Nevertheless, smaller companies, particularly community-based ones, continue to flourish due to their local appeal and ability to maintain a viable infrastructure base. Thus, while there is a standard modus operandi for delivering armed response, there is also diversity within the sector, with companies working and portraying themselves differently depending on their marketing strategies and policing ideologies.

Yet despite these differences between companies, there are three core features that define the sector at large. The first is the predominance of males: Like the private security industry as a whole, armed response is regarded as a man's world in which attributes deemed to be feminine are considered unsuitable. The industry (re)produces masculinization processes that profile the sector as a collective of masculinities. This gives rise to a particular style of policing that cultivates and rewards masculine qualities.

The second key issue is the division between management and operations. Although this distinction may be less stark within community-based companies where owners tend to be more involved in the operations, hierarchical relations are nonetheless a ubiquitous feature of the sector. The division is generally marked by race, with management being predominantly white and operations predominantly non-white. Once again, this rule does not necessarily apply to community-based companies, as evidenced by the Indian-owned firm whose owners, managers, and armed reaction officers were all Indian. Even in this company, however, most of the security guards, who were "managed" by the Indian armed reaction officers, were black. The security industry is structured according to apartheid-like racial hierarchies. These racial distinctions are obviously a legacy of the apartheid past, and the maintenance of this hierarchy reproduces particular understandings of race and often incites feelings of envy, oppression, and mistreatment.

In addition to race, the armed response sector is defined by various mechanisms of surveillance for instilling obedience. Companies employ numerous strategies to ensure that armed response officers are "good" and "do as they're told." This use of these strategies reveals a degree of suspicion on the part of the company owners, who feel they need to control their employees' behavior. For management, then, surveillance measures are conceived as a part of the policing game. Operational staff, however, perceive them as coercive and oppressive, and the racial differences between management and operations deepen this difference of opinion.

These three features of the sector cultivate an occupational culture that encourages armed response officers to operate in public spaces. Given the diversity of the sector, I do not claim that all reaction officers always engage in twilight policing practices. However, I contend that particular attributes are collectively cultivated that promote punitive, disciplinary, and exclusionary policing practices. Although the performance of twilight policing primarily emerges through local security networks comprising other actors, such as clients and state police officers, the occupational culture of the armed response sector plays a significant role in determining how armed response officers police the streets.

More importantly, the occupational culture encourages practices in which the sector at large mimics the state police both operationally and symbolically. Although there are many similarities between the private security industry and the state police as a whole, as discussed by Loyens (2009), I argue that these similarities are more prevalent in the armed response sector for two reasons. First, response officers are armed men who patrol communities; they are not security guards who stand outside shopping malls. With firearms, uniforms, and vehicles resembling those of the state police, they are reproducing particular notions of statehood and transmitting them to the public. Second, the sector was founded by former police officers who operated one-man shows inspired by the mentality and strategies of the state police. Although the movement of state police personnel into the sector is diminishing and the industry is increasingly "cutthroat," in which competition and profit making have come to overshadow policing methods, I claim that the attempt to reproducing particular notions of statehood still dominates the armed reaction sector and will perhaps be accentuated in the near future as demands for a return to "old school" policing tactics (Chapter 2) become more vociferous.

CHAPTER 4

"Wanna-Be Policemen"

Being an Armed Response Officer

December 2008

I was visiting Thomas, a dear friend of mine, in one of Durban's townships. We were standing against his car outside his mother's house, listening to some tunes and shooting the breeze over a few Black Labels.[1] As the night progressed, more and more of Thomas's friends joined us, and talk turned to how my research was coming along. Thomas and his friends readily disclosed their opinions about private security, namely, that it was for rich people or those who couldn't look after themselves properly. Their views contained not only an underlying sense of contempt but also of envy because, as they eventually admitted, if they had the financial means, they would install alarms and employ security guards in a heartbeat.

As the conversation proceeded and I started to analyze their words, it became evident that their ideas about and experiences of private security were in absolute contrast to those of my friends in the suburbs. The stories coming out of suburbia were of sleeping guards, irritating car guards, and armed reaction officers who arrived too late, only after they had already been robbed at gunpoint. Although such accounts and sentiments were not foreign to my township acquaintances, it was not the stories of the consumers that they shared. Rather, it was the stories of the workers, the men on the ground who perform security. It was in the townships that the experiences of the security officers were narrated, because it was here that the majority of them resided.

We talked all night about being a security officer: the training, the long hours, the poor pay, the suspicious clients, the dangerous sites, and the professional hierarchies. The vicious and underhanded aspects of the industry permeated their accounts: not being paid after months of hard work, working for "fly-by-night" companies, criminals offering bribes to look the other way, and managers yelling at them after falling asleep on duty. They told me that for many, it was a shameful job—not one to be proud of—but one with economic prospects. I then asked the most obvious question: So why do you do it? As I had expected, there was one common answer: "I needed a job."

. . .

In South Africa, security officers do not have a great reputation. As will become clear throughout the remaining chapters, they are often distrusted and suspected of misconduct. When I told people about my research, they frequently made condescending remarks about private security officers and voiced concern that I was placing myself in constant danger by working with such "criminals." This sentiment is echoed by several other studies on private security officers.[2]

The aim of this chapter is to provide a description of the lives of armed reaction officers and the main factors that play a role in their line of work. The previous chapter looked at the different companies that comprise the armed response sector, their various policing styles, the forms of discipline and surveillance they implement, and how race and gender shape the occupational cultural of this line of work. In this chapter, I look more closely at the lives, motivations, backgrounds, and perspectives of the reaction officers.

The first objective of this chapter is to examine how reaction officers view the social, cultural, and organizational aspects of their work and their position within the sector and the industry as a whole. The second aim is to show how armed response officers define themselves in relation to other security officers and the state police. I demonstrate that armed response officers strongly differentiate themselves from other types of security officers, such as Thomas and his friends, and instead, associate themselves with the state police. This is crucial when understanding why and how armed response officers are increasingly policing the public realm.

"JUST A JOB" AND "CRIMINALS IN UNIFORM"

The literature on private security officers has suggested various categorizations of such workers based on their motivations and the type of security they provide.[3] Although each classification is different, they all point to the same spectrum of security officers, ranging from low-skilled employees who are in the industry because they have few (or no) other options at one end, to skilled and dedicated security officers at the other.

In South Africa, the public and members of the industry tend to use three main labels to describe private security officers: the "just a job" officer, the "criminal in uniform," and the "wanna-be policemen." For many of my friends in the townships, security work is "just a job," yet because of the diversity of private security officers in South Africa, applying one label would be reductive. There are five general types of security officers in South Africa: car guards, security guards, national key point protection officers, armed reaction officers, and cash-in-transit officers.[4] These five types constitute a security officer hierarchy, with car guards at the bottom and cash-in-transit officers at the top. The strata of this hierarchy reflect different types and levels of motivations, training, and wages. Armed reaction officers occupy the second highest position on the ladder; they rank higher than security guards, but fall behind cash-in-transit officers on account of the greater risk associated with that form of work.

The "just a job" reputation is common among car guards and security guards, which is supported by the recent work of Sefalafala and Webster (2013). Although there are also armed reaction officers who started with the mentality of "just getting a job," entering the armed reaction sector is a more time-consuming and costly affair, because it demands more skills and training, such as firearm competency. A likely scenario is that an individual starts as a security guard and slowly works his way up to armed reaction. The second and perhaps more ubiquitous characterization of security officers is that they are "criminals in uniform." Whenever a crime takes place, security officers are the first to be blamed. Although such suspicion applies to all private security officers, its degree and intensity are dependent on the officer's position in the security hierarchy; car guards, for example, are mistrusted substantially more than cash-in-transit officers. In South Africa, this suspicion is not entirely unfounded: Security officers are regularly convicted of engaging in criminal activity, both on and off duty. It is for this reason that PSIRA conducts a criminal record check for each prospective employee. In 2010–11,

PSIRA rejected almost 12,000 applications from individuals who were guilty of a "disqualifiable criminal offence" (PSIRA 2010–11, 31).[5] Unfortunately, PSIRA annual reports do not provide further information on the exact amount and types of crimes that lead to the rejection of applications.

Despite PSIRA's evaluation and additional police checks conducted by the companies, some security officers with a criminal past are able to enter the industry undetected and commit crimes after registration. Between 2010 and 2011, 168 registrations were withdrawn when the individual concerned was convicted of a criminal offense after registration. Compared to the nearly 12,000 dismissals before registration, we can conclude that dismissal for criminal activity after registration is uncommon. In several cases, companies turn a blind eye to past criminal activities. In February 2009, I crewed with Barry, an Indian reaction officer in his late twenties, who told me about his criminal past as a (unconvicted) drug dealer. Apparently he had informed his employers about his past, but they had been willing to give him a fresh start. Toward the end of my fieldwork, however, Barry, who was still working as an armed reaction officer, started dealing drugs again. Several other reaction officers admitted to being involved in drug dealing, illegal gambling, fraud, theft, and other crimes. This criminal activity was generally conducted outside their work and was not connected to their occupation.

The reputation of private security officers as "criminals in uniform" is based less on their own involvement in crime than on their possible connections to criminals whom they meet while on duty. When certain crimes take place in South Africa, particularly those closely related to the work of private security such as theft, most people's initial suspicion is that they are "inside jobs."[6] All employees are considered potential insiders, but security officers are the first to be suspected, because their low wages are perceived to make them more susceptible to bribes and corruption. Because most of the security officers live in the townships, areas widely regarded to be home to criminals, collaborative efforts are seen as eminently feasible (see Chapter 7).

Yet collaborating with criminals is more difficult in the armed reaction sector, because it would require the coordination of numerous individuals (e.g., controllers, technicians, officers) from the company's various departments. I heard a few stories of armed response officers working with criminals to stage an armed robbery or some other type of crime, but I did not see any evidence of this during my fieldwork. However, I did know of numerous reaction officers who were dismissed for engaging in criminal activity, most commonly stealing from clients or the company.

"WANNA-BE POLICEMEN"

The "just a job" and "criminals in uniform" labels are therefore not unfounded, yet I argue that armed response officers can best be described as "wanna-be policemen." This description is both assigned to them by the general public and a means by which armed response officers describe themselves.

Many studies have shown how working as a security officer provides an opportunity to gain the experience and expertise necessary for eventual employment in a public law enforcement division (Button 2003; Manzo 2009; Rigakos 2002; Wakefield 2003). Indeed, the majority of the armed reaction officers I met during my time in Durban initially wanted to be policemen. Kenny's experience was fairly typical:

> Every since I was a child, I wanted to be a police officer. I always loved the action, you know, fighting and catching the bad guys. I tried to enter the force, but it didn't work. So I became armed reaction. It's not the same, but it's close. It was the closest thing at the time. I still feel like I'm experiencing that thrill, you know. And that I'm helping people, that I'm doing my part to fight crime and protecting people from the bad guys. And eventually, I'm quite happy about it really. I would never become a policeman now, hell no.[7]

Many reaction officers describe fighting crime as a passion and a "lifestyle." For example, Michael left the industry to work in a call center, where he earned double the money for half the hours. Yet within six months he was back working in armed response; he explained why as follows: "It is my dream to fight crime, to catch the criminals . . . so although I was earning more and living more of a normal life back there, I wasn't happy. This work, it kept calling me back. This here, this is what I must do with my life."[8] This passion to fight crime is particularly prevalent among those who have themselves been the victim of violent crime. Frank, a senior Indian armed response officer in his late forties, was one example:

> About ten years ago, I was running a taxi for a while, and one day, four guys came in as passengers, but as soon as I drove off, they pulled out their guns and held up all of us, the passengers and me. They put a gun to my head, robbed all the passengers of their possessions and started throwing them out of the taxi while I was driving, even a pregnant woman. . . . When all the passengers were out, they made me stop by the road. They forced me out of the

taxi, beat me all over, and tied me up. For a long time, they discussed about whether to kill me or not. They decided no, because of the noise. . . . So they poured petrol over me, dumped me into a garbage bin and set it on fire. And they drove off, left me there to die. The bin was moist and wet, so I escaped and survived. But you can see the scars [he points out the numerous scars on his body]. The next week I started the security training. I decided then: this country is going to hell with the crime, and it is my role, as a citizen, to do something about it.[9]

As discussed in the previous chapter, many private security companies encourage a proactive policing style, and this, I argue, promotes a wanna-be policemen mentality among reaction officers. To understand this process, one must consider the historical background of the armed response sector. The ex-policemen who operated the one-man shows of the 1980s portrayed themselves as men who wanted to fight crime and protect their community. Others described them as men who went "out of their way" to go "the extra mile." This description is linked to a policing style that is often referred to as "old school," an oppressive form of policing steered by the "*skop, skiet en donder*" attitude that prevailed under apartheid rule (see Chapter 2). Because its practitioners were white reaction officers, old school policing also had a racial dimension. According to a white female controller who had been in the industry for many years, the situation was better in the past:

> I don't mean to be racist, but it was more fun with the white guys. They used to chase cars on the highway, really go after it. Now they don't do that anymore. When their shift is up, they stop, no matter what's going on at that time. It's just different. No heart, no passion. The old school style has gone, which is sad.[10]

"Old school" therefore refers to particular policing practices, and because of its association with apartheid, it also refers to the racial identities of the individuals engaged in these practices.

Because the term "old school" policing refers to a style that prevailed some twenty years ago, many of those involved in it are now at least in their early forties. As elsewhere, the majority of security officers in South Africa are between twenty and forty years old (Button 2007; Rigakos 2002; van Steden 2007; Wakefield 2003). According to PSIRA regulations, all private security officers must be at least eighteen years old. In the armed response sector, the minimum age for officers is twenty-one because of legal stipulations regarding the use of firearms in South Africa, as outlined in the Firearms Control Act 60 of 2000 (Berg 2003: 190).

Armed response officers in their early forties or older, who experienced old school policing practices, are now therefore in the minority. Brian, who had been working in the sector since the early 1990s, described how old school officers differ from their younger counterparts during one of our conversations in November 2008:

Brian: The old school guys, we have passion for this work. We saw how it was back then: this work was more intense; gun laws were different. . . . Everybody knew each other; we were friends, no matter which company you worked for. But now it's different, these new guys are different.

Me: Are there other differences between the new and old guys?

Brian: Hell yeah! Man, the new guys, they are lazy. Lazy. For them, this job is classy, they just like to drive around and look cool, like they got game. They lack the passion, that drive to go further. . . .

Me: And why do you think that is?

Brian: Because the industry has just changed. Back in the day, there weren't many of us, so we really had to fight for it. There was more crime, and well, the streets were different then; they were rougher, and security, we could do more. But now it's like, we drive a car, we cool, you know? It's more about money and looking good than wanting to catch criminals. . . . So when the shit goes down, I rely on the old schoolers, 'cos I know they're good backup.

Brian's explanation highlights how old school policing practices are no longer deemed to be as important by those in the armed response sector. At the same time, there is also evidence that the public is increasingly demanding a return to old school policing practices. I therefore argue that the legacies of old school policing continue to shape the armed response sector. For most armed response officers, then, it is not "just a job;" rather, their main motivation for entering the sector is fighting crime.

"A DOCTOR AND A DENTIST"

The armed response officers' passion for fighting crime further explains why most of them associate themselves with state police officers rather than with other types of security personnel, as Nick explained to me:

A lot of people see us like they see policemen: someone that puts his life on the line for you; someone you treat with respect. Someone you should take seriously. But a security guard doesn't get that. People see him as someone that just stands there at a place and doesn't really do anything. He's useless. We are not security guards; there is a really big difference.[11]

In fact, many armed reaction officers are insulted when people refer to them as security guards. The South African term *machinjingilani* (isiZulu for "marching the line") is a derogatory word for security officers that is used to express disrespect and contempt.[12] Armed response officers are especially insulted by this term, because they feel that they are "worlds apart" from security guards.

This distinction between armed response officers and other types of security workers is made not only by the reaction officers themselves but also by the industry as a whole. According to several of my informants, guarding and armed response have always been two separate worlds: They are like the difference between "a doctor and a dentist."[13] The white former owner of an armed reaction company described this division as follows:

> The industry is pretty much split. It has always been like that. I mean, the security guards guard property, are paid a pittance, but the reaction guys, they have guns, drive around in vehicles, and they earn much better. There is a difference in caliber, with the reaction guy having more training, more skills. . . . Armed reaction and guarding were always separate things. Now you've got companies that are doing both, so it seems connected, but they're not.[14]

The following sections discuss two important factors that distinguish armed reaction from guarding: training and wages.

"We Can Do Much More"

Across the industry, members complained about the poor quality of the security training and claimed that this was the main reason for the negative reputation of security officers. Other studies of security work have reported similar low standards of training (Button 2007; Manzo 2004; Sefalafala and Webster 2013; van Steden 2007; Wakefield 2003). For example, Hobbs et al. assert that the training for bouncers in the United Kingdom is a "short, awareness-raising programme rather than comprehensive occupational training" and that, because of fierce competition, the schools (and companies) are forced to stick to a "minimum standard of learning" (2002: 365).

After completing security training in October 2008 and visiting other training facilities throughout my fieldwork, I believe that the poor standards identified by other scholars also apply to South Africa. Despite the differences among the 530 accredited training centers (PSIRA 2010–11), the quality of the security training is generally poor. In addition, cheating among students is widespread, instructors readily accept bribes from students, certificates are often falsified, and it seems that many participants simply memorize what is taught to them without actually understanding it. Yet perhaps this is not so surprising. There are few formal requirements for those wishing to undergo training, and they are rarely checked. The training is inexpensive (completing grades E, D, and C costs approximately R 700 in 2009) and thus attracts many individuals who fit the "just a job" profile.[15]

Originally, the Security Officers Board (SOB) Training Regulations were the training standards of the private security industry (Berg 2003). When the SOB was transformed into PSIRA in 2001, the training standards were also transferred. However, PSIRA came under increasing criticism from security employees for failing to inspect the training schools in an efficient manner. On July 4, 2005, the Safety and Security Sector Education and Training Authority (SASSETA) took over the regulation of security training. Since then, SASSETA has been responsible for inspecting and accrediting the training schools and instructors, ensuring the legitimacy of the certifications, and recognizing prior learning of those who had already undergone the training.

Although the transfer of the regulation of training from PSIRA to SASSETA has been welcomed throughout the industry, security training continues to attract criticism as being inadequate and is therefore currently being redesigned. In 2008, when I went through the training, it was divided into five skill levels, from "grade E," the lowest, to "grade A," the highest.[16] The training for each level comprised a week of classroom instruction and practical instruction in skill development. The ranking system creates a series of unified strata within the industry, such that a grade E security officer in company A possesses the same skills as a grade E security officer in company B, and so on. For armed reaction officers, the minimum entry requirement is a grade C certificate combined with additional armed reaction training. The additional training introduces the essentials of armed reaction: crime scene management, dealing with "strangers" on clients' premises, handling victims, issuing statements, and participating in court procedures. Additionally, armed reaction officers must have a driver's license and a firearm license.

In addition to the instruction provided at the training centers, many companies provide their own supplementary in-house training, which primarily focuses on the guidelines of that specific company. Several companies also have their own courses. BLUE Security, for example, runs an additional biannual armed response training session called Hellsgate, which includes shooting exercises, vehicle chase/driving courses, obstacles courses, and house protection and entering exercises. Participants are also given additional legal training and take part in an array of team-building exercises. Furthermore, most companies implement a type of "peer training." When armed reaction officers are first recruited, they must undergo a trial period in which they ride with senior personnel before being allowed to operate their own vehicles. During this trial period, the officers get a firsthand perspective of the occupation and are taught about the rules and requirements of the company in question.

The structure of private security training is based on, and further strengthens, a hierarchy of security officers that places armed response officers and security guards in different categories. This hierarchy reinforces the prevailing mentality among reaction officers that "we can do much more."

"We're Not Graphing for the Money"

Training levels also determine wage rates. Table 3 presents the monthly salary rates of security officers from 2009 and 2012, as stipulated by the Department of Labor. The poor reputation of security officers is largely driven by the low wages (Button 2007; Manzo 2006; Micucci 1998; Rigakos 2002; van Steden 2007). Let us compare these wages rate to those of other sectors in South Africa. In 2012, domestic workers (i.e., housekeepers, gardeners, and drivers) working more than twenty-seven hours per week had a minimum hourly rate of R 8.95, resulting in a monthly salary of at least R 1,746.[17] That same year, employees in the hospitality sector had an hourly rate of R 11.49 and a monthly rate of R 2240.6.[18] By looking at Table 3, we can conclude that low-level security officers (grades E and D) therefore earn more than domestic workers but less than those in the hospitality sector, yet security officers also work longer hours.

Table 3 does not show the wage rates for armed reaction officers, because these rates are determined not by the Department of Labor, but by the companies themselves. Armed reaction officers generally earn between R 3,000 and 8,000 per month, depending on their rank and employer. Each company has an entry-level wage of around R 3,000–4,000 per month. Monthly wages increase the longer one works for a company

TABLE 3   MONTHLY SALARY RATES FOR SECURITY OFFICERS IN SOUTH AFRICA

Grade level	Monthly rate 2009	Hourly rate 2009	Monthly rate 2012	Hourly rate 2012
Car guards	R 2,024	R 10.38	NA	NA
Grade E	R 2,101	R 10.10	NA	NA
Grade D	R 2,195	R 10.55	R 2,519	R 12.11
Grade C	R 2,367	R 11.38	R 2,691	R 12.94
Grade B	R 2,887	R 13.88	R 3,211	R 15.44
Grade A	R 3,334	R 16.03	R 3,658	R 17.59

SOURCE: PSIRA website (www.psira.co.za).

NOTE: In the wage determination, there is a geographical demarcation into four areas, with rates being higher in the urban areas. These rates refer to Area 1, which covers the Magisterial District where Durban is situated. The rates for 2012 were in effect from September 1, 2011, to August 31, 2012. Table 3 also shows that grade E was nonexistent in 2012.

and when one is promoted to a higher rank. The lowest monthly salary I encountered was R 3,000, while the highest (earned by a high-ranking officer with eighteen years of experience) was R 8,100. These monthly salaries contain a "bonus incentive" of between R 200 and 600 that armed response officers receive if they perform well. However, if they perform poorly, such as by arriving late on duty, an amount is deducted from this bonus as a penalty. If a company owner states that the firm's reaction officers earn R 6,000, this means that they earn about R 5,600 per month with a R 400 bonus incentive that they may or may not receive. The wages of armed response officers have decreased substantially since the 1980s and early 1990s, when armed response officers earned more than their counterparts in the state police. As the sector expanded and the demand for reaction officers grew, the supply grew to meet the demand and salaries fell rapidly.

Because the armed response sector is effectively an oligopoly, wages are generally the same for all companies, and if one of the big players increases its wages, the rest tend to follow. Where there is divergence, however, even a slight difference in wages can motivate a reaction officer to move from one company to another. In some rare cases, however, officers choose to work for a lower wage in a small company where they feel more appreciated, as was true for Kenny:

> I can go and work for one of those big companies; they've asked me to come over before. But I like it here. I'm not a number. I know the boss, the big man, personally. If I need something, I just ask him, and don't have to talk to four levels of management before I get there. Yes, we *graph* [work] more here, money is less, fewer days off, but it's the personal connection that does it.[19]

Although reaction officers earn substantially more than other security officers, the wages are not their main motivation to work in this sector. Many continually complained about their salaries, and several stated that "we're not graphing for the money." This dissatisfaction with their salaries is exacerbated by additional financial difficulties associated with their occupation. The first concerns the equipment they must pay for themselves. Although PSIRA stipulates that companies must provide uniforms and necessary gear, the reality is that many reaction officers are forced to buy their own equipment, such as batons, jackets, and bulletproof vests. This gear is generally paid for in installments deducted from the officers' salaries. The second financial challenge involves the lack of overtime pay and the need to attend work-related events, such as court appearances and company meetings, on their days off.

The third and largest financial difficulty concerns the costs that "come with the job," such as speeding tickets and bail money, which most armed response officers feel should be paid by the companies, not by them. For example, if an officer receives notification that a client may be in danger, he will race over to the client's premises and will thus risk getting a speeding ticket. Officers claim that this is a Catch-22, for if they fail to arrive at this premises promptly they are likely to be penalized for not assisting the client properly. In turn, several managers cited vehicle costs as their largest financial strain and claim that reaction officers are too reckless and "behave like idiots on the road." One Indian manager of a medium-sized company claimed to have spent R 1.8 million on vehicle repairs in 2008–09.[20] Managers argue that insurance policies cover such costs if a reaction officer is not at fault, but reaction officers dispute this, claiming that the costs are always deducted from their salaries. For many reaction officers, the situation is so dire that they are in major debt to their employers. I met several officers who had debts of between R 10,000 and 30,000, which would take them the rest of their lives to pay off. Some jokingly stated that they had become "silent partners" in the company.

It is primarily for this reason that many reaction officers actively seek additional sources of income. In November 2008, I went on a day shift with Gayle that began with a visit to a business client who had been robbed during the night. Having only been on duty for a couple of weeks, I was surprised to see Gayle transform into a sales agent and technical expert. He started by explaining to the client why the criminals had been able to rob his business and what was lacking in terms of security appliances; he then outlined an array of extra equipment the client *needed* to ensure this crime would not happen again. Gayle was convincing: The client listened intensely and eventually purchased some of the equipment that Gayle had recommended. When we got back into the car, Gayle had a massive grin on his face. Initially I thought he was just happy about his performance, but then he explained that if the client went through with the purchase, he would get a percentage of the payment.

Receiving commission from the acquisition of new clients or the installation of additional equipment is one of the most common ways for armed response officers to earn supplementary income while on duty. For some reaction officers, this source of income is crucial, and they will go to great lengths to try to win over new clients. They work especially hard to earn commission from collective clients, actively encouraging community members to join the group (see Chapter 6). Another source of income stems from informal ties with other businesses, such as tow trucking companies and vehicle repair shops. Armed reaction officers strike deals with such companies to receive a margin of their earnings from client referrals.

However, the most common way for reaction officers to earn additional income is by moonlighting. "Moonlighting" is a generic term; some in the industry use it to refer to any form of work that officers engage in outside their working hours, while others apply it only to security-related work conducted while off duty. Many of the armed reaction officers I knew were involved in other businesses, often with family members. Matthew, an Indian officer in his forties, worked with his family selling food products at local markets, while William assisted his wife in her retail business. Manual labor, such as tiling, was another common source of income. The general rule employed by most companies is that reaction officers must report any off-duty work activities to their managers, who will then decide whether they are permissible, as the following statement from a white operations manager of a medium-sized company highlights:

> If a guy helps his wife on a Sunday selling fruits and vegetable, or is doing some construction work, I've got no problem with that. If it doesn't interfere with his work here and he tells me about it, I'm fine. The problem is when it does affect their work for us, when he's got clients that are our clients, or when he's showing up to work exhausted. And the big problem comes when he's doing security work. That is not tolerated, at all.[21]

Despite this alleged lack of tolerance, numerous armed reaction officers are engaged in other security-related activities. In addition to his drug dealing, Barry also sporadically worked as a bouncer for a nightclub in his area and as a bodyguard for a relative's company. Dirk, a white reaction officer in his forties, was regularly involved in VIP protection, and David, another white reaction officer in his forties, was frequently recruited as a debt collector. Several armed response officers were police reservists or were engaged in security-based community initiatives in their own neighborhoods. Most did not believe that security-related moonlighting affected their main work, and many felt entitled to "outsource" themselves for extra money.

However, there were also cases of security-related work that emerged from encounters on duty. Tim, a white reaction officer in his late forties, worked as a bouncer on his off days for a bar that happened to be a client of his employer. Although he stated that he never worked as a reaction officer and a bouncer simultaneously, he obviously gave preferential treatment to this client. Everybody at the company knew about this, even the managers, so it seemed that the situation was tolerated. The same applied to Sanjeev, an Indian armed response officer in his early thirties, who did "extra chores" for certain commercial clients in the area that he had patrolled, such as providing security when opening and closing their businesses.

Thus, whether it is by signing up new clients, networking with related businesses, or moonlighting, many armed reaction officers actively seek extra income to improve their financial circumstances. Yet, though they do not become reaction officers for the wages, they know that they are paid better than other security officers, a fact that they habitually use to differentiate themselves, as evidenced by statements such as "we can do more" and "we earn more." However, armed response officers primarily define themselves (particularly in relation to others) according to the nature of their work: they patrol the streets, possess a firearm and vehicle, and, in their eyes, "actually fight crime."

ON THE ROAD

December 2008

Gayle, an area supervisor, picked me up at 5:30 a.m. to start the day shift. He was a little late, since he had had to wait for a client to go to a site that had been broken into during the night. Not a lot had been stolen, but they had had to get all the paperwork sorted before the police could take over. We started the shift by monitoring the openings and closings of several businesses of one of their "special projects" and then headed to a gas station frequented by other officers from Gayle's company to grab a coffee. Gayle told me the night shift was quiet—mainly false alarms and two minor break-ins. We then received a call-out about an alarm activation nearby. We went to the site in question: The client wasn't there, we conducted a perimeter check, realized it was a false alarm, left behind a call slip, and then departed. Over the next few hours, we attended two more call-outs, both false alarms. We spent time patrolling areas where a lot of clients were based or where there had recently been more incidents of crime. Every so often, Gayle pulled up next to one of the other officers working in "his area": He inquired whether everything was fine, checked their records of the day, and picked up the necessary paperwork, which included the statement written by Mark, another Indian armed response officer in his late twenties, about yesterday's break-in. We had lunch with Mark at a small grocery store while we waited for the next call-out.

After lunch, Gayle sighed and said we had to see Leonard, a white armed reaction officer in his early fifties, who had been late to work several times in recent weeks and was known to have an alcohol problem. Gayle needed to give him a written warning and to "have a talk" with him about his tardiness. When we saw Leonard, he acted rather cool about the whole situation. He admitted that he had been late, but didn't really give any explanation. He did seem concerned about the written warning, but then just shrugged and accepted the letter without any resistance. Gayle and I then headed over to the company office to deliver all of the paperwork to the armed response manager. Afterward we conducted two more call-outs—both false alarms—before finishing up for the day. Gayle dropped me off at home and then headed out to pick up his replacement for the night shift.

. . .

The preceding account, which is a summarized version of my field notes, describes one of my day shifts with a large company. It excludes various details and observations, such as the numerous conversations I had with Gayle and the other reaction officers. Although there is much diversity within and between companies, the intent here is to illustrate a typical day on duty as an armed response officer. It should be noted, however, that Gayle is a senior armed reaction officer—an "area manager"—and therefore has tasks, such as checking up on his colleagues working in his area, that armed reaction officers of lower rank do not have.

This section discusses two features that define a typical day on the road. The first is that the majority of call-outs are false alarms. With most companies, "positives" (i.e., incidents of crime) do not happen on a daily basis, and when they do occur, they tend to be break-ins that took place before the reaction officer arrived on site. Arriving at a scene while a crime is in progress is not part of their daily routine. Yet some companies face more "positives" than others, and certain periods, such as weekends after payday and Christmas, are particularly busy. The second feature is that armed response officers spend most of their day sitting alone in their vehicles.[22]

One of the main complaints that armed response officers have about their job concerns the working hours, an issue identified in other research on security officers (Button 2007; Manzo 2006; Micucci 1998; Rigakos 2002; Sefalafala and Webster 2013; van Steden 2007). Like other policing bodies in South Africa, armed reaction officers operate using a system of day and night shifts. Most companies employ a "3 day, 3 night, and 3 off system," which means that officers work three day shifts and three night shifts before having three days off. Each shift lasts for twelve hours, and officers are generally expected to report in approximately thirty minutes beforehand.

Each company has its own system for rotating armed reaction officers, but many place their officers in a certain geographical area for a substantial amount of time. This allows the reaction officer to get to know the specifics of the area, such as the road names and client details. Each area has its own rules and guidelines that are primarily determined by the clients. Companies work with "standing-down" points, which are particular locations where a vehicle must stand still, often during stipulated time slots. Managers claim that these points are chosen for strategic reasons, yet they are clearly also selected for marketing purposes, since they are found at busy intersections with high visibility, rather than in the remote corners of residential areas. Some companies demand that officers actively patrol areas, while others encourage them to remain at an easily accessible point. Some firms expect that the vehicles be washed on a daily basis. Some companies demand that certain clients are monitored regularly. Therefore, when a reaction officer is stationed in a new area, he is provided with rough guidelines regarding standard protocol in that locality. Reaction officers also have preferences for certain areas.

For example, Gayle loved working in quieter residential areas while Mark preferred the busy city center.

After working in an area for a period of time, reaction officers often establish close relationships with clients. Managers both encourage and restrict these relationships. In December 2008, I met with the community manager of a large company to talk about collective clients (see Chapter 6). We started talking about Keith, one of the armed reaction officers working for that company, and his popularity in the neighborhood of one of their collective clients. When I mentioned how clients were enthusiastic and appreciative about his performance, she tensed up and made a pained expression. "Well, he's popular," she mumbled, "but we can't let him get too friendly." When I asked her what she meant by this, she explained that she did not want the community to get too attached to Keith, because "anything can change in the near future." Evidently, she was worried he might leave the company and work directly for the community initiative. This would mean that the client (i.e., the community initiative) would no longer require the services of her company. She was also apprehensive that he would perform favors for clients and that he might engage in some form of moonlighting or find other work in the area. In the eyes of the companies, the more time an armed response officer is stationed in an area, the more susceptible he is to moonlighting. To prevent this, companies have a rotation system whereby officers are regularly reassigned to new localities. However, armed response officers generally prefer to stay in one area so they can build up relationships with clients as they provide them with social interactions and "shape up" their shifts.

The daily routine of a reaction officer is thus highly dependent on the rules of his employer and the area in which he works. Yet all reaction officers regarded their work as lonely and boring. If there are no incidents for an entire day, reaction officers end up spending the entire twelve-hour shift alone in their vehicle. The risk of danger is ever present, but boredom and mundane routine work are a large part of this occupation, as they are for other armed forces (Grassiani 2013; Reiner 2000). For this reason, social interaction with colleagues stationed nearby is highly valued. Reaction officers often develop friendships with one another and hang out together on their days off, especially if they live in the same area and work the same shifts. Yet, arguments between reaction officers are not uncommon. However, although I knew many reaction officers who disliked some of their colleagues, I only witnessed three cases of colleagues coming to blows over work-related issues.

One aspect of the armed response sector that particularly stood out is the lack of interaction and cooperation between armed response officers from different companies. It seemed as if the competition between companies has trickled down to the ground level, since reaction officers are discouraged from engaging with those working for other companies, which had not always been the case, as Brian explained:

> Before, we always used to park off together and chill. Many times, there'd be a few vehicles, all different companies, parked off at the same place, catching up. We were friends; we made jokes. We worked for different guys, but we were the same at the end of the day. And we helped each other, told each other about things going on, any crime updates, it was good. But now, it's not allowed. Management says we shouldn't do it. It's not good for the company image, or something like that. So now it happens less. And the new guys, they don't know better. So there's more distance, more competition . . . and it makes it even quieter in the vehicle. But us old schoolers, we still do it, 'cos it's in our system.[23]

This minimal level of social interaction also leads officers to badmouth other companies. Many reaction officers were quick to belittle the policing practices of their competitors and frequently made comments to the effect that "we are better" or "you don't want to be one of their clients."

However, despite the decreased camaraderie and increased competition between employees of different companies, there is still a general sense of unity among reaction officers. This became evident when I talked with my informants about the risks and dangers involved in armed response work. Everyone referred to the recent death (during the time of my research) of Dick van Eyck, an armed reaction officer from BLUE Security. Although they worked for different companies, my informants described Dick as "one of us," and the majority knew the exact details of his death. These elements of group loyalty and social inclusion are also deeply rooted among police officers (Loyens 2009).

Although this sense of unity among armed response officers has diminished over the years, group cohesion still occurs when a "they" emerges. The "they" in question is any group from which armed response officers look to distinguish themselves, such as management. This cohesion is particularly apparent when other armed reaction officers are guilty of misconduct, such as coming on shift late or drinking alcohol on duty. Although such behavior is generally frowned on and armed response officers gossip about such activities among themselves, it is very rare that they report such misconduct to management. For example, in December 2008, rumors reached the management of one company that three of its reaction officers were repeatedly getting drunk together while on duty. The managers questioned all of the reaction officers about these allegations, but all denied them, despite some of them knowing the rumors to be true. Loyalty among reaction officers is even stronger when they are friends and work the same shift. If armed reaction officers do tell on each other, they will do so generally to the reaction officer(s) of higher rank, who can then choose whether to inform management.

This sense of cohesion highlights how reaction officers collectively feel that they form a distinct group that operates independently of management. As in the scenario I observed at the Armed Reaction Man Competition in 2010, there is very little interaction between management and operations in their daily routines. The following example attests to this separation. When I returned to Durban in April 2010, I visited one of the large companies that I had worked with the year before. I was immediately introduced to the new assistant armed reaction manager who had been hired a few months earlier. When I joined some of the reaction officers in their vehicles, I asked them what they thought of their new manager, but to my surprise, it turned out that only two of them—both of higher rank—had actually met him. In many companies, particularly the large ones, management and operations rarely meet, as reaction officers conduct their shift changes on the road rather than in the office. In small companies, however, shift changes often take place at the company office, and managers are more involved in day-to-day matters.

The division between management and operations is also evident when reaction officers are promoted to higher ranking or management positions. On the rare occasions when this happens, the relationship with the other armed response officers changes, because he is now "closer" to management. In 2008, I frequently went on patrol with Nick, an Indian senior officer at a large company, who was very close with several of the reaction officers. When I returned to the company in 2010, however, I found that Nick had been promoted to assistant armed response manager and was now working from the office. Unfortunately for Nick, his close relationship(s) with the other reaction officers had turned sour, and many felt that he had changed, since he was now "on the other side" and was working against management, not alongside them.

"TOOLS OF THE TRADE"

In the literature on private security, one of main points of discussion concerns the legal rights and powers of private security officers (Boghosian

2005; Button 2007; Joh 2005; Thorburn 2008) and how they relate to the officers' various "tools of the trade" (Mopas and Stenning 2001). With a few notable exceptions, security officers worldwide do not generally possess powers beyond those of ordinary citizens. This is the case in South Africa, where the Criminal Procedure Act 51 of 1977 compels individuals in the security industry to operate within the parameters of state law. Thus, security officers may only use powers granted to "private persons." Singh neatly summarizes the powers of security officers under the Criminal Procedure Act (51 of 1977) in South Africa:

> [Security officers are] empowered to arrest, without a warrant, anyone seen to be engaged in an affray and anyone "reasonably" believed to have committed *any* offence and who is fleeing a pursuing individual who "reasonably" appears to be authorized to effect an arrest for that particular offence. The term "reasonable" is open to wide interpretation. Private security may also, without a warrant, arrest and pursue any person who commits, attempts to commit or is reasonably suspected of committing any Schedule 1 offence. [Discussion of Schedule 1 offence] Further still, as agents of the owner, occupier or manager of property, private security may arrest without a warrant any person found committing *any* offence on or in respect of that property. In order to effect an arrest in any of the above circumstances, security personnel are authorized to break open, enter and search any premises on which the person to be arrested is known or reasonably suspected to be. Furthermore, they are empowered to use reasonable force, and lethal force in relation to Schedule 1 offences, where an arrest can not be effected by other means and where resistance occurs, or where the suspect flees. (2008: 50, italics in original)

According to Singh, the rights bestowed on citizens in South Africa are "far-reaching" when compared to international standards since these rights were conceived during the apartheid era, when citizens were granted powers "to defend the state against threats to its sovereignty" (Singh 2008: 50).

Numerous other studies have also highlighted the significant powers enjoyed by security officers (e.g., Button 2007; Rigakos 2002; South 1988; and Stenning 2000). Braun and Lee, for instance, argue that the "private police enjoy extensive powers which enable them to perform functions analogous to public police activity" (1970/71: 582). This claim is based on two premises. The first is that the legal rights of private security officers cannot be compared to those of citizens due to differences in access to and possession of this legal knowledge. As Joh (2005) argues, citizens are often unaware of their rights to arrest suspects, whereas security officers are trained in this knowledge and regularly invoke it.

Button (2007: 14) refers to this access to information as "knowledge tools" and notes how effective use of these tools provides security officers with more confidence and ability to obtain authority.

The second premise is that the authority and legal rights of private security officers are bestowed through private relationships and contracts. By entering into contractual agreements with clients, private security officers have the right to search people and property, carry out various surveillance techniques, enforce sanctions, determine access, and evict individuals from private premises (Button 2007; Mopas and Stenning 2001; Stenning 2000). By restricting the access of particular individuals to certain spaces, security officers are exercising a power that lies "beyond those universal rights all citizens possess" (Button 2003: 230). The legal powers of the private police thus stem from a "legal relationship they have both with those who employ them (the property owners) and with those whom they police (persons using the property)" (Stenning 2000: 332). Therefore, when citizens or businesses subscribe to an armed response company's services, they enter into a contractual agreement that bestows certain rights of access and conduct on armed reaction officers on their premises.

The legal rights of security officers are therefore fairly wide ranging (although unquestionably less so than those of the state police). There are also several other "tools of the trade," including institutional, physical, personal, and symbolic tools, that private security officers can employ.[24] Mopas and Stenning (2001) emphasize how symbolic power is essential in ensuring the public's compliance. Much like the public police (Loader 1997a), private security officers obtain authority from the symbolic nature of their uniforms and equipment. In fact, Stenning argues, private security officers make more use of symbolic power than the public police, because they "are much less closely oriented towards, and reliant upon, the formal criminal justice system" (2000: 334). By driving in marked vehicles, wearing customized badges and uniforms, and possessing a firearm, officers exhibit a symbolic authority that ensures compliance. It is the possession of firearms, in particular, that signals this authority and the powers that accompany it (Button 2007: 11). In their study on the powers of bouncers, Hobbs et al. (2002) employ the term "bodily capital" to analyze how these individuals display their ability to use force to deny access. Based on the work of Goffman (1959), these authors discuss how bouncers cultivate an intimidating and authoritative appearance to perform their duties. This is clearly the case for armed reaction officers, whose entire appearance is designed to exude influence and authority. Elsewhere (Diphoorn 2015), I have demonstrated how armed response officers experience particular parts of their "gear," particularly bulletproof vests and firearms, as a part of their body and how they are very reliant on such equipment to ensure their own safety and to acquire (symbolic) authority amidst violent circumstances. The bodily capital of armed response officers is thus their most important tool of the trade.

It is generally argued that, in comparison to the public police, private security officers rely less on coercive tools and use less physical force (Mopas and Stenning 2001). Stenning argues that private security officers are more reluctant to enforce their legal powers through coercion because of a "legal regime which treats them less favourably than it treats public police" (2000: 335). Stenning further argues that the prominent role of technological hardware in the private security sector leads to less direct human contact, making coercive confrontations far less likely than in state policing. In contrast, I argue that coercion and violence are essential parts of the occupational culture of armed response, which is a "culture created around violence and violent expectation" (Winlow et al. 2001: 537). This does not mean that private security officers encounter or employ violence on a daily basis—quite the contrary. However, armed response officers possess a firearm and are trained to use force when necessary. Like the state police, their entire appearance is intended to convey a willingness and ability to employ coercive tools. Martin (2013) refers to this as "force capital," which is the "ability to deploy or threaten to deploy force across space" (153). Force capital includes both physical resources, such as personnel and weaponry, and nonphysical resources, such as training and reputation, and is employed both directly, such as through the use of physical force, and indirectly, such as through intimidation. The combination of bodily and force capital is essential in "the cultivation of an authoritatively intimidating appearance and demeanour" that accentuate an individual's ability to commit violence and underline his position of "authority and dominance within the milieu" (Hobbs et al. 2002: 357). Similar to the finding by Hobbs et al. (2002) relating to bouncers, the ability to fight is the most crucial attribute for armed response officers.

As discussed in the previous chapter, different companies promote different policing styles and therefore instruct their armed reaction officers in different ways, particularly concerning the use of force. Some companies encourage their armed reaction officers to avoid situations that may lead to physical confrontation, whereas other companies actively press their officers to chase suspects. Although the latter companies do not promote violence as a policy, they generally encourage the use of violence in "getting the job done." As one white owner of a small company explained to me, "I encourage my guys to shoot. If they're being threatened or their lives are in any form of danger, they must shoot. It's an order."[25] Paul, an Indian owner, openly admitted that he recruited men based on their ability to fight and shoot:

> I employ these guys based on the fact that they're fucked up, that they're screwed up somehow. It makes them good and hard workers. And you have to be kind of messed up to do this work. And you gotta know how to fight, how to hit hard. You can't be fragile, too kind or sensitive. They won't survive. No matter what their past or background is—if they have passion and are ready to do the hard work, I'll employ them.[26]

The cultivation of force and bodily capital therefore plays a prominent role in the armed response sector and is closely linked to its masculinization processes. This does not mean that force is always used, but simply that the sector fosters policing practices that center on the *ability* to use force.

Although the use of violence is explored in more detail in Chapter 7, let me point out here that armed reaction officers frequently use intimidation and coercion to ensure complicity and authority. In fact, the threat of force is inherent in their policing practices. Having previously described that violence is the source of sovereign power (Chapter 1), I reiterate here how the ability to impose punishment and inflict violence on other bodies is cultivated by the occupational culture of the armed response sector.

OCCUPATIONAL HAZARDS

When I returned to Durban for my second period of fieldwork in April 2010, my first meeting with one of my informants proved to be a grim reminder of what had occurred in my absence. Although I expected that some things would have changed in my absence, I was not prepared to hear that some of my informants had died. And while none of these deaths occurred in the line of duty, several were indirectly associated with the occupation, which highlighted the occupational hazards associated with armed response work.

"Cannon Fodder" and "Thrill Seekers"

The most recent armed response officer to die on duty at the time of writing was Dick van Eyck from BLUE Security, who was killed in December 2007.[27] The death was mourned by all in Durban's private security industry, in particular the armed response officers, who all knew the exact details of the fateful call-out that cost him his life. In December 2008 during one of our patrols, Brian explained to me the impact of Dick's death:

Me: Are you ever scared about a call-out?

Brian: I used to be, but not anymore. When we know something is definitely going down, you feel adrenaline, but not like it used to be, when I first started doing this work. But it's good to be a little bit scared—it keeps the edge on. You have to treat every call-out seriously. Although the majority are false alarms, you never know when there can be a positive.

Me: And what about the other guys?

Brian: Hell yeah, especially the new guys. You can tell that many are just too chicken shit, but those guys won't stay in the industry too long. At one point they won't be able to take the pressure. When Dick died, many of us got worried. We all started to think: shit, this is serious, what's gonna happen to our families if something happens to me? His death really made us realize that this is a very dangerous job, no jokes. When the shit goes down, it goes down, for real he. But now that time has passed, the guys are more relaxed again; nobody has been seriously hurt in a long time. As soon as that happens again, which it will, you'll see them tightening up again, getting that look on their face.

Me: What look?

Brian: That look of shit: this job is dangerous and I'm doing it.

Although Dick is the only officer I am aware of to have been killed on duty since 2007, the risk of danger is ever present for armed response officers, as it is for the state police (Reiner 2000). Even though this threat is generally regarded as being less pervasive in the private security sector, studies increasingly show that violence, verbal abuse, and intimidation are frequent occurrences (Button 2007; Loyens 2009; Rigakos

2002). During my fieldwork, violence and danger were certainly not daily occurrences, yet I witnessed numerous violent and fearful incidents in the field that further attest to the constant risk of violence. As the "first line of duty," reaction officers are usually the first persons to respond to a crime scene. A police reservist once mentioned to me that armed reaction officers were the "cannon fodder" of the policing business, and many informants supported this description.[28] The main risk for reaction officers is becoming victims of crime themselves, particularly since they possess firearms, which are in high demand among criminals and make them an attractive target. During my fieldwork I heard of numerous cases where firearms were stolen from reaction officers.

The danger is heightened by the fact that reaction officers operate alone in their vehicles; this practice stands in stark contrast to police officers, who usually operate in teams. As one operations manager said to me, "These guys are like the police except they're all on their own."[29] When I asked my informants what aspect of their work was most in need of improvement, they all stated that working with another officer would be not only more enjoyable but also safer and more efficient. Numerous reaction officers provided examples of instances where they were together in a vehicle by chance (such as during a shift change) and were more successful in apprehending suspects, because they were able to operate as a team.

Just like the "canteen talk" (Waddington 1999) among the public police, for whom storytelling and reminiscing about certain incidents are core parts of the job, reaction officers habitually recollect violent incidents. These recollections become habitual primarily because of the mundane nature of their work, which affords plenty of time to "just hang around." Retelling these stories reinforces the perception that danger is imminent.

In addition to the potential risks to the lives of armed response officers, injuries on duty are also common. Every single reaction officer I encountered had experienced some form of work-related injury, which ranged from small cuts to gunshot wounds. The armed response officers of one large company had experienced 167 "serious" on-duty injuries that required hospitalization between 2007 and 2009. Such serious injuries generally occurred while chasing suspects on foot, climbing over high walls or fences, or during car accidents while chasing criminals.

In their own social environments, reaction officers are sometimes threatened, pressured to engage in crime, and confronted by acquaintances who are "on the other side." In November 2008, Craig, a black technician working for a small company, told me about his experiences while working as a reaction officer:

Me: Why did you stop with armed response?

Craig: *Eish*,[30] the danger! When I was an armed response officer, there was an incident, a nasty one. There was an armed robbery and two of my colleagues, armed response guys, shot two of the suspects. And I knew these guys, the suspects.

Me: How did you know them?

Craig: They also come from my township. See, about a month later, while I was working, I was called out to that same house, where that armed robbery was before. I did a check, the window was broken, but nobody was on site, so I assumed that all was fine. That same day, when I got home, these two guys [the suspects] came up to me and said, "Hey, we didn't know you are working for that company." The thing is that my car didn't have the name of the company on it, so they didn't know. So I asked them, "How did you find out, what do you mean?" And they said, "We saw you today. We were at that house. We were waiting for those two guys that shot our friends. We wanted to shoot them, we were ready for it. But then we saw it was you." The next day I resigned. I thought, *eish*, this is too much. Too much danger. Just too much.

Me: And what did you tell the manager? Did you tell him this story?

Craig: No! I told them I wasn't happy about my salary, which was true.

Me: But do things like this happen often?

Craig: What do you mean?

Me: Well, that you're confronted with suspects that you know while you're at work?

Craig: *Eish*, many times. Because the truth is: The intruders do come from the same place as us, the guards, the security guys. You see, anybody can become a guard. It's easy. And we live in the same area as the guys who rob these houses, who jack the cars, you know? So this suspicion—I hate it, but it's true.

Me: Have you had any other similar problems?

Craig: So many. Let me tell you another one. When I was a guard, I arrested a guy for shoplifting and the police came and picked him up, sorted it out. But he was let go very quickly.

Me: How come?

Craig: I don't know, they probably paid him; *eish*, that happens all the time. Guys are always let go. Anyways, when I arrested him, I thought he looked familiar, but I wasn't sure. I thought I knew him through other people. So a few weeks later, I heard from some other guys that this guy that I arrested and his friends were looking for me. Everyday I tried to avoid them, but one day I just couldn't. I saw them in the same taxi and I knew they were gonna jump me, jump me hard. When I got out of the taxi, they started following me, but I kept my back turned and just kept walking, relaxed, acting like I didn't know. Then all of a sudden, one of the guys grabbed me from behind and the three of them started beating me, beating me hard. Luckily the police just happened to show up in their vehicle, so they stopped and I ran away. But the police car left quickly, so they started running after me again. One guy picked up a brick and he was about to throw it at me, but then the police came back. I was able to get away.

Me: And what happened after that?

Craig: The next week I heard that the guy I arrested was shot by the police and he died. His friends gave up on me.

Me: So it stopped?

Craig: Yeah, it stopped, but it happens so often. To these guys, criminals, we are the enemy! Really, the enemy, like the police.

Another black armed reaction officer, Themba, described to me in detail how some men from his neighborhood had approached him on the street and threatened him with a knife, because, as a security officer, he was associated with working for the police/the authority/the government. These associations force individuals such as Themba to lie about their occupation. They are also the cause of the "criminals in uniform" stigma. Most reaction officers experienced such encounters as threats to their lives or those of their family members and acquaintances living in the same community.

Another common cause for concern among reaction officers and some owners is retaliation by criminals. This threat is particularly problematic for community-based companies with closer ties to local citizens. I spoke with two owners of community-based companies who told me numerous stories of how they and their reaction officers were habitually threatened by criminals living in or close to the areas they patrolled.

One of the owners, Paul, had been threatened on countless occasions and had experienced several attacks on his life, such as when his home was looted and set on fire a few years before. For safety purposes, he now hid the details of his personal residence from his employees and did not walk around the neighborhood with his wife and children. Michael, an armed reaction officer working for the same company, was targeted while driving his personal car. He was dragged out of the car and attacked with beer bottles. In fact, retaliations against this company were so common that all employees, including the controllers, were instructed not to wear their uniforms when coming to and leaving work. Retaliation is not the norm for the armed response sector, however, and many of my informants claimed that only companies working on the fringes of the black townships or that actively encouraged the use of force experienced such incidents.

Officers working for those companies that actively encourage the use of force are often described as being "trigger-happy" and "thrill seekers." Although not applicable to all armed reaction officers, this reputation is not unwarranted. Like the public police (Chan 2007), armed reaction officers often see danger as a perk of the job. Many become addicted to the action and adrenaline and regret missing out if a crime occurs during their days off. I even recognized this thrill seeking within myself: Although the thrill of violence was certainly not my initial motivation for this research, the research was addictive and frequently incited adrenaline and feelings of invincibility. On days when "nothing" happened, we sat around in anticipation for the next prescription of action and adrenaline. It is a world into which one is easily drawn and in comparison to which everything else seems boring and mundane.

Indeed, it seemed that some of my informants had an overt passion for physically apprehending and reprimanding suspects. Many were not shy about expressing their enthusiasm for getting into fights. In fact, it appeared that armed reaction officers sometimes provoked violence in order to have some "action for the day." Comments such as "I want some fresh meat today," "Today can't be another hit-free day," and "Let's go loiter and stir so we can hit someone" were not uncommon.

I often asked my informants why they claimed to take so much pleasure in violence, and a few responded by referring to their own broken backgrounds and abusive pasts. One example was Michael, one of the most violent and trigger-happy armed reaction officers I encountered during my time in Durban. When Michael was thirteen, his father was hijacked and murdered. Shortly afterward, his mother married an alcoholic who repeatedly physically abused Michael and his brother. When Michael was sixteen, a group of armed men robbed his family's house and assaulted his mother in front of him. After that, Michael became caught in a spiral of drug use and crime, and his dream of becoming a police officer slipped away. When he was nineteen, he saw an advertisement in the local newspaper for a private security company that was recruiting reaction officers; he applied for a job, was accepted, and never looked back. For him, this work was his savior. Although Michael was a rather extreme case, many armed reaction officers had similar stories.

Michael also claimed that "violence is the answer" to fighting crime. Many other reaction officers shared this opinion, talking about violence as if it were "no big deal" and a normal part of life. Gayle, Michael, David, and Barry, among others, explained to me how violence had always been a part of their lives and was "all they knew." David's view was typical:

> You see, where I come from, the way of the fist is how the job is done. My father taught me to fight, literally, fight for what I need and want. It's what I know how to do. It might not always be the right thing, but it's what I know and it's what I can. And I have to feed my family at the end of the day.[31]

The notion of a "culture of violence" (Altbeker 2007; Kynoch 2005; Scheper-Hughes 1997) is often used to describe South African society, where violence has become normalized, tolerated, and even accepted as an everyday part of life. Although I find this concept highly problematic, I do concur that individuals repeatedly exposed to violence in numerous spheres of life start to experience such violence as normal. Many of my informants grew up in violent homes, and some, such as David, were taught that violence was a means to achieve one's goals. This unquestionably influenced how they policed the streets.

"It's Part of the Job"

While the risk and danger inherent in armed response work are for many a source of excitement, they also give rise to physical and mental scars. Most companies, particularly the large ones, have direct contact with counseling agencies, such as the Careline Crisis Center, which are on hand to assist clients. Although some managers state that these counseling services are available to armed reaction officers, I did not know of any officers who had actually made use of them. Discussing traumatic experiences is not common among armed reaction officers. When I inquired about particular traumatic episodes, common responses included the following: "I can handle it," "It's part of the job," and "I've toughened up." In fact, the ability to "just deal with it" was seen as an essential attribute for an armed response officer. Once again, these abilities were conceived of as masculine, whereas "getting emotional" and "talking about feelings" were perceived as feminine and therefore ridiculed and condemned.

As time passed, however, several armed reaction officers opened up to me about their difficulties in dealing with the stress of the job. As I discuss elsewhere (Diphoorn 2013), this often happened because I purposely discussed my own emotions and experiences, which created space for them to share theirs. For example, in May 2010, I was hanging out at the office of one of the companies during the night shift when we heard that Michael's cousin had just died of an asthma attack. Out of compassion for Michael, Paul, the owner of the company, suggested we visit the cousin's residence. When we arrived, the whole family was present and extremely upset. Feeling like an intruder in this private matter, I remained outside in the garden. We had been told that Michael's cousin was already dead, so I was surprised to see that several family members were calling an ambulance in the hope of reviving her. On my last trip to the Netherlands following my first phase of fieldwork, I had completed a basic first aid course that included instruction in mouth-to-mouth resuscitation, so when Michael asked the crowd for help in resuscitating his cousin and nobody responded, I stepped forward.

With my heart racing and wracked with nerves, I approached the victim. She was lying on the floor in the middle of the living room surrounded by approximately twenty family members, who were all staring at me and begging me to save her. When I knelt down beside her, I felt that her body was ice cold and that she had no pulse. My training told me that she was already dead, but my lack of medical qualifications and the pressure of the family members forced me to perform mouth-to-mouth resuscitation. As soon as I placed my mouth on top of hers, it was like I had tasted death; a horribly foul and rotten taste slipped from her mouth into mine, and a wave of vomiting reflexes engulfed me. Although I was guided by a qualified person on speakerphone and assisted by a family member, I was outright petrified about aggravating the situation. My urge to vomit and concerns about expressing my revulsion were eventually overpowered by the mechanical act of resuscitation. When the paramedics arrived after what felt like hours, I felt I could finally breathe, as if I myself had just been resuscitated.

After the paramedics took the girl's body away, I resumed the night shift, but I could not shake off what had happened and continued to retch uncontrollably. I also became angry with Paul and the other officers on the scene for not being able to perform mouth-to-mouth resuscitation themselves, and I started demanding (rather rudely) that Paul provide such training for all of his employees. As happened in incidents described by Campbell (2002) and Punch (1986), when I got home early in the morning after the shift, I went straight to sleep, but woke up a few hours later, drenched in sweat, to vomit. For weeks I had recurring nightmares of the woman's face floating out of a bathtub and coming toward me, on the verge of vomiting over my body.

While on a night shift a few days after this incident with Brian, who works for another company, I told him about the incident, how I vomited afterward, and my recurring nightmares. He initially expressed awkwardness about my openness; he avoided eye contact, continuously shifted in his seat, and changed the topic at the first opportunity. But a few hours later, while we were parked by a gas station, he took the initiative and shared what he called "the heaviest shit" he had seen:

> The most hectic thing I saw, it was a case of attempted suicide. So it wasn't dangerous, but it was disgusting. The guy had shot himself, a client, and bits and pieces of his brain were lying everywhere. I almost had to vomit. I had nightmares of that image for weeks and weeks. I didn't sleep properly for a long time. I will never forget that image. It fucked me up, it fucked me up, it fucked me up.

There was a long silence. He looked at me, shrugged, and then continued:

> But hey . . . then you see something new and it just softens. Every time comes something new, and it goes on and on. Your nightmares are replaced, or something like that.

Something similar happened during my interactions with Gayle. It was during a day shift in February 2009, and we had just left the house of a female client who had been robbed. She was very shaken up by the incident, and Gayle had repeatedly tried to convince her to seek the assistance of the company's counselors. She refused, and this irritated Gayle; he felt that she needed help to deal with what she had seen, because "flashbacks" would start to haunt her, as they had done to him:

> You see, flashbacks of these traumatic incidents, they only come after a few days. The first few days, you're still in a state of shock; maybe you're a bit more alert or nervous. Some people start rambling a bit, others just stop talking. . . . But later, they come, the images, and you can't sleep. I had it after a

call-out where a woman was raped and badly beaten, I mean bad. There was blood, she had bite marks, all that sort of stuff. I was shocked when I saw it, but I didn't feel so bad then. But a few days later, that image of her . . . I didn't want to come to work. I was tired, depressed. I had no idea who this woman was, but I kept seeing her face, her bloody body. . . . But slowly, it went away. And the more often you experience shit like this, the faster they come, but the faster they disappear. Your system, your body, builds a system to deal with this shit.

In July 2010, Anthony, a white reaction officer in his late twenties, resigned after receiving several written warnings from management about his performance; he had been acting rather turbulently. His behavior was linked to an incident that had occurred a few weeks earlier, when a citizen had threatened him with a gun. When I spoke to him a few weeks later, he explained that he could no longer handle the pressure:

> I became paranoid. That incident with the gun, I couldn't shake it off. Anyone who moved their arm up or made any movement, I started to think they were grabbing their firearm and wanted to shoot me. To me, they were all criminals. I just can't see clearly between who is a suspect and who is just walking down the street. It's affecting my life at home, I'm starting to think everyone is out to get me. I'm just done, done.

Bringing the Work Home

Anthony's description of how his work affected his life at home was not unusual; many informants had similar tales to tell about the impact of "bringing the work home." One day in May 2010, David picked me up for the night shift, seeming very irritated. At first he acted like nothing was wrong, but after I repeatedly asked him what was wrong, he admitted that he had just had a big fight with his wife, but did not want to talk about it. We continued on with the shift, and a few hours later, when it was quieter and we were parked and drinking coffee, he told me about the fight. Although he made some mention of the content of the argument, David seemed most upset about his wife's lack of understanding and the exhaustion he experienced from this work. When I asked him whether such fights happened often, he told me the following story:

> One day, I came home and I was finished. It had been a very, very long day, two armed robberies, running around like crazy. . . . I finally got home at ten and all I wanted to do was bath, eat, and sleep, but she [his wife] wouldn't have it. She was screaming at me for being home late, for not being a good husband. . . . And I just jilted. I went off. . . . I took the plate with hot food and threw it right at her face. I punched in her face; she was bruised for days.

The next day, I was sorry and felt bad about it, but at the same time . . . I understood why I did it. After such a heavy day, my home is supposed to be a place of rest, of understanding. At work, so much is going on, there's no time to think about it, what you are actually doing, but when you come, it all comes together. And I know that if there's anything I can do, is . . . I can hit. I'm very good at that. I know that by hitting someone at work, I solve whatever is going on. And it works at home too. . . . It is horrible to say it, but it's what goes on in my head. I am sure that everyone here has it, everyone has at some point hit their wives or something . . . if they haven't, I want to know what their secret is. Because you can't just shut off, you stay in this same hunting mode.[32]

Many informants shared similar stories about the difficulties of "turning off" after a day's work. For most, getting into fights while off duty in their own social environment was fairly common, and several suffered from alcoholism. Many discussed being impatient with their wives, not being able to communicate with their families, engaging in various forms of domestic violence, and having extramarital affairs to escape their "failures at home." Some reaction officers also seemed to be overbearing and overprotective husbands and fathers who imposed strict rules on their family members. Although establishing rapport with the wives and family members of my informants was slightly difficult, some did confide in me how they wished their husbands had a different job, one that could "give him more peace." Gayle's wife once told me that she knew not to "nag at him" when he got home and that he only "became himself during his off-days."

In his research on the state police, Herman Goldstein speaks of the "moral cynicism" that afflicts policemen because of their continuous exposure to crime and violence: "The average officer—especially in large cities—sees the worst side of humanity. He is exposed to a steady diet of wrongdoing" (1975: 25). I observed this same cynicism in many reaction officers, who had strict moral frameworks that they applied to their personal lives. Daily encounters with crime had made many informants see morality in black-and-white terms, with criminals conceived as the "bad guys" and them as the "good guys." They often described criminals as evil people with no compassion who are out there to steal, kill, or hurt others and must be stopped. For many, exposure to crime on a daily basis had transformed their perspectives on violence, as was the case with Charlie, an Indian armed response officers in his mid-thirties:

When I started working, about five years ago, I never got into fights and it was difficult to see; I never hit anyone, anything like that. I didn't like the idea of being violent. And when I would ride out, I'd try to stop the others from hitting. But now, it has changed me. I love to hit. It gives me a rush. After everything I've seen, all the crime . . . it has changed me.[33]

I was fascinated by how reaction officers often expressed a passionate disdain for violence and crime while at the same time justifying their own use of force and arguing that "violence solves crime." Whenever I questioned (or criticized) their use of violence (both on and off duty), I was treated to long and ornate answers replete with moral precepts and propositions, as illustrated by the following excerpt from a discussion with Michael:

Me: And what makes you so different from the criminals?

Michael: What do you mean?

Me: Well, your view is that criminals are bad, because they rob people, hit people unnecessarily, etcetera, but yesterday you also hit someone.

Michael: But hitting a criminal is different. You see, the criminals hit and rob innocent people, people that haven't done anything wrong. But we're hitting someone that has done something wrong.

Me: But how do you know that for sure? Like yesterday, you don't know for sure if those guys actually did it. You had suspicions, but you weren't sure. What if they hadn't robbed that house? That you were wrong? Then in fact you're also hitting an innocent person, or not?

[Long silence]

Michael: If it were so, then yes. But you see, with *kaffirs*,[34] you're almost always gonna get a guilty one, because all of them are criminals.

Me: But isn't that up to the court to decide? Who's guilty or not?

Michael: The courts don't do fuck all. There's no point in relying on that—can't trust them.[35]

The conversation then turned to corruption within the police and the judicial system at large, triggered by a case in which two of Michael's colleagues had been recently arrested for assault:

Michael: You see, those policemen, they are corrupt, jealous, and out to get us. That's why they punish us. But what they're doing is wrong! It's up to the court to decide whether we are guilty or not.

Me: But earlier you said that the courts can't be trusted to decide who is guilty or not, and now you are saying that the courts are the ones to decide.

Michael: But it's different, because that was about criminals. They are a different story.

I tried to probe further, but Michael made it clear that he did not want to continue.

I frequently had conversations like this with armed reaction officers, particularly toward the end of my fieldwork, and it was the closest I came to being able to openly criticize some of their perceptions. As has been suggested by Goldstein's (1975) work on "moral cynicism," I argue that holding such narrow conceptions of right and wrong appear to be necessary for reaction officers to do their work. When they questioned their own actions or doubted their moral compasses, which sometimes happened during our conversations, it confused and angered them. This was particularly true for those with a criminal record. Many presented that record as "the past" and explained how they had changed from being a criminal to a "crime fighter." Ultimately, all invoked their own work experiences to justify their use of violence, as the following quote from Gayle exemplifies:

> I know what you're gonna say: Violence is not the answer, blah, blah, blah. But I do believe that violence is, in some way, the answer, the way to deal with it. You see, with the crime and violence in this country, it's completely out of control and people are sick of it. I know, it's difficult at first, so I understand why you think what you think. But if you do this work, after years of this shit, and it really is shit, and you see it day in, day out, you change. Your vision, on beating and hitting and stuff like that, it changes. It just changes. I can't explain it. I will bet on it; if you would do this, what I do, for years, you would start to think like me.

CONCLUDING REMARKS

Gayle's description of how his work as an armed reaction officer had shaped his views attests to the centrality of violence in my informants' experiences. The aim of this chapter was to show how armed response officers define and perceive their occupation, particularly in comparison to other forms of security work. Although armed response officers are commonly associated with the "just a job" and "criminals in uniform" labels, I argue that the "wanna-be policemen" tag is more appropriate, particularly because they identify themselves with state police officers. This association is based on the origin of the sector, the officers' motivations for doing the work, and the divergence in training (and thus wage) levels between armed reaction officers and other security personnel. Yet the main reason why reaction officers distinguish themselves from other security officers concerns the nature of their work: They are armed men who patrol communities in vehicles.

This chapter presented a general idea of what it means to be an armed response officer, discussing false alarms, boredom, loneliness, financial problems, working in different geographical areas, and the importance of social interactions. Furthermore, it argued that, even though reaction officers possess few legal powers, their use of other tools —particularly the cultivation of bodily and force capital—allows them to obtain authority and legitimacy. The constant danger, the element of thrill seeking, the problems with "taking the work home," and the officers' perceptions of violence all shape their profession. This chapter showed how armed response officers experience the prominence of masculine attributes in their work and the distinction between operations and management, thereby expanding on the two main claims from the previous chapter.

All of this points toward one main argument, which is that the occupational culture of the armed reaction sector bears more resemblance to the state police than to other forms of private security in South Africa. Although armed reaction officers are private security personnel and occupy a specific position in the private security hierarchy, they feel closer to the state police and regard themselves as semi-policemen. As individuals, they aspire to act like state police officers. This is a major reason why they are increasingly policing the public realm, the cornerstone of twilight policing.

CHAPTER 5

"It All Comes Down to Them"

Daily Interactions with the "State"

May 2010

After a long morning of patrolling the streets, Michael and I arrive back at the office and see a young, black male standing outside in the heat of the sun. He is crying, sweating profusely, and reeking of alcohol. Michael approaches him, and the young man tells us that he was just robbed in a bar by people he knows. He asks Michael if the armed response officers can come to the bar and arrest those responsible. Michael informs him that they can only consider helping him after he makes an official charge at the police station. When the man complains, Michael sternly instructs him to go to the police station. The man eventually leaves.

A few hours later, the man comes back, but with an entirely different demeanor and appearance. His eyes are no longer teary and bloodshot; instead, he smiles and wears a carefree expression. He tells us that the policemen at the station referred him back here for assistance, because they were preoccupied and his case was not "worth it." I ask him why he's smiling, and he explains that he knows that the company will help him now, as he had originally hoped. Unfortunately for him, the reaction officers are in the process of a shift change, so he is asked to wait. He quickly grows impatient and eventually leaves without being assisted.

After the shift change, I discuss this incident with Michael and several other armed response officers. One of them thinks that the police didn't want to assist him because he was obviously drunk. Another defends the police, claiming that they probably *were* too busy and had more important things to do. Gavin, a senior armed response officer in his mid-thirties, then says, "You see, this is the main problem we have with the police. So many people who go to the police are sent to us, by them. Now, if we don't do anything, then people think we don't wanna help the community, and the police will milk it and talk nonsense about us only wanting to make money . . . but if we step up and it gets ugly, you know, then we get the shit, get charged with assault, that we went around the law, you know, those long stories. It's a big game. And you never win or lose; you don't know when you start. The rules are different every day. It's like gambling—you don't know how much to put in, how much you're gonna get back."

. . .

In the preceding vignette, Michael's acknowledgment that the police must be informed before he and his colleagues can assist the man points toward a subordinate role for armed response officers in relation to the state police. Yet, because the police officers referred the man back to the armed response company, we also see that this role is not firmly established. For many armed response officers, this ambiguity cultivates what Gavin described as a "gambling" sensation, which refers to the constant sense of uncertainty and unpredictability that pervades their interactions with police officers.

In attempts to understand the relationship between the state and the private security industry, many studies focus on state-centered national policies, such as state regulation. State regulation of the industry, which is the mandate of the Private Security Industry Regulatory Authority (PSIRA) in South Africa, is analyzed as a means whereby the state "outsources" its sovereignty and stipulates the (legal) conditions under which the industry must operate. The first section of this chapter examines PSIRA's role in regulating the industry and the corresponding legislation, which, though comprehensive, is heavily criticized by various parties. The second section of the chapter discusses the "partnership policing" of the post-apartheid state, a strategy that allocates the private security industry a junior and supportive role in formal partnerships.

The third section, which forms the heart of this chapter, analyzes the informal and ad hoc interactions in the local security networks comprising police officers and armed response officers when policing the streets of Durban.[1] I define police officers here as state representatives responsible for everyday law enforcement and public policing. With reference to various empirical case studies, I examine how the sharing of crime intelligence, divergent policing goals, divergent and similar policing mentalities, perceptions of corruption, moonlighting, social networks (i.e., old boys' networks and old boys' feud), and the use of violence define these local security networks.

In the course of this analysis, I make three claims. The first is that the relationships between armed response officers and police officers are multifaceted, context and person dependent, and thus unpredictable, resulting in a sense of "gambling" for most armed response officers. The second claim is that the distinction between state and nonstate is increasingly blurry on the ground. Police officers, as performers of "state" policing, and armed response officers, as performers of "nonstate" policing, increasingly encroach on each other's domains through relationships that are simultaneously competitive and collaborative. A twilight zone is thus created through daily policing practices in these local security networks. The third claim is that police officers play a large role in creating the twilight zone by actively entering the private realm and pulling armed response officers into the public realm. This chapter concludes by arguing that police officers are the arbiters of these local security networks. Since it is they who are able to wield state sovereignty, they ultimately determine the nature and outcome of local security networks.

A "TOOTHLESS BULLDOG": STATE REGULATION OF THE INDUSTRY

In South Africa, state regulation of the private security industry requires that all companies and personnel in it must be registered with PSIRA. Along with other state bodies, such as the Department of Labor, PSIRA determines how the industry must operate. If a service provider is not registered or does not operate in accordance with PSIRA's regulations, a charge of misconduct is opened, with the penalties differing according to the case. Comparatively speaking, South Africa's regulation system is very comprehensive.

In the Private Security Industry Regulation Act No. 56 of 2001, PSIRA's broad scope is exemplified in its definition of a security service provider, who is "a person who renders a security service to another for a remuneration, reward, fee or benefit and includes such a person who is not registered as required in terms of this Act" (PSIRA 2001). A security service ranges from the protection of property to the installation of security equipment. Other parts of the act also attest to the wide scope of regulation, such as its zero-tolerance policy, which dictates that any form of malpractice leads to a penalty. Another example is the consumer liability clause, which states that any person who knowingly or without the exercise of reasonable care contracts security services and provision that are contrary to the act is guilty of an offense (Berg 2003).

However, despite international acclaim for South Africa's regulation scheme, members of the industry, police officers, and even PSIRA employees are heavily critical of PSIRA. My informants regularly described PSIRA as a "toothless bulldog" that was incapable of enforcing its wide-ranging legislation. Such criticism centered on five claims: a lack of representation from the private security industry, inefficiency, a lack of collaboration with other state bodies, corruption, and poor employee vetting procedures. First, many members of the security industry experience state regulation as a form of punishment imposed by an unrepresentative body. As discussed in Chapter 2, the growth of the private security industry was advocated by the apartheid state, for which it functioned as a complementary armed force. The creation of the Security Officers Act of 1987 (SOA) was the result of this alliance, and the Security Officers Board (SOB) consisted of ten members, of which six were from the private security industry.

This changed with the advent of the post-apartheid state, whose representatives felt that members of the security industry were overrepresented in the SOB. When the SOA became the PSIRA, a new governing council was created that lacked any security industry representation. The current council consists of a chairperson, a vice chairperson, and three councilors, all of whom are appointed by the Minister of Safety and Security and do not have "direct or indirect financial or personal interests in the private security industry or represent in any way the interests of those within the industry" (PSIRA 2001). Many members of the industry feel that regulation has been "hijacked" by the state, that it does not represent their needs, and that it damages the industry rather than protecting it, as one owner of a security company said to me: "PSIRA is taxation, not representation."[2] The monthly registration fees exacerbate this sentiment.

Second, similar to other government bodies, PSIRA is criticized for being understaffed and inefficient. In 2009, PSIRA inspected 6,971 (93.45 percent) of the 7,459 active security businesses, equivalent to 202 businesses for each of its 37 inspectors. As a result of these inspections, 1,568 security providers were charged with misconduct. These figures point toward an active inspection and regulation system. Nonetheless, many of my informants (members of the industry, police personnel, and others) still described PSIRA as ineffective, particularly with regard to inspection. The persistence of "fly-by-nights" was frequently used to substantiate such claims. Furthermore, many respondents claimed that most inspections were based on tips and that PSIRA does not take a proactive approach. Companies also use these tips to badmouth other companies; indeed, one PSIRA inspector felt that PSIRA was "used as a battleground for companies to fight against each other."[3]

Third, criticism is leveled at the relationship between PSIRA and other government bodies, such as the Department of Labor, which determines wages and employment standards, and SASSETA, which monitors security training. Many of my informants claimed that referrals to other departments, particularly the SAPS, were not adequately handled. According to one PSIRA inspector I spoke to, the problem lies chiefly with the police, who do not prioritize their cases of illegal misconduct by private security personnel.[4] In 2009, PSIRA filed 177 cases with the SAPS, resulting in a total of 962 pending criminal cases that still had to be dealt with.

Fourth, many industry personnel accuse PSIRA inspectors of corruption, of favoring certain companies over others, and/or of inspecting only the "easy" companies; that is, those that are reputable and easily accessible rather than those that require more effort because of their geographical remoteness. PSIRA is seen as guilty of "under-inspection," whereby inspectors fine companies for minor matters, such as incorrect attendance registers or posting sheets, while disregarding larger problems, such as unregistered firearms.[5] Some informants even alleged that the government was unwilling to "straighten PSIRA out" because members of the government have interests in the industry and use their political connections to acquire contracts.[6]

During my interviews, PSIRA inspectors denied allegations of corruption and favoritism. Without investigating the veracity of such allegations, I do know of several private security companies that were guilty of numerous, easily identifiable forms of malpractice, such as underpayment of security officers, which were not detected during inspections. Various informants discussed cases of inspectors assisting their friends in the industry while punishing their rivals. Though no managers openly admitted to giving bribes, they hinted at the occurrence of such practices with statements such as "we have friends there" and "just treat them nicely and everything will be fine."

Fifth, PSIRA is criticized for the inadequacy of its employee database and criminal record checks. Given that the raison d'être of the industry is fighting crime, criminal activity among employees is seen as a serious problem. When individuals register with PSIRA, a criminal record check is conducted, yet this excludes "unrecorded" criminal activity. Furthermore, checks are not conducted on an ongoing basis after registration. The fact that I interviewed numerous private security employees—both officers and managers—who were or had been engaged in illegal activity shows that these checks are far from foolproof.

As this discussion makes clear, the South African state has a comprehensive regulation system that enables it to maintain a degree of supervision and control. Yet the criticism directed at PSIRA from across the policing field suggests that much of this regulation exists on paper, not in practice. The reality is that the regulations are not always enforced and illegal practices persist. Furthermore, though armed response officers are registered with PSIRA and pay their monthly fees, many do not feel represented by it and regard it is "just another government body that I must pay for."[7] PSIRA legislation stipulates how armed response officers must operate, yet many of those I spoke to felt that it did not determine how they acted during their shifts. When I asked them how the "state" influenced their occupation, most of them only referred to the state police. For them, the police was the state body that most defined how they operated.

"PARTNERSHIP POLICING"

In the literature on public-private policing partnering, most studies identify a "junior partner" model (e.g., Button 2007; McManus 1995; Nalla and Hwang 2006; Wakefield 2003). It is characterized by a strict hierarchical structure in which the public police are the senior partner and private policing bodies are the junior partners. As Berg and I have argued elsewhere (Diphoorn and Berg 2014), this model has also been the doctrine of the post-apartheid South African state, primarily outlined in the National Crime Prevention Strategy (NCPS) of 1996 and the 1998 White Paper on Safety and Security. The NCPS delineated a "multi-agency approach" (Singh 2008: 14) whereby the government would work alongside other partners, such as community members, businesses, and the private security industry, to combat crime. Although the post-apartheid state was initially suspicious of the private security industry due to its alliance with the former regime, it also recognized the need for collaboration.

The "partnership policing" strategy determined the structure for security networks between the state police and other policing bodies. However, this vision for partnership policing was to be directed by police officers (Minnaar 2005). Although the police regard private security companies as "their 'natural' allies and partners" (Marks and Wood 2007: 150), this partnering strategy implies that "the SAPS 'runs the show'" (Berg 2004a: 113) and that private security firms function as "force-multipliers" that play an "adjunct role" (Manzo 2009: 199). The South African state thus envisioned the multi-agency approach not as an equal partnership but one in which the police are the senior partner and the security industry is the junior partner.

The junior role designated to the private security industry was further defined through the outsourcing of particular tasks to it. Within a larger process of liberalizing crime management, the SAPS embarked on a "more managerialist approach" (Berg 2004b: 227), as exemplified by its change of name from a police "force" to a police "service." It outsourced two activities to the private security industry: the guarding of government buildings, such as police stations, and vehicle tracking. In 1996, the SAPS entered into a national partnership with Tracker, a vehicle-tracking company. Tracker installs tracking systems in certain SAPS vehicles and aircraft, links them to the SAPS system, sponsors the computers in the SAPS aircraft and vehicles, and provides vehicle-tracking training to police officers (Minnaar 2005: 106). This contractual relationship implies that both parties (i.e., the police officers and the Tracker recovery teams) have an obligation to search for any stolen vehicles.[8] However, except for the outsourcing of guarding and the Tracker-partnership, there is "no formal national co-operation agreement in existence between the SAPS and the private security industry" (Minnaar and Ngoveni 2004: 55).

Local Partnering

Due to the lack of a national agreement about formal partnerships between the SAPS and the private security industry, partnership policing primarily occurs through operations established by local municipalities and police stations (Minnaar 2005: 99). In Cape Town, city improvement districts (CIDs) have been implemented as part of a larger urban strategy, in which private security companies are contracted to provide security (Abrahamsen and Williams 2011; Berg 2004b; Samara 2010). A Durban equivalent of the CIDs is the urban improvement precinct (UIP), a public-private partnership set up by Metro Council, whereby property owners in a specific area pool resources to contract companies to provide a variety of services, including security.

These formalized public-private partnerships are platforms for police officers and security officers to work together indirectly, but there are also local partnerships that are more direct. In Gauteng, one acclaimed partnership is the Honeydew Project, an initiative facilitated by Business Against Crime (BAC) to enhance communication between the industry and the SAPS. Initiated in October 2008, the Honeydew Project is labeled as an "alliance" between the security industry and the SAPS, comprising five police stations in the Honeydew Police Station Cluster and eleven private security companies.

There are also locally based partnerships that center on a specific operation or police station. In 2009, a police station in Chatsworth, a former Indian township in Durban, founded an initiative called POLSEC, which is aimed at fostering police efforts with numerous companies working in the area. The initiative includes weekly meetings and joint operations between the police station and seventeen "qualified" companies.[9] In the Bluff, a residential area in the south of Durban, the state police requested assistance from several private security companies from the area to assist in two operations in 2008 (Operation Clean Up and Operation November) focused on raiding squatter camps in search of drugs and stolen goods.[10]

"To Talk and Share"

These initiatives are just a few examples of locally based policing partnerships between the private security industry and state police in South Africa. In the course of my fieldwork, the most common form of official cooperation between the state police and the private security industry that I encountered occurred during Ground Operational Coordinating Committee (GOCOC) meetings.[11] These weekly meetings are organized by local police stations and attended by "outside members" such as representatives of private security companies, ward councilors, and chairpersons of community organizations, who are invited to "talk and share." I regularly sat in on the weekly GOCOC meetings. Although the composition of the participants varied between stations, the general structure and order of events were similar: First, the police officers would present the crime trends of that week, often with specific crime statistics for the area in question, and then outside members would provide relevant information pertaining to crime.

These meetings are used to share "security data" (Lippert and O'Connor 2006: 53), discuss problems, and improve joint-policing efforts. They act as platforms where various stakeholders, particularly the police and private security companies, share information in order to enhance policing efforts. During these meetings, there is a well-defined hierarchy among the participants: The SAPS are clearly in charge while the outside members are guests, although the potential contribution of the guests and their subordinate role differ per area. Additionally, some companies, often the larger ones, are represented at numerous GOCOC meetings, while others, usually the smaller ones, are not represented at all. In Sydenham, for example, the GOCOC list of outside members for November 2007 included twenty-three private security companies, but only five attended regularly. Larger companies are vested in more areas and have the financial capacity to employ individuals to attend these meetings. The result is that a particular group of men hop from one meeting to the next and constitute a small network of knowledge brokers between the SAPS and the industry. Thus sharing information only takes place with a small segment of the industry, and this group is not representative of the entire industry. This means that local security networks between companies and the state police are not uniform, particularly with regard to sharing crime intelligence.

MEETING ON THE STREETS: INFORMAL AND AD HOC ENCOUNTERS

The lack of uniformity and consistency within the relationships between police officers and armed response officers is both the cause and the reason for the large number of informal relationships and ad hoc encounters that occur. In this section I do not focus on a particular police station or company, but instead examine local security networks between armed response officers (and companies) and police officers from various companies and stations throughout Durban.

As presented elsewhere (Diphoorn and Berg 2014), these networks are also predominantly framed by a junior partner model, but are much more multifaceted and function more as "negotiated tactical alliances" (Baker 2010: 35). In agreement with Crawford and Lister (2006: 175), I argue that there is considerable heterogeneity in these local security networks due to divergent and changing circumstances. At times, armed response officers supplement and assist the police, while in other situations, they compete with and undermine the role of the state police by encroaching on their domain. More importantly, these processes of collaboration and competition very often occur simultaneously. The networks are therefore not linear and straightforward, but are multifaceted, constantly in flux, and shaped by social networks and individual preferences and personalities. The result is that a twilight zone is created, in which it becomes unclear who is responsible for what and where. The following subsections present empirical cases that permit further analysis of several factors that shape the diversity of the networks and the process of blurring between the private and public policing domain.

Sharing Information

February 2009

Around 6 a.m., Gayle and I received a call informing us that a client's son had been carjacked as he was driving out of his driveway. Anthony, a white armed response officer and Gayle's colleague, was already at the scene, and we dashed to the premises to assist him. On arrival, we encountered a middle-aged couple and their daughter, who provided us with the details of the carjacking. They told us that the son had been kicked out of the car by the side of the road and had fortunately found help to phone them. The father was rushing out to pick up his son while the tracking company continued to look for the vehicle. There was not much that we could do apart from staying with the clients and waiting for the police out on the driveway. Gayle and Anthony complained about the long wait for the police, both in front of and with the clients. During this discussion, the clients, Gayle, and Anthony openly criticized the police and the South African government in general, so that when the police arrived approximately forty-five minutes later, the situation was rather tense.

The police inquired about what had happened and were shocked to hear that the boy had been carjacked. Apparently, the company's control room had informed the police that this was a case of vehicle theft, not carjacking. The latter implies that the owner or driver of the vehicle is inside when it is stolen and is thus present when the crime occurs, whereas vehicle theft implies that no one is present and, thus, that it is less likely that the victim will be hurt. The police therefore prioritize carjackings over vehicle theft. Clearly frustrated by the situation, the police officers began to quarrel with the armed response officers. They accused the armed response officers of being "stupid" and "useless" and not doing their "job properly." One of the police officers explained to me, "If we would have heard hijacking, we would have run here, been here like now. But we heard vehicle theft, so there was no need to rush."

The police officers then encouraged the client to report the case, telling them, "Even though the car will be found, please report the case, so we can keep up our stats." When the police left, annoyed, the armed response officers told the client that the police officers had lied, that the control room was not to blame, and that the police used it as an excuse to justify their late arrival. Additionally, the armed response officers discouraged the client from reporting the case, saying doing so was "a total waste of time."

. . .

Private security companies have a certain degree of control over the flow of information to the police (Hobbs et al. 2002; Shearing, Farnell, and Stenning 1980: 197–98). Since many companies do not keep statistical records of the crime they encounter, tapping into this information is difficult, however. Because the security industry primarily serves clients, "networks may serve to exclude public police from important sources of information about security incidents, concerns, problems and responses to them" (Lippert and O'Connor 2006: 60). According to one Indian station commander, the private security companies working in his area refused to share their crime records, yet demanded that the SAPS share theirs.[12]

During my research, I knew of many crime incidents that were not reported to the police. Although clients and citizens often made these decisions of their own volition, the carjacking incident discussed earlier shows how armed response officers also discourage clients from reporting crime because "there is no point" and "the police can't help you anyways." For example, in an attempted housebreaking where nothing is stolen and citizens choose not to report the case, private security companies will not report it either. As one owner said to me, "There is a lot of crime that goes on without the SAPS even knowing the slightest thing about it. Completely out of their hands."[13] This implies that the state police do not possess a monopoly on knowledge and expertise on crime, which undermines their dominant and "senior" position.

This carjacking case also serves as an example of miscommunication between the two policing bodies. The police officers perceived that the armed response officers (or the company) had purposely withheld and/or conveyed incorrect information. Many police officers accuse armed response officers and others in the industry of purposely providing false information to consolidate the poor reputation of the police. They claim that companies deliberately denigrate the police to remind clients of the need for private security. As one police officer told me, "These guys [armed response officers], when they come to a client's house and there was a break in, something was stolen, or what not, they often tell them not to phone us; they say we'll never come or that there's no point. And they keep many clients like this."[14]

"Clients over Crime"

May 2010

I was accompanying police officers on a day shift when we received a call from another police station asking us to check out an apartment in a nearby apartment complex. When we got to the lobby, the guard refused to let us in. He stated that the client, the property owners' association, had instructed him to refuse entry to anyone without direct permission from the resident in question, and this included the police. Hearing this, the two police officers became extremely annoyed and demanded to be let in, repeatedly asserting, "We are the police!" One of the officers then ordered the guard to call his supervisor, and eventually, after a rather intimidating phone call, the guard let us in.[15] For the police officers, this was a prime example of private security officers obstructing them in their line of work, as one of them said to me afterward:

> The main problem with these guards, or with private security, is that they protect their clients. They only care about the interests of who pays them. I am here to protect the public, I serve the South African people, but he [a guard] serves those that pay. . . . They listen to their clients more than they listen to us. I mean, it's fucking ridiculous! You won't let the police come in because the client says no? Since when do they decide what goes down here?

. . .

Although state police officers have far more legal powers than their counterparts in the private security industry, through their contractual agreements with clients, private security officers are permitted to search people and property, carry out various surveillance techniques, enforce sanctions, deny access to individuals, and evict individuals from private property (see Chapter 4). As the incident at the apartment complex shows, these powers can undermine the authority of the state police. Furthermore, the two policing bodies often have different objectives: The security industry operates with a client-defined mandate, while the state police serve the general public. As argued by Dupont, security networks do not always consist of a "shared objective or value, but instead a myriad of over-lapping interests brought together by informal, voluntary, contractual or regulatory ties" (2006: 39).

Many armed response companies have a strict policy of first and foremost ensuring the safety of the client and then attending to other matters. Because of this principle, it is often not possible to arrest or chase a suspect, particularly when there is limited manpower. Many in the state police resent this policy, as one officer explained:

> For them, it's all about the client; it's about client over crime. Now if they hear about an armed robbery, or anything like that, and even if they know the client is okay, because he phoned in, what these guys do—they go straight to the client, but don't think, "Hey, these guys could be driving around somewhere, let me see if I can find them." That's how a cop thinks. And this frustrates us: Many guys get away, we never catch them.[16]

Because of this (presumed) consumer focus, members of the industry are often not seen as real "crime fighters." Police officers often accuse owners and managers of companies of not putting "their heart into it" and only "listening to the jingle of their pockets." Another frequently heard statement—"They make money out of crime; we fight to get rid of crime"—highlights how police officers differentiate themselves from members of the industry.

Police officers often feel that armed response companies cite their relationship with the police to increase sales; they use it "as a marketing tool—borrowing, as it were, the symbolic power of the police as a means to enrol customers and boost sales" (Goold et al. 2010: 15). Many police personnel expressed resentment about this, yet appeared to direct it toward management so it did not influence on-the-ground interactions between police officers and armed response officers. Although the latter unquestionably played the marketing card, police officers did not accuse them of "making money out of crime," because they were aware of their poor working conditions and low salaries. In fact, police officers often expressed pity for private security officers and claimed that their managers abused them.

In contrast, private security companies see themselves as being exploited for financial reasons. Many industry members claimed that the state police initiated relationships with them solely to use their financial resources and that they were threatened if they did not comply. The manager of a guarding company told me about an incident that occurred when his firm won the contract for guarding a new shopping mall. Several police officers from the local station had requested "sponsorship" from him; when he refused, officers from that police station stopped patrolling that area and turned up late whenever a crime was reported.

During a GOCOC meeting in June 2010, the discussion centered on the organization of a new community-awareness event to increase participation in the local community policing forum (CPF). Throughout this conversation, the police officers repeatedly highlighted their lack of funding and the need for "donations." After the meeting ended, I spoke to some of the representatives of the private security companies who were clearly irritated by the police officers' call for financial assistance. One participant summarized his fellow armed response officers' frustration as follows:

> This sponsorship talk, these donations—that's all we're good for. They don't give our guys more power, on the road, to actually fight crime, but it's okay if we donate cars or computers. There's no problem with that? At these meetings, when we come, they start seeing money signs and sponsors, not partners, people to fight crime with.[17]

The police feel that private security companies should provide crime intelligence and financial resources, and tensions emerge when they do not do so. In turn, private security personnel are willing to share their knowledge and resources, but they become frustrated when they feel that their contributions are abused and unappreciated.

"Getting in on the Action"

June 2010

During a night shift with David, the control room informed us that the police had requested our assistance with a "dangerous operation." David and I rushed off to the police station, where we were told that they had received a tip that someone in one of the adjacent townships was in possession of a large stash of illegal firearms. The police were planning a raid and would need backup from David and the other armed response officers on duty at the time. For the remainder of the night shift, David was extremely excited and kept driving by the station to see whether there was any progress. He kept repeating that he wanted to "get in on the action." For the rest of the night shift, David shared with me several past incidents when the company had assisted the police by providing additional vehicles, manpower, and firearms. Unfortunately for David, the raid never occurred.

. . .

David's enthusiasm is not uncommon: Many armed response officers are eager to assist the police and to "get in on the action." This sentiment predominantly derives from the "wanna-be policemen" culture of the armed response sector, as discussed in Chapter 4. Because many armed response officers initially wanted to be policemen or are supervised by former policemen, they thrive on incidents where they are allowed to do more than simply patrol. Statements such as "we are policemen; we just don't do all of the boring paperwork" and "we are policemen; we just do a certain part of it" testify to this mentality. I therefore concur with a common claim in the literature that private security officers are generally supportive of and excited about cooperating with the police (Berg 2004a, 2004b; Manzo 2009 Nalla and Hwang 2006; Wakefield 2003). In fact, as Hummer and Nalla (2003) argue, security professionals are more positive about working with police officers, hold the police in high regard, value ongoing partnerships, and propose more police cooperation for the future than police officers do.

Armed response officers and police officers face many of the same challenges in their respective lines of work, such as a lack of power to combat crime, an inability to please the public, a fear of legal prosecution, and various occupational hazards and risks. These similarities shape a shared policing mindset. In her analysis of the "bandit-catching" mentality of a particular group of private security officers in Cape Town, Berg (2010: 295) argues that these officers acted like the police and had a similar mentality. The police do not feel threatened by armed response officers, therefore, because both parties are operating with the same mindset. Indeed, police officers can be highly complimentary about armed response officers; although they generally feel that the latter are "below" them in the policing hierarchy, many also regard them as "partners in crime" who face similar problems. It was common for me to hear police officers claim that "we can use all the help we can get." As one police officer stated, "We're fighting the same war: the war on crime!"[18]

Yet despite these perceptions, armed response officers often feel unappreciated by the police. They claim that police officers do not realize that their role is indispensable. Common statements such as "we are always on the scene before them" and "we arrest the bad guys for them" indicate how armed response officers place value on the work they do for police officers. The "wanna-be policemen" mentality can also create friction, because their eagerness can lead to armed response officers overstepping the supportive role. One of my key informants, whom I refer to in Chapter 6 as an "active policer," explained this problem as follows:

> You see, all of them have a different part to play; from the car guard on the street to the national police commissioner. But there is hierarchy within the food chain of policing, and armed response officers are lower than police officers. They are above the security guards, and for some communities, they are very often the police, but they will never reach the same part of the chain . . . there is simply not room for both of them there. But when they [armed response officers] try to be there, or maybe when a police officer doesn't look out or slips up and brings one of them there, then there's a problem. Because then they don't know who's boss, who's in charge. . . . It is here where personal vendettas start to play; it is here when the manhood is threatened, when men become boys.[19]

Conflicts arise when armed response officers do not comply with the junior role envisioned for them. In such cases, police officers may perceive them as obstructive and disruptive. For example, police officers frequently voiced concern over the poor management of crime scenes, even after several police stations organized crime scene management courses for armed response officers.[20]

"They're a Bunch of Criminals"

The mutual perceptions of police officers and private security officers are also shaped by events outside their work, a dimension that is often ignored in the literature. This section discusses how both parties characterize the other as "a bunch of criminals."

The SAPS generally have a negative reputation among the South African public, and as citizens, many armed response officers share public perceptions of the police as corrupt, understaffed, and inefficient. On the one hand, their perceptions of the police are more positive than those of the general public, because they do similar work and face comparable challenges. On the other hand, their views are more negative when they witness corruption and other police failings firsthand and experience these problems as an impediment to their own work. Armed response officers often described the police as exceptionally corrupt. My informants gave numerous examples of cases in which they had arrested suspects who were subsequently released by the police and whose statements had "miraculously" disappeared. In November 2008, Gayle shared an incident that had occurred a few years before, when he had arrested a young man for drunk driving and illegal possession of a firearm, only to find out a few days later that the suspect had been released and the charges dropped. Apparently, the young man in question was the son of a police officer from a neighboring station. Since then, Gayle had purposely taken photos of each suspect he arrested for use as evidence.

This perception of the police as corrupt and inefficient was even held by police officers themselves. During my patrols, interviews, and interactions with the state police, many officers discussed how they did not trust their colleagues, as the following cases illustrate. While I was conducting a roadblock with the state police during a night shift in August 2010, two senior police officers told me of several occasions when they had arrested officers from other stations for drunk driving but that other police officers had not charged them. During a GOCOC meeting in July 2010, several police officers openly discussed the leaking of important information from police stations and the corruption of officials. Another example derived from a residential area where I often patrolled with armed response officers. In this area, several police reservists and police officers had established an active neighborhood watch that included regular patrols. They worked closely with the armed response officers in the area, primarily by sharing information. Interestingly, the members of the neighborhood watch (i.e., police officers and reservists) did not disclose this information to the local police station. One police reservist explained this decision to me by noting that the police officers working at that station were untrustworthy and corrupt, claiming that "I trust these guys [i.e. armed response officers] more than those." In May 2010, I spoke with an inspector, who explained how the lack of commitment and competence among policemen was one reason why he was supportive of the private security industry, especially armed response:

> Go to the police station on a Tuesday night at three; you'll see are a bunch of sleeping policemen. And the worst part is that they're putting people out on the streets, because they can't do paperwork. Now, see, a lot of the guys, especially the Blacks, they are not good at writing statements and general office work. So they are put out on patrol. So now you've got the guys that *can* write statements, like ourselves, stuck in the charge office. But what's more important? Admin work or actually catching the criminals? And this is why we need these guys [armed response officers] to work the ground for us. They can do the work, they can patrol, arrest criminals, even better than some policemen. And many of them, such as these two [two armed response officers present], I trust them more than the guys sitting inside with a uniform.

In contrast to this inspector, however, many police officers share a common perception of private security officers as "criminals in uniform" (see Chapter 4). While this aspersion is most often cast on other types of security officers, such as car guards and security guards, it is also applied to armed reaction officers. For police officers, however, this negative stereotype is associated less with the armed response officers' professional activities than with their off-duty engagement in illegal activity, as one policeman explained:

> The whole inside job thing, that happens with security guards, car guards, that level. For an armed response officer to be directly involved in an inside job, it's difficult . . . it happens, but it's rare and he's gotta plan it out properly, from control room to the top. So if I say an armed reaction guy is a criminal, I don't mean in his work, but I mean outside work, back home, in the *location*.[21] There they are drunks, smoke marihuana, visit prostitutes, have kids all over the place . . . that kinda thing. That's why they [are] below us.[22]

Armed response officers also hold disparaging views of one another. Indeed, while an individual officer will be quick to assert that he is not a criminal, he will not be shy about accusing his colleagues of that charge. During a focus group discussion with several armed response officers in March 2009, we discussed the possible granting of more legal powers to security officers. They all agreed that this was dangerous and said they understood the government's hesitation in granting these powers, as the following quote from one armed response officer points toward:

> The problem is that not all of us are good at our job. You see, I've been doing this for 10 years. I know the law; I understand it. And I'm not stupid. But [name of fellow armed response officer]; he's nineteen, did his training a year ago, and hardly has any experience. I don't think he even knows what to do with an armed robbery. Now you can't go and give him more power, because he'll fuck it up, completely. Some of these guys are just stupid, and some will abuse [the additional power]. Will use the power for their own sake, you know? For their own games, to help out their friends . . . many guys can't be trusted.[23]

Allegations of corruption and participation in illegal activities therefore occur in both directions of the local security network; they are fragmented, multifaceted, and often based on personal experiences of corrupt practices and personal relationships. Police officers may work closely with some armed response officers, but distrust others, and vice versa. Furthermore, members of both policing bodies direct these accusations toward their own colleagues, trusting some and suspecting others. The willingness of police officers and armed response officers to work together is therefore more often based on social networks and individual preferences than on whether they belong to a "state" or "nonstate" policing body. This is also evident in the practice of moonlighting.

Moonlighting

December 2008

At the start of a night shift with Brian, while we were parked on a busy street, I noticed a white male standing outside a grocery store having a heated argument with someone over the phone. When I pointed this out to Brian, he casually commented that the man was a police detective who guards the store for the owner, a friend of his, "on the side." Brian explained to me that many police officers of all different ranks are engaged in security-related work to earn extra money. He told me it's what they call "moonlighting."

. . .

Moonlighting is a phenomenon that is defined differently across the globe.[24] In Chapter 4, I described moonlighting as security-related employment undertaken by armed response officers outside their main job. In this chapter, however, I use "moonlighting" to refer to *police officers* who are engaged in undocumented policing or security-related activities outside their work, such as owning a private security company or working as a bouncer. It does not refer to "user-pays policing" (Ayling and Shearing 2008) or "privately paid public policing" (Gans 2000), both of which operate with consent from the larger state police apparatus. Rather, moonlighting here implies security-related work that is prohibited and does not appear in official records or occur through official channels.

According to my informants, moonlighting was nonexistent in South Africa before the 1970s, when many police officers primarily earned their extra income in other sectors, such as construction work. With the tremendous boom of the private security industry in the 1980s, however, demand for security personnel increased, and those with expertise and high levels of training were preferred. Many police officers left the force to work in the industry, but some stayed with the state police and engaged in moonlighting as an extra source of income. One former police officer explained his reasoning for to me:

> We were asked to do this, because of our expertise. But also because of the image, the symbolicness, you know? When collecting a debt, a man in a police

uniform was more effective; people assumed you would arrest them. We basically used our role as law enforcement officers to persuade people to do things, to enforce our authority in other areas. And people paid us nicely for it. It was good income for us. It was perfect for many of us who didn't wanna leave the police but needed the extra money. I wanted to do both, and I could . . . so I did.[25]

During the 1980s, many policemen worked as bouncers, bodyguards, or armed escorts or were engaged in debt collection or the eviction of squatters. Bouncing was the most common entry point to moonlighting; in the 1980s, most doormen were policemen who earned between R 80–100 per night. Although bouncers were dressed in civilian clothing, people knew they were policeman. It was not talked about, however; as one former police officer told me, "Back then, all policemen did it; it was a normal part of the job, it's what you did on your off days, but nobody talked about it, explicitly . . . it remained hush-hush."[26] It is for this reason that the majority of my data regarding moonlighting originates from interviews with former police officers who were willing to discuss the issue. Many of these former officers were working in the private security industry at the time of this research.

The situation changed in the early 1990s, when moonlighting began to receive a lot of negative publicity. With the explosion in taxi violence at the start of the decade,[27] news surfaced that many policemen were directly involved in this situation, because numerous police officers, both black and white, owned taxis or had invested in them.[28] This situation worsened when more cases surfaced of policemen using their firearms off duty. The Ministry of Safety and Security intervened by changing the "standing orders" of the Police Act. This amendment stipulates that police officers are allowed to engage in other income-generating activities, but that they must apply for permission from their station commander. Additionally, it forbids employment in certain sectors, such as the private security industry.[29]

However, violations of these rules are not severely punished. If a policeman is engaged in security-related activities or in employment that he has not requested permission for, he is departmentally charged with "misconduct" or "failure to disclose other employment."[30] The punishment is usually a fine; dismissal is very rare and only occurs in the event of a serious crime that occurs during the act of moonlighting. One informant told me of a police officer from a specialized unit who had his own private investigations company: he was charged departmentally and instructed to stop with a final written warning.[31] In addition to the amendment forbidding the employment of police officers in the security industry, PSIRA regulations also prohibit it. If police officers are registered as security providers, the first step is to deregister them. If they continue to operate, they are charged with operating an unregistered company. However, because PSIRA prosecutions are eventually referred to the SAPS, the majority of these cases are never dealt with. As a PSIRA inspector said to me, "eventually it is up to the police to police their police; we police the industry—must we now also include the police?"[32]

SAPS and PSIRA legislation prohibit moonlighting because it sets up a potential conflict of interest. Police officers can easily use their authority to acquire clients; they can attend a crime scene as a police officer one day and return the next day as a sales rep to sign up the client. A police reservist provided an example of such a conflict of interest:

> Take the case of a bouncer. Where is his loyalty? Let's say the club he works for is raided for whatever reason, such as possession of drugs or under-age drinking, or whatever. Will the police officer work as a policeman and assist the raid or will he lay allegiance to the owner and assist him?[33]

The questions raised in the quote are of even more significance when police firearms are involved. Despite the legislation, many police officers and members of the industry approve of moonlighting. It was regularly described as "a part of the policing game" and as a way of assisting each other. As one owner of a company told me, "I ask a lot of policemen to do work for me. I need the expertise; they need the money. It's a great deal, so why not?"[34] Yet many informants were reluctant to talk about moonlighting. During a joint interview with two informants, one of them said to me, "It's not safe to talk about it—they'll have you arrested."[35] Whether or not this is true, such claims highlight the clandestine nature of moonlighting.

One police reservist claimed that police officers could earn up to R 5000 per month through moonlighting.[36] The most common forms of contemporary moonlighting are body guarding, business inspections and consultancies, working as a bouncer, debt collection, and vehicle tracking. Body guarding pays approximately R 250–1000 per day, and working as a bouncer pays between R 300 to R 600 per shift. Guarding, particularly for large events, is also common: Police officers wear company uniforms and are paid approximately R 500 for a few hours' work.[37] Private investigation is another common form of moonlighting; it is often referred to as a system of "lick, stamp, and mail," which implies that private investigators do the work and then send the results to the police.[38]

In turn, police officers also provide private investigators with assistance. In fact, many informants claimed that most private investigative work is based on active cooperation between private and public bodies, either as a paid service or through reciprocal exchanges.

The type of moonlighting that raises most concern involves police officers who own private security companies. A few ex-police officers provided me a list of names of policemen who owned companies at the time of my research. I knew several individuals on this list; in fact, two of them were informants whom I spoke to regularly, yet who had denied any engagement in moonlighting. One of them once stated to me, "I am very proud to say that I have never been engaged in any form of moonlighting. I have always been able to keep the two [state policing and private security] completely separate." However, other informants mentioned this same police officer as an example of someone who engages in moonlighting: "He's been doing it for years—everyone knows it. You can see him, driving around in his police vehicle, checking up on his guards."[39]

Most of the companies owned by police officers are guarding companies. One ex-police officer once told me, "All policemen have a few guards—it's almost like their uniform."[40] Police officers who own such businesses generally employ a small number of guards, approximately ten to twenty, so that their moonlighting activity is not too obvious. Monitoring the work of guards is easy, because it can be done during the company owner's shifts. To get around PSIRA legislation, these companies are not registered in the officer's own name, but rather in that of a relative, a police informant, or a friend.[41] As one police officer explained, "You're not allowed to own a company or do the physical work, but you can manage it."[42] Registering the company in someone else's name is referred to as "fronting" and is claimed to facilitate illegal behavior.[43] The only way to uncover the true ownership is to analyze the flow of money through financial audits. Although PSIRA has the legislation to implement such audits, this is rarely done.[44]

Although my informants concurred that moonlighting remained a common phenomenon, several stated that it had diminished as corruption increased. One police officer explained that extra income was now generated through "spot fines;" that is, demanding a fine (i.e., a bribe) on the spot. As he indicated, "Why work as a doorman for R 500 if you can make a *docket* go missing for R 10,000?"[45] Other informants noted how "sponsors" have replaced moonlighting. This practice refers to policemen demanding that private security employees provide "sponsorship," such as a portion of a guarding salary, in exchange for "police assistance."[46] One police officer framed this practice as a form of "policeman influence":

> For example, the owner of a hotel or bar wants to know where the road blocks will be on a certain night, so I'll offer to give him that information every week, as long as he'll have the bouncing and guarding done by a company that I suggest. If he says no, I can play a very dirty game and he knows it. . . . So they almost always do it.[47]

This police officer further shared how the company he "suggests" will provide him with a kickback. Policemen tied to certain companies can also exert power over other police officers. On this subject, many informants referred to a high-ranking police officer who was also the owner of a large company and was known to have

> bought out the whole station; all those guys are working for him, protecting his clients and his interests. They're not policemen anymore, although they wear the uniform. They do police and private security work at the same time. That station is filled with corruption, political games, all money. Money from the industry is leading them, not passion.[48]

One of the contemporary claims made regarding moonlighting is thus that police officers no longer earn extra money by conducting security-related work themselves; instead, they use their authority as police officers to arrange financial deals with the private security industry.

For many, the difference between moonlighting and corruption is racially tinted; as one police officer put it, "White policemen do security work; black policemen do spot work."[49] Many informants claimed that white policemen were more involved in moonlighting because of their ties to the old boys' network. Additionally, due to the government's Black Economic Empowerment (BEE) standards, white policemen have fewer promotion prospects and are more dependent on extra income generated from moonlighting.[50] Because of affirmative action policies, their jobs are more at risk, and they perceive moonlighting to be less dangerous than corruption.

Moonlighting is a direct form of "boundary-crossing" (Davis 2009: 240), an explicit example of a practice that blurs the boundaries between public and private policing. This makes it increasingly difficult to distinguish between public and private officers, as one police reservist explained:

> It's difficult to separate with all this intermixing between the forces; guys from SAPS are connected to the private security, and private security guys are doing police work, it's all mixed up. It doesn't have to be a problem—we are all

here to fight crime. But it becomes a problem when there's a conflict of interest, when someone steps on someone else's shoes . . . uses their position on one side to influence the other. It's a problem when the law no longer matters.[51]

Moonlighting contributes to creating the twilight zone, a sphere of uncertainty about the boundaries between public and private policing. It is an explicit example of state police officers engaging in private policing practices, of police officers themselves creating and participating in the twilight zone. The junior partner model thereby becomes untenable in the face of backdoor networks and social ties that continuously cross the public and private borders. Moonlighting also shows how personal links and social contacts between individuals from different policing bodies play a crucial role in shaping local security networks. Furthermore, it is based on "hidden" social connections between various individuals that may not be evident at first, but that do shape how policing is performed on the ground. I develop this claim further in the next two subsections.

The Old Boys' Network

May 2010

I'm on the night shift with David, and we're on the trail of a suspect who threatened the relative of an important client with a firearm about an hour ago. At one point, we spot the suspect's vehicle coming toward us on a small windy road in a residential area. David drives into the middle of the road to cut the driver off, jumps out of the vehicle, and yells at me, "Put your head down, Tessa; put it down!" He then commands the man to get out of his vehicle. At this point, Matthew, our backup, arrives at the scene, and he searches the vehicle while David searches the suspect. The suspect is clearly intoxicated; he is unable to stand up straight, and his speech is slurred and incoherent. After a round of questioning, the suspect admits to having a firearm, which he duly hands over to David. David then contacts the complainant (i.e., the client's relative) to ask him to come to the scene and identify the man.

When the complainant arrives, he immediately runs up to the suspect and punches him in the face. The two men start yelling at each other, and David and Matthew are forced to intervene. Matthew then handcuffs the suspect. We step aside, and the complainant says to David, "Let me just fuck him up a little bit, come on. A few slaps here and there." David and Matthew answer with a firm "no" to ensure that the complainant does not hit the suspect. Matthew then turns to me and explains, "We can't let him do anything because he is related to one of our clients. We can't risk him getting into trouble. Normally, we let them go ahead, but we can't take a chance to lose the client."

The next step is to contact the police, but the control room promptly informs us that the police cannot come to the scene because they only have one vehicle for the night and it is engaged elsewhere. Matthew and David become irritated and go off on a rant about the police. They then consider their options. The first is to wait, which they are loath to do since they had had to wait for the police for three hours following a vehicle theft during last night's shift. The second option is to contact another police officer. David provides the control room with a list of phone numbers of police officers whom he knows throughout the province, but all of them are either off duty or engaged elsewhere. The third option is to take the suspect to the station themselves, but they could get charged with "kidnapping" if they did this.[52]

While Matthew and David are discussing their options, we suddenly spot two police vehicles driving toward us. David whispers to me, "Let's hope we have a good shift tonight." As the cars come closer, David starts to smile. He sees that the inspector on duty is Manesh, an Indian policeman he knows very well, who is part of the "good shift." Manesh steps out of the vehicle and says playfully, "Why didn't you guys just bring him to the station? Why did we have to come all of the way out here?" While the other police officers attend to the suspect and complainant, Manesh chats with David and me. With a smirk on his face, he asks David, "How come this guy looks so good?" They both start laughing.

Shortly afterward, the police take the suspect back to the station, and David also goes along to make a statement. I go with him, assuming that we will be there all night, but we are out of the station in fifteen minutes. David then says to me, "What happened tonight was good. We arrested a guy, got the SAPS out here, they helped us, I wrote my statement, and now I'm out, ready to continue my work, to arrest the next guy. No hours of waiting at the station, no funny questions asked. But we were lucky, because Manesh was on duty. Tonight was the good shift."

. . .

In addition to the observations that David and Matthew patrolled the public realm and ensured that the complainant did not use more violence, the main point I want to make here concerns the use of social networks. David is a white armed response officer who previously worked in the apartheid armed forces. Because of his background, he knows many police officers in the area in which he works, whom he calls on "in times of need," as he did in this incident. David describes Manesh as part of the "good shift," which refers to a group of police officers at the local police station who regularly collaborate with the armed response officers from the company David and Matthew work for. The members of the "good shift" have a positive attitude toward the company, appreciate its officers' work, and assist them when possible, which sets them apart from those belonging to the "bad shift."

The distinction between good and bad shifts is primarily based on social connections that stem from the old boys' network (Hummer and Nalla 2003; Rigakos 2002: 39; Shearing and Stenning 1983). As discussed in Chapter 2, the "old boys' network" refers to a pool of white men within the industry and the apartheid armed forces, the connections among whom facilitated the entrance of former policemen and soldiers into the private security industry (Shaw 2002; Singh 2008). Because many of the members of this network had worked together as police officers, collaborative relationships between the two policing bodies continued after several left to work in the private security industry. Such relationships were particularly common in the armed response sector, because many police officers started armed response companies as one-man shows.

Another example of a collaborative police-armed response relationship that I encountered in the field was that between the owner of a community-based company and a police officer who had previously worked in the police force together. The two men frequently conducted night patrols and responded to incidents together; in fact, the owner of the company would rarely go out on patrols unless his "police friend" was on duty. They claimed that cooperating was enjoyable and led to more efficient policing. However, this friendly working relationship also involved some shady practices. For example, by sharing a police radio, the owner had direct access to police communication and was therefore able to choose which crime scenes he would respond to.[53] His presence at particular, often high-profiled, crime scenes was publicized in the local newspapers and functioned as a marketing strategy for the company, which further highlights how security firms often engage in "symbolic borrowing" (Thumala et al. 2011: 294) from the state. As the owner stated, "I'm a small company, not so many clients, so this here, this radio, this keeps my clients; it makes me look good." But more importantly, the owner also used his police connections to cover his tracks. If he acted outside the parameters of the law, which he was renowned for doing, he always had a police witness to uphold his narration of events.

In other cases, the personal connections between police officers and members of the industry are less obvious. One example used by many informants was a local Tracker project. Due to the success of the national partnership between the SAPS and Tracker, the head of Tracker in KwaZulu-Natal implemented a pilot project in 2009 called the "private user programme," whereby private security companies acted as additional response teams to assist Tracker in retrieving vehicles. Tracker identified four companies to work with based on their reputation and location.[54] However, when I discussed this partnership with other informants, many claimed that it was based on social ties between a group of former police officers. Apparently, the owners of the chosen companies and several employees at Tracker were all former policemen who had worked together at the same police station. The partnership was thus regarded by many as a self-serving scheme to ensure that these former colleagues could work together within a new structure and with different titles. Although this partnership did not result in any direct financial gain for the companies, it enhanced their reputation and fed the eagerness for armed response officers to "get in on the action."

In their study on security intelligence networks in Ontario, Canada, Lippert and O'Connor (2006) argue that interpersonal connections based on the migration of personnel from the public police to the security industry no longer play a major role in the sharing of security intelligence. In my research, moonlighting was also claimed to be less prominent than in the past. The first reason for this claim is that it is currently rare to find armed response officers who are former policemen; David is an exception in this regard. Currently, policemen who enter the industry do so in more lucrative sectors, such as investigations or tracking, or at the management level. Although their policing mentality may trickle down to operations (see Chapter 4), it does not define on-the-ground interactions. A second alleged cause of the demise of moonlighting concerned racial issues. Because the old boys' network stems from the apartheid era, it necessarily comprises white individuals. The decrease in the number of white police officers has reduced the frequency of interactions between policemen and private security personnel, thereby lessening the opportunities for moonlighting. As the white owner of an armed response company shared with me,

A lot of white cops have left . . . I'm not gonna be received with open arms
by a black policeman who wants to help me out. If the police still had a lot
of Whites, or if more companies had black employees, or representatives,
then the relationship with the SAPS would be much, much better.[55]

In contrast to the claimed demise of moonlighting as largely stemming
from the decline in the strength of the old boys' networks, I conclude
that they continue to shape local security networks. In addition, past
professional and social connections can also lead to hostile relationships, where the old boys' network can better be characterized as an
"old boys' feud." The following section analyzes a case involving the
same company that David works for to show how social connections
can create a "bad shift."

"Old Boys' Feud"

June 2010

During a shift change, a bunch of us are sitting outside the company office and chatting. At one point, an armed response officer arrives and
hands over a plastic bag to Paul, the owner of the company. I ask Paul
what's inside and he says "drugs." I initially assume that he's joking, but
then a guard from the company appears and Paul shouts at him and slaps
him in the face a few times. The guard is taken downstairs to the outside patio. Upstairs, we open the packet and find eight small packets of
marihuana. Paul quickly gives me the background to this story: In response to mounting suspicions that the guard was selling drugs at his
site (a high school), Paul instructed some of the armed response officers
to investigate the situation, and their fears were soon confirmed. The
managers decided to bring the guard to the office for disciplinary action.
Paul was clearly frustrated about the situation, saying things such as
"Here we are fighting crime and this guard is wearing our uniform and
selling drugs to schoolchildren" and "we have to take action and defend
our reputation."

As a group, the officers discuss what to do next. One option is to
phone the police and hand the guard over, but everyone is against this
option. They believe that the police will not deal with the case properly
or that they will only charge the guard for possession of drugs, rather
than for distribution. They also feel that it is their responsibility to deal
with the matter. They decide to resolve this case without the help of the
SAPS by finding the supplier of the drugs. Apparently, the guard pro-

vided information about the supplier's whereabouts to two of the armed response officers and offered to guide them there. In actuality, this information was likely obtained under duress; when the guard is brought back upstairs, he has obviously been physically assaulted as he is covered in cuts and bruises.

In two vehicles, we head off to a neighboring Indian township, where we stop at a shack adjacent to a brick house. When we get out, a crowd of people immediately surrounds us, and it gets bigger throughout the entire ordeal. The "supplier" is not at home, but the company employees search the shack extensively for drugs. While I remain outside and try to deflect any attention, I hear things breaking and people being pushed around inside the shack. A few seconds later, the armed response officers all walk out of the shack; one of them holds up a bag that they found inside a drawer that contains thirty-eight small packets of marihuana. At this point, the guard's wife and family arrive at the scene, and a family dispute erupts, with the wife hitting the guard several times. Paul turns to the crowd and declares, somewhat piously, that the company employees will need to take the guard to jail to set an example. He repeatedly stresses that the company will not tolerate this type of behavior. Before we leave, one of the armed response officers is instructed to hide any evidence of their search of the shack.

Now that they have found more marihuana, they collectively agree that they have enough evidence to go to the police, who will be forced to charge the guard with drug dealing. The three armed response officers who initially arrested the guard (and brought him to the company office) proceed to take him to the police station to make a statement, while the rest disperse to continue the night shift; I join David on his patrols. A little while later, we hear over the radio that the three armed response officers are still at the police station, so David and I go there to find out what is going on. When we enter the charge office of the station, we see the three officers standing in a cell: they have been arrested for "assault GBH": assault of grievous bodily harm.

As we step outside the police station, we come across two policemen whom we know. The more senior one explains to us how stupid we are: "I can't believe you did this. You guys took the risk for something so small? You fucked the guy up completely and then bring him here for marihuana? You don't bring in a guy bleeding like that and then say that nothing happened. At least be smart enough to give a statement that makes it look like you had to use the force you did; then it's fine, but like this, come on!!"

The rest of the night shift is filled with speculations, chatter, and gossip about what happened, and when I return home as the sun starts to rise, my thoughts keep me from sleeping. Although I am worried about the armed response officers in jail, I also sympathize with the police. I may not have actually witnessed any of the armed response officers hitting the guard, but I am certain that they inflicted physical pain on him. I am deeply torn between empathizing with my informants and judging their behavior.

It is not until two days later during a day shift that the three armed response officers in question tell me what happened that night.[56] Apparently, they were framed. They first reiterate their innocence by stating that, although they had arrested the guard and taken him to the company office, they were conducting patrols when the rest of us visited the supplier's shack and had therefore not been a part of the entire ordeal, which I realize is true. They then tell me that, when they arrived at the police station, the guard was arrested and taken into custody by the police. However, the commanding police officer questioned him about his visible wounds, and the guard stated that he had been assaulted by Paul, but not by any of his three escorts. The commanding officer then instructed the guard to change his statement to say that all three of the armed response officers had also assaulted him. The guard was convinced to change his statement by the commanding officer's promise that he would only have to pay a small fine and would then be released. The guard went along with the plan, which resulted in the arrest of the three armed response officers. I was initially reluctant to believe this story, because it implied that the commanding officer had unlawfully arrested them and purposely altered the guard's statement. Yet over the next few days, I spoke to other police officers who were also on duty that night, and they each confirmed the response officers' account.

. . .

Whether the armed response officers were really framed is not the point I want to make. Rather, what I want to show here is that the hostile relationship between this particular police officer and the armed response officers was shaped by previous interactions and can only be understood in the light of background information about the company and police station in question.

During my time in Durban, I heard from various sources—police officers, employees of the company, community members, and so on—that there was a very hostile relationship between the owner of the company, Paul, and a high-ranking Indian police officer, Robert, which stemmed from the time when Paul worked as a police reservist. One theory for this enmity was that Paul was often guilty of illegal misconduct as a police reservist, primarily due to his excessive use of force. He continued such practices with his own company, and the police regarded this as vigilante behavior. The second theory was that Paul was an efficient police reservist who chalked up a lot of arrests, which incited jealousy among other police officers. Paul claims he was "bullied away" by a specific group of police officers, of which Robert was the ringleader. This encouraged Paul to start his own company, which has gradually become a successful one that plays a large role in policing the community. Therefore, rather than constituting an old boys' network, the social connections here resulted in a competitive and hostile relationship.

Furthermore, various interlocutors told me that moonlighting also played a role in this antagonistic relationship, because Robert owned a guarding company that was registered under his wife's name and that competed directly with Paul's company. Two different forms of competition thus shaped this hostile relationship: that between the private security company (and its employees) and the police, and that between two private security companies, one of which is owned by a public official. The conflict of interest resulting from Robert's moonlighting entered the domain of public law enforcement and had a tremendous impact on the overall relationship between Paul's company and the police station. I want to stress that obtaining information about this issue was not easy because many informants were very reluctant to discuss it publicly, as is shown by the following comment from a member of the local CPF board:

> I would like to tell you about it, but I can't, it's too risky. But what I can say is: It's not about two organizations; it's about individual and personal fighting and problems. And if the situation doesn't get better, then innocent lives will go to jail. We need to come up with a solution or the situation is going to burst.[57]

Although the animosity between Paul and Robert was extreme, hostile relationships between particular police officers and members of the industry are not uncommon. Thus, social ties between the two policing bodies do not always mean that a local security network is more efficient and appreciated. Old social connections, what I have labeled here as an "old boys' feud," can also be the source of rivalry and competition between different policing bodies.

We therefore see two contrasting local security networks between one company and one police station, referred to by David as the "good shift" and the "bad shift." These contrasting relationships are a main source of the "gambling" sensation highlighted by Gavin in the chapter's introduction. In both cases—the incident involving David, Matthew, and Manesh and that of the guard selling marihuana—we see how armed response officers contemplate whether or not to involve the SAPS when an incident arises. Both episodes required the armed response officers to weigh their options. Although their eventual decisions were based on numerous factors, the likeliness of encountering the "good" or "bad" shift was pivotal. This also highlights how armed response officers and other members of the industry are aware of their subordinate role in relation to the state police, who ultimately define the outcome of an incident. The dominant position enjoyed by police officers is also evident when armed response officers use violence.

"They Do Our Dirty Work"

November 2008

During a day shift with Gayle, we received a strange call from a client about a young boy who was tied to a tree. We were given an address, but when we arrived at the scene, we couldn't find anything. After back-and-forth communication with the control room, we learned that the tied-up boy was somewhere nearby, close to the client's residence. We drove around the neighborhood for a while and then saw two middle-aged black women hailing us to stop. As the car slowed down and we came closer, we saw a young black male with his hands tied behind a tree. He was only wearing shorts and had obviously been beaten, as he was bleeding from several places and had numerous scratches on his body. A strand of mucus hung from his nose, and saliva streamed from his mouth. He was making incomprehensible noises, moaning, and speaking gibberish. The two women were laughing and yelling at the boy. They told us that two boys had robbed them on the street, but they had chased after them and were able to catch one of the culprits, whom they then beat and tied up.

Shortly afterward, the police arrived on the scene. The three police officers, Gayle, and the two women all laughed at the boy and called him a "retard" because of his appearance and obvious speech impediment. I felt rather out of place. One of the police officers then stepped toward Gayle and me and said with a smile on his face, "You had fun with this one, didn't you?" Another police officer then untied the boy and smacked him a few times before handcuffing him, at which the police officer next to us then said, "Don't worry; we'll make it that he got out of hand."

. . .

In this case, the police officers not only assumed that Gayle had hit the boy but also openly condoned it, stating that they would cover it up for him. This "covering up" was also evident in the example in the previous section, in which a senior police officer reprimanded the armed response officers not for their use of violence toward the guard but for not being "smart enough" in covering their tracks. This raises questions about how police officers perceive and act on armed response officers' use of violence.

In many studies on policing, particularly those conducted in Europe and North America, police officers are defined as enforcers of the law who represent the "legal" side of policing, particularly in incidents when private security officers use violence. In their case study, Sharp and Wilson highlight how the public police felt negatively about a particular private security company because it was "taking the law into their own hands" and operating "on the fringes of the law" (2000: 127). In his case study, Noaks also shows how the public police were unwilling to work with certain private security officers due to the latter's "tendency to come in all guns blazing" (2000: 154).

Although I experienced a few instances where police officers stepped in and arrested armed response officers for malpractice, such as assault, I mostly experienced the opposite, when police officers condoned or even encouraged the use of force. I frequently saw suspects handed over to the police with clear signs of assault, which the police duly ignored. The incident involving David, Matthew, and Manesh was one example, with Manesh, the police officer, expressing his surprise that the suspect still "looks good." In addition, David and Matthew stopped the complainant from hitting the suspect for the primary purpose of retaining their client, not out of fear of punishment by the police. Many police officers voiced sentiments such as "they [armed response officers] do our dirty work" and even claimed to be grateful that they (the police officers) didn't have to "get their hands dirty." As noted by Baker, the "state police may outsource their 'dirty work' to nonstate agents that, as the police, they are not entitled to perform" (2010: 33). According to this perspective, the use of violence by armed response officers does not undermine the role of the state; rather, it is a form of outsourcing.

In Chapter 1, I discussed how violence is the source of power, the means to create and maintain a particular social order. I also discussed how state law primarily defines sovereignties based on the use of violence. This was exemplified with reference to the distinction between vigilantism and private security, whereby violence used by vigilante organizations is defined as illegal and violence used by private security officers is generally regarded as legal because they operate within the legal parameters of the state. However, this case of the tied-up boy and many others that I observed in the field show that this distinction is not always clear-cut. Although Gayle did not use violence on the boy, the police officers assumed that he had and tolerated it. And as shown in Chapter 7, the use of violence by armed response officers does not always operate within the legal parameters of the state. Yet if it is tolerated or even encouraged by state officials, can we define it as illegal? Furthermore, can we assume that police officers always represent the state? Jensen (2003, in Baker 2010: 34) argues that state representatives often "shed their stateness" and act independently from state rules. Can the condoning of violence by a police officer therefore be seen as a practice of state sovereignty?

Furthermore, I want to highlight here that interventions on the part of police officers are very often based on their social connections with armed response officers, as several cases in this chapter have shown. Such connections often determine whether police officers decide to enforce the law. In the case of the tied-up boy, Gayle told me afterward that he did not know the three police officers personally, but that his boss (i.e., the owner of the company) was a good friend of one of the high-ranking police officers at that station. The company as a whole was therefore viewed positively by these police officers. Perhaps the police officers would have acted differently if armed response officers from another company had responded to this incident.

CONCLUDING REMARKS

In this chapter, I analyzed the relationship between the private security industry and the South African state. I first examined state regulation of the industry by PSIRA and argued that, despite its comprehensive nature, it is subject to severe criticism. Furthermore, state regulation does not necessarily determine the daily interactions of armed response officers with the state. Rather, armed response officers are defined by their encounters with police officers. The state can therefore implement a far-reaching regulation scheme that empowers various government agencies to oversee different parts of the industry, but the impact of state regulation on the actual policing practices of armed response officers is largely dependent on the practices of state police officers. As a former member of PSIRA's council put it, "How can PSIRA address illegalities in the private security industry if police officers are the ones doing it and encouraging it?"[58] It therefore seems that overseeing the private security industry is not only a matter of regulating it but also about regulating the practices of state police officers.

This chapter showed how the South African state envisions interactions between armed response officers and police officers as occurring within the framework of a senior-junior partnership. Yet, because of the lack of a national agreement that outlines how "partnership policing" should occur, interactions between armed response officers and police officers are very often informal, ad hoc, and based on social networks. We saw how private security companies engage in policing activities that occur without police supervision. Moreover, I showed how the state police may not always be in possession of all available crime data and may not determine or control all of the mechanisms and processes that occur in local security networks, which threatens their dominant and senior position. As armed response officers increasingly enter the public realm and engage in "state-like performances" (Buur and Jensen 2004: 144), they challenge the state's role and incite feelings of competition between the policing bodies. Furthermore, with decreasing public confidence in the state police and clients demanding to have their own police force, the role of the public police is becoming increasingly peripheral. Meanwhile, private security companies, which are often regarded as more reliable and efficient, continue to grow in popularity.

However, the eagerness of private security personnel to cooperate with the police shows that the state is far from obsolete. Private security employees actively build alliances with the police, particularly through social connections. Armed response officers also mimic the state and thereby (re)produce its "procedural and symbolic forms of legitimacy" (Buur 2006: 750). Security networks between police officers and armed response officers are thus "negotiated tactical alliances" (Baker 2010: 35) that are simultaneously competitive and collaborative.

All this points toward the performance of policing practices in an ambiguous domain, namely the twilight zone, and this chapter showed the active role of police officers in creating and participating in this zone. This is particularly evident in the instances of moonlighting, whereby police officers engage in private policing practices. Engagements in moonlighting show that private and public bodies can be differentiated by their uniforms and other aspects of their appearance, but that their motivations and actions do not always match this physical distinction. Determining whether a practice is "public" or "private" is increasingly difficult. A police officer may represent the state in uniform, but if he is motivated by financial gains or by acts of reciprocity within a social network, then what and who does he represent? And if an armed response officer is managed by a former police officer and regularly works with police officers and supports the latter's actions, then how "private" is his position and performance? With citizens increasingly claiming that the two policing bodies are essentially the same, is there even any need to make such a distinction?

Ultimately, however, I conclude that it is the state police who decide if and how networks remain in play, either through front door, official channels or through backdoor operations and informal mechanisms. Schmitt's (1985) idea that the sovereign power of the state rests in the monopoly to decide, rather than the monopoly to rule, implies that police officers are the "deciding" actors who determine how a network unfolds. I therefore concur with scholars such as Loader and Walker (2004, 2006), who argue that it is ultimately the state and its representatives that determine the course and nature of local security networks. It is the state that "structures the security network both in its presence and in its absence, both in its explicit directions and in its implicit permissions" (Loader and Walker 2004: 225). Although there are "multiple sovereignties" (Bertelsen 2009), this research concurs with Rigi's claim that representatives of the state are "the final arbiters" (2007: 41): They have the final say about which sovereign practices are honored.

However, this decision-making process is not always steered by "state-based policies": Social networks, financial gains, and individual personalities play an equal, if not greater, role. This does not diminish the role of police officers as "arbiters;" it simply makes the process much more complex. And because the policing practices in these networks are often informal and ad hoc, they are continuously in flux, which further attests to the precarious and unpredictable nature of twilight policing. This creates immense uncertainty for armed response officers, because they often have no idea how the police will react to their actions. This uncertainty is encapsulated in the "gambling" sensation described by Gavin in the introduction, which also highlights the subordinate position of armed response officers in relation to the state police. As Nick, an armed response officer, once said to me, "It's all about the guys at the station. We're always willing, but no matter what we think or do, they decide. It all comes down to them."[59]

CHAPTER 6

"Getting Connected with the Community"

The Beneficiaries of Armed Response

December 2008

It's one of my first night shifts with Brian, and we head out to meet a client who's just reported a break-in. Another reaction officer, Mark, is waiting for us at the client's premises. On our way there, Brian emphasizes that this client is the leading member of one of the company's "special projects" and therefore needs "extra special attention;" we will need to be on our "best behavior," he explains. When we arrive at the scene and begin talking with the client, I observe how Brian is indeed on his best behavior and treating this client differently—better—than others.

A few hours later, while we're having a cup of coffee at a gas station, we hear over the radio that Tim, one of Brian's colleagues, has just escorted a female client from her workplace to her residence. Over the radio, other reaction officers are making crude jokes, complaining about her demands, and mocking her "paranoid" behavior. Brian explains that this client requests escorts frequently and is "a bit of a pain." A few minutes later, a white male in his late forties knocks on Brian's window, and they strike up a conversation about the current crime situation in the area. The man fills Brian in on recent crime activity and what he and his colleagues need to look out for and also asks Brian for any relevant crime updates. When the man leaves, Brian explains to me that this man isn't a client of the company but is someone who conducts patrols in this neighborhood and "helps us out."

A few days later, Brian and I are reflecting on this particular shift. I question him about these different interactions with clients and citizens, and he replies as follows:

> You see, every client, every person, needs a different approach, and when you're in the game long enough, you know this. Now, you don't know exactly how to be with every single person coming up to you, but with every company, there are different types of clients that need a different type of way. And if you work for a company long enough, you suss it out, you start to feel it, it becomes a part of it all, this work. Some clients want more; some want less. Some clients want to be treated like they own the fucking world; others want you to do your job and just get out of there. Some guys think what we doing is worthless; others look out for us and take the time. But at the end of the day, they're all clients, or people that the company wants to be clients, and they tell us what to do. That's the same, no matter where you go.

. . .

This extract from my field notes shows the different types of clients and the variety of encounters between Brian and citizens in one single shift: a client who needs "special attention," another who who is "a bit of a pain," and a supportive citizen engaged in his own policing efforts who "helps us out." This chapter analyzes various forms of interactions and relationships between the armed response sector and citizens (mainly clients) and how they shape the foundation of the twilight zone.

Citizen-based initiatives for fighting crime, both individually and collectively, are plentiful in South Africa and range from individual patrols to entire "communities of security." These initiatives, which are often categorized as forms of "self-policing," "citizen policing," or "community policing," have been extensively studied in the South African context.[1] However, only a few studies have analyzed the interactions and relationships, both formal and informal, between citizen-based policing initiatives and private security companies worldwide (Brown and Lippert 2007; Clarno and Murray 2013; Crawford and Lister 2006; Marks and Wood 2007; McManus 1995; Noaks 2000), and none does so ethnographically. This chapter thus sheds light on a largely unexplored terrain in studies on private security, for South Africa and beyond.

I make this contribution by analyzing the various interactions and relationships between armed response companies—at the level of management and operations—and citizens, particularly clients, through the local security network framework (Dupont 2004). Although I examine the perspectives of clients and managers, my primary focus is the experiences and perceptions of reaction officers. I distinguish between formal security networks, which are networks based on an official partnership between a client and a company and governed by a contractual agreement, and informal security networks, which are networks in which the interactions are not based on an official contractual agreement. Formal security networks consist of "clients" (i.e., paying citizens), while informal security networks consist of both clients and nonclients (i.e., nonpaying citizens). I further differentiate between high-maintenance, collaborative, and competitive local security networks, which can be both formal and informal. On the one hand, these categorizations highlight the tremendous diversity of local security networks. Yet on the other hand, they are all similar, in that they show the pivotal role that clients and citizens play in creating the foundation for twilight policing.

This pivotal role has two causes. First, clients are undoubtedly the "dominant actors" in these networks. I concur with Shearing and Stenning (1983), Lippert and O'Connor (2006), and Wakefield (2003) that clients play a vital role in determining the nature of security provision. The second reason concerns the main contemporary trend of the industry, namely the establishment and growth of "collective arrangements," an issue also discussed by Clarno and Murray (2013). These are (in)formal schemes whereby citizens "club" together to benefit collectively from armed response. Through these arrangements, armed response companies are increasingly serving "communities of security" that mandate them to operate in public spaces. Due to the dominant position of clients and the growth of various collective arrangements, armed response officers are engaged in an array of policing tasks that occur in the public realm. Clients are therefore also responsible for creating and perpetuating the twilight zone.

The first section of this chapter analyzes the general demand for private security and elucidates why citizens subscribe to private security companies, particularly armed response, and why they increasingly are establishing collective arrangements. It examines how fear, particularly the fear of crime, shapes the (perceived) need for private security and the desire to upgrade into a collective, how the state police has encouraged this trend through the neoliberal profiling of citizens as "responsible citizens," and how certain marketing strategies used by the industry have accelerated the establishment of collective arrangements. The second section analyzes various types of formal and informal local security networks, which I then further distinguish between high-maintenance, collaborative, and competitive networks to show their diversity. The third section examines repercussions of the growth of collective arrangements in creating (imagined) borders between communities. Armed response officers are ascribed the role of "gatekeepers" to police these borders, yet are continuously negotiating their own position along them. This chapter ends with some concluding remarks that emphasize how "getting connected with the community" sets the stage for the performance of twilight policing.

UNDERSTANDING THE DEMAND

An analysis of the demand for private security is needed to understand the vast size of the private security industry and the growth of collective arrangements. This section explores how citizens, state police officers, and the private security industry create this demand.

"It Makes Me Feel Safer"

July 2010

I accompanied Sally, a white female in her late thirties who is a sales rep in a large armed response company, for a day to analyze her work. Her third call of the day was a young woman who had recently moved back to Durban after living abroad for more than a decade. She was a new client and wanted to install a completely new security package in her home, so Sally inspected her residence and advised her on the type of technical installation she would need for maximum security. At one point the client and I were standing outside, and she told me that she had been back in the country for just a few days and that this was her first "homecoming" task, because she perceived it to be the most pressing. I asked her why she was so eager to set up a private security system. She explained that she had left the country to study abroad and while there had been horrified by the stories about crime on the international news. Since her return, her friends and family had recounted numerous incidents of violent crime and had urged her to employ the necessary security measures. She then elaborated as follows:

> Of course I've heard all the stories; I've been back to visit a few times and I know all the stories. But I haven't lived here for a while, so I'm no expert. But look around [she points to the houses on the same street as hers]; everyone has it, don't you? I mean, that must mean that it's necessary. Why else would have everybody have it? So I'm just trying to be smart and do what I

think I should. And with all these stories you hear all the time, the media, it just makes me feel safer that I've done what I can.

. . .

This client was new to armed response, yet her perceptions of private security were fairly typical and highlight the collective impact of fear. The purchasing of private security or taking part in any type of security initiative is always instigated by an incident of crime, whether felt close by or experienced "at a distance" through social acquaintances, rumors, or media reports (Brown and Lippert 2007), that feeds into the "talk of crime" (Caldeira 2000). Whenever I asked clients why they subscribed to private security, crime was the primary explanation.

Chapter 2 briefly analyzed South Africa's high crime rates and showed how crime is a real societal problem. Yet the (perceived) need for private security is primarily based on perceptions of crime, fear of crime, and feelings of insecurity. The biggest boom in the industry occurred around the time of the political transition. Although crime rates increased then, the era was predominantly marked by uncertainty about the direction of the post-apartheid South African state. The fact that South Africa has the largest private security industry in terms of GDP (Abrahamsen and Williams 2011; Singh 2008) cannot be explained solely with reference to the high crime rates, but must incorporate the complexities of fear, especially collective fear.

Fear is primarily understood as an emotion or feeling that is associated with particular images, events, and people and is felt and expressed during particular moments. Although fear is also a biological response, it is given meaning through representation. It can be regarded as a text and cultural artifact, because it "acquires meaning through cultural language and rites" (Geertz 1973, quoted in Bourke 2005: 7). The experience and meaning of fear are intrinsically connected to the social environment in which it is evoked (Reguillo 2002). Fear is a social construction; it is society, with its encompassing social logics, structures, and practices, that constructs fear and notions surrounding fear, such as risk, death, and danger (Beck 1992; Douglas 2002; Merry 1981). When I asked Durbanites about their fears and what they felt they needed protection from, their answers centered on crime. However, substantial literature shows that fear of crime primarily revolves around fear of *becoming* a victim of crime, rather than having actually *been* a victim (Lemanski 2006; Merry 1981).

Combining the cognitive perception of risk and the emotional dimension of fear, the perspective used here is that fear of crime and discourses of crime are embedded in larger social issues (Rountree 1998). The concept of crime operates as a condensed symbol comprising more general perceptions of fear and insecurity within one's social environment (Douglas 1986; Jackson 2004; Lemanski 2004, 2006; Louw 2007; Merry 1981). Throughout my fieldwork, I was frequently astounded by South Africans' perceptions of crime and the numerous "practices of security" (Rotker 2002: 13). I often felt that they were paranoid and that their fear of crime was rather disproportionate to its incidence. Yet the reality is that many South Africans have experienced traumatic incidents of violent crime. All my acquaintances had been victims of violent crime or knew people who had. Tales about having a gun pointed at one's head, being physically forced out of a car, or being tied up were widespread. The traumatic nature of these experiences and their impact on one's perception of crime should not be underestimated or trivialized. Furthermore, the talk of crime feeds into a larger, collective understanding of fear and a perception that private security is a basic need. A study conducted in South Africa by Roberts (2010: 270) found that 43 percent of respondents stated that a burglar alarm system was "essential" and 31 percent defined armed response as "essential."

The consumption of private security is a practice that reacts to fear and gives it meaning. Goold et al. argue that security products cannot be compared to other forms of mass consumption because they are not "a significant part of mainstream consumption" (2010: 10), are not on substantial display, and do not constitute a part of "routine" shopping. Rather, security occupies "a marginal place in contemporary consumer culture" (10) and provides little satisfaction and joy: It is a grudge purchase. Although I concur with some of these claims, nonetheless, I argue that private security does *not* occupy a marginal space in South African society, but is very prominently on display. Driving through any South African city, the dominance of private security is inescapable: High walls topped with spikes, broken glass, or barbed wire; electric fences; boom barriers to control vehicular access, and emblems of private security companies are in abundance. In a neighborhood where everyone displays a subscription to a private security company, the one house without such an emblem is regarded as the weakest link and easiest target.

Given the emotional element of fear (Loader 1997b), security must be analyzed subjectively and be understood as "the hopes and fears of those who are willing, in ever increasing numbers, to purchase it in the market-place" (Spitzer 1987: 46). Purchasing security to mitigate fear should be seen as "an investment based on faith" (47), making people feel protected, empowered, and responsible (Brown and Lippert 2007; Buzan, Wæver, and de Wilde 1998; Loader 1997b, 1999; Noaks 2000). In my fieldwork, many clients claimed that purchasing private security was a means of empowerment, as the following quote from a white male client illustrates:

> I know that an alarm system in my house and car, an electric fence, burglar bars, whatever, it's not going to stop the guy. Even if I carry a panic button with me wherever I go, I can still get jacked. So I know it doesn't really work, it doesn't really protect me. But it does make the chance smaller, it does give me some protection. . . . And it makes me feel safer. When I come home and lock up the doors and put on the alarm, I know that I am not 100 percent safe, but I am safer than if I don't do anything; then I wouldn't be able to sleep at night.[2]

For many, private security acts as a deterrent and provides assurance and peace of mind (McManus 1995; Sharp and Wilson 2000). This effect is experienced not only at the individual or household level but also, and more intensely, at the collective level in a social environment that encourages the consumption of private security.

As the case of the new female client discussed at the beginning of this section illustrates, the phrase "everyone around me has it, so I need it too" is a powerful way of reasoning and highlights the collective nature of fear and the workings of social pressure. Private security is an individual *and* collective mode of consumption (Loader 1999), which explains the proliferation of collective arrangements: They are social "fear-management strategies" (Lemanski 2006) that amalgamate individual practices of security to produce a collective one. I view collective arrangements as a form of upgrading one's security in a context with endless possibilities. If security depends on the *absence* of something "risky" and "dangerous" (Brown and Lippert 2007; Sharp and Wilson 2000), then it is an industry with never-ending prospects (Bauman 2001; Buzan et al. 1998; Spitzer 1987). This is particularly apparent when a product fails the client, such as when one's house is broken into despite having a security system. An upgrade to collective arrangements is very often the result of such incidents. The inference is not that the security measures did not work, but that there simply were not *enough* of them, as one marketing manager emphasized:

There is a never-ending supply. . . . First it starts off with alarms. Then people realized, and I feel exactly the same way, I don't want the *oak* standing in front of me, I want to know in the garden that he's already there and about to come into my house. So then came the beams. But then that wasn't enough, and then came the CCTV cameras, so we can see exactly what is happening around our house. And now, clients are thinking: Hey, let's get together and create a system together, so we can control what's going on in our neighborhood and act together.[3]

Upgrading to a collective arrangement is also believed by many to strengthen social cohesion and order. Crime is associated with disorder; it erodes trust, security, and social interaction. Mobilizing residents to create a collective entity with a common objective (i.e., in this case, fighting crime) is regarded as a means of (re)establishing trust and social cohesion (Cohen 1966). The formation of collective arrangements is thus a practice that represents and gives meaning to the collective experience of fear and is perceived to create a sense of community and order.

"The Police Won't Do That for Me"

This need for empowerment ties in with the perception that the state has failed to provide security for its citizens. In survey after survey, "crime" is the main reason that people give for subscribing to private security, and this response is automatically linked to a view of a failing state police force. The police force is one the least trusted institutions in the country (Mattes 2006; Roberts 2010). For example, 41 percent of those interviewed by Roberts (2010: 270) expressed distrust toward the state police.[4] During my fieldwork, the state police was habitually described as worthless, corrupt, understaffed, and incapable.[5]

One day in November 2008, I was on duty with William when we received word of an attempted break-in. When we got to the residence, the clients—an elderly white couple—showed us at great length where the suspect had tried to get in and what he was after. After a casual chat about crime in the area, William asked whether he should notify the police. The elderly clients were adamant that they did not want police involvement. When I asked why, the woman narrated a convoluted story about a previous break-in at her neighbor's house and the subsequent involvement of the police. She ended her story with the following remarks:

The police are not the answer to the crime; they are the criminals. I am sure that that one policeman at the station—that young, black man with the funny teeth—he helps the criminals with the break-ins in this area. So no! I do not want them here. I will just bring trouble on myself.

Regardless of whether such stories are true, they feed into the "talk of crime" and reproduce images of the police as unreliable, inadequate, and criminal.

Although I claim in this book that the state-failure argument is insufficient for explaining the proliferation of nonstate policing worldwide, I do concur that the provision of private security "bridges the gap between public expectations of security services and the existing reality of police protection" (McManus 1995: 118). With the armed response sector, there are three main factors that bridge this gap: quick response, visible patrolling, and personal service. My informants repeatedly cited the poor response times of the police as a grievance. In the Victims of Crime Survey report (2011: 23), 68.1 percent of respondents identified the fact that police "don't respond on time" as a primary reason for being dissatisfied with the way the police deal with crime. The following quote from an Indian male client highlights the allure of quick response:

> If something happens to me or my family, if some criminal comes into my home, and hurts one of us, or takes anything, I want somebody to be here right away. Not after three hours to take my statement and try to get some fingerprints, but I want them here when the guys are still inside my house . . . at the point when one of them has a gun to my head and the other is walking outside with my flat screen. That's when I need help and that's what I'm paying for, because the police won't do that for me. But armed response, they're here within a few minutes; they respond much quicker. That's their job—to be here as soon as possible. That's what I pay them for.[6]

In addition to quick response, patrolling is also appealing to clients. Patrolling functions as a physical and symbolic form of public assurance. The patrolling of public spaces is citizens' main motivation for forming a collective arrangement, whereby armed response officers are requested to actively patrol a given area and look out for anything suspicious. It resonates with an increasing global demand for visible policing, whereby state police and private security officers are encouraged to be proactive rather than reactive.[7]

Additionally, private security companies provide personal service and cater to clients' specialized needs. Clients often mentioned that the state police didn't "care for them" or "take the time" to address their needs. Private security, in contrast, offers a personalized service that allows clients to feel "heard" and "taken care of." Security officers are seen as willing to deal with personal issues and to take the time to "sort things out;" this personal service provides clients with a sense of ownership and allows them to make demands, unlike the state police, which makes them feel that they are "put on hold" and "one of the many."

"Take Back Your Streets!"

Quick response, visible patrolling, and personal service are the three key elements of armed response that differentiate it from the state police in the eyes of citizens. The allure of private security is strengthened by encouragement on the part of the state police. In the current neoliberal era, states are increasingly framing people as "responsible citizens" (Johnston 1992).

Since 1994, crime has played a distinctive role in the formation of citizenship in South Africa (Bénit-Gbaffou 2008; Singh 2008). During community policing forum (CPF) meetings, police officers repeatedly call on citizens to take the initiative in combating crime. They encourage people to "take back your streets," to create neighborhood watches, to "know your neighbor," "to be a survivor, not a victim," and to be "vigilant," as made explicit during a CPF meeting that I attended in February 2009. When the crime trends and hot spots of the area were discussed at that meeting, a particular street was identified as a "problem" due to the large number of recent break-ins. The police officer coordinating the meeting then issued the following warning:

> If no one in that road does anything, they will get punished. They will get robbed, or even worse. And then if that happens, they will come crying to the police and blame us for not being there. But this is not only our responsibility: you are responsible for your road; you cannot expect us to do everything.

This statement shows how citizens are encouraged to assume at least some responsibility for their own safety. However, such views also result in feelings of guilt if crime does occur. While I patrolled with police officers, they frequently blamed citizens for particular incidents of crime and repeatedly described them as stupid, apathetic, and irresponsible in ensuring their own safety. Police officers often felt that citizens relied too much on them and that they needed to take matters into their own hands, with subscribing to a private security company being the most obvious course of action. Almost all of the police officers I interviewed supported citizen-based security initiatives, such as collective arrangements with the private security industry. State officials are thus sending out a message that citizens are "responsible" for their own security and therefore to blame if they do not take preventive action. This process of blaming instills tremendous feelings of guilt in people and consolidates a constant security-related state of mind, which is strengthened by the marketing strategies of the private security industry.

"Who's in Your Bed while You're at Work?"

June 2008

I was walking through the grand halls of Securex, a large convention for the private security sector that is held annually in Johannesburg and caters to industry members from across the globe. At one point I spotted a large red banner that read, "Who's in your bed while you're at work?" and I laughed out loud, assuming that this was a clever pun or exaggeration of some sort. All of a sudden, an elderly white salesman came up to me and said, "Yes, you can laugh all you want, but you never know who can enter your house, who is talking to your wife or what your kids are doing while you're at work. You need to be aware of your surroundings at all times." I was shocked by his statement, which my face apparently betrayed as the salesman continued to explain to me at length how I, as a young woman, was not safe in this "dangerous world." He urged me to realize that I could easily fall victim to "the sick evil of this world" and that protection through an array of gadgets was my only hope of salvation. I was left slightly stunned and disgusted by the content of the message and the way the salesman was trying to "sell" his products.

. . .

Although my conversation with the salesman was an extreme case, it underlines how members of the industry commonly portray security as essential. The sales and marketing sector is a huge part of the industry that cannot be overlooked when analyzing the demand for private security and the growth of collective arrangements. In the world of private security, clients are labeled as "the cornerstone" of every company, and firms invest heavily in marketing strategies and customer service training for their employees. They also devise powerful marketing strategies featuring slogans such as "Always Peace of Mind;" "There First, There Fast, There for You;" and "We Serve and Protect."

Private security firms are regularly scrutinized by the public for profiting from and consolidating fear (Thumula et al. 2011). High crime rates in South Africa maintain a demand for private security, and companies tap into the fear of crime as a marketing strategy, as the marketing manager of a large company explained:

> Yes, the fear factor does play a role in how we sell and we do work with this. But without fear, people wouldn't need us anymore, so it has to be done. We do try to be more subtle, but it is still there, yes. It is not our main push, but it is underneath it all, a basis of sorts.[8]

This focus on fear is also evident in company monthly newsletters that offer safety tips and updated crime statistics. The following two extracts from the digital newsletters of a large armed response company show how crime and (in)security are framed:

> Living in South Africa is a lifestyle decision, part of that decision is to take appropriate measures to ensure your safety and that of your family. (November 2010)

> Sad to say, but many of these crimes were committed because the work of criminals was made easy—yes, you got it, criminals gained access to homes through open, and in some cases, unsecured windows with devastating consequences. . . . We can change our behaviour by taking the power for ourselves and accepting that there is a lot we can do to prevent crime. (February 2011)

These extracts reveal how subscribing to private security is framed as a "lifestyle decision" that allows citizens to take "the power for ourselves." Significantly, this framing resonates with the "responsible citizenship" message propagated by the state.

Entering the "Community"

Around the turn of the twenty-first century, armed response companies began to target middle-class and lower income segments of society as potential clients. This strategy was accompanied by a general rebranding of the industry from a military-style force into "community policing groups." Although some companies still identify themselves by using militaristic symbols, there has been a general shift toward companies portraying themselves as having a "community orientation." Many firms want to be seen as "friendlier," comprising "community policing officers" who cater to the needs of citizens and are not solely interested in profiting from crime, as a marketing manager explained:

> We wanted to move away from the whole combat, military-style, because we were starting to see that people didn't want that anymore, they were done with it. They wanted a friendly professional to assist them. So we researched it and

created a "community policing force." . . . We invested in everything: new uniforms, new vehicles, new symbols, you name it, and it worked, because our sales went through the roof.[9]

This shift was primarily orchestrated by the marketing sector of the industry, which rebranded armed response officers as committed and trained individuals who "care about the community." This branding was promoted through the usual channels, including newspaper advertisements, radio commercials, newsletters, and flyers. Companies also began offering anti-carjacking and "domestic watch" training,[10] and company representatives started attending community policing forum (CPF) meetings and operational meetings run by police stations. Yet the main strategy for "getting connected with the community" was (and continues to be) the establishment of collective arrangements, as is made clear by the following quote from a marketing manager:

> It's not about price anymore . . . all of us charge about the same. As a company, you need to differentiate yourself through your service, through making your product stand out. So we invest money into the community. The message is: We care about your safety. So we invest in the community policing forums, sponsor local crime newsletters, provide free security trainings, provide free monitoring to schools, all of that. It costs us a hell of a lot of money, but it pays off, because our signage is everywhere, it's visibility, and people think: They really care for the community, and so I want to be their client. This is what we're targeting, this process. . . . And this really comes out in these client projects, these groups of clients that come together. This is what we invested for and these special projects are the fruits of this investment we made years ago, and we now focus on this, getting these clients.[11]

Collective arrangements are highly lucrative and regarded as the most efficient means of procuring new clients. Let me provide a simple example of how they work. The residents of a certain street want to establish a collective arrangement and are in the process of selecting an armed response company with which to partner. Let us say this street has twenty-two households, of which eleven are clients of company A, four belong to company B, and seven are linked to other companies or are nonsubscribers. Because its clients are in the majority, company A is the most obvious choice of provider and will invest heavily in winning this contract. It may offer a "reduced fee" to its existing clients and nonclients and promise to deliver "specialized service." In most cases, company A will be successful in gaining the contract; it will thus retain its existing clients while also gaining new ones.

Collective arrangements match the companies' community-oriented profile and provide financial benefits. They are therefore a key source of competition between companies, as the marketing manager explained:

> It is a very competitive market. As soon as a community organization springs up or a road or area wants to set up something, we all jump, and we jump high! It literally happens like me phoning him, offering him so much money, then the next company will offer more, then I will offer something else. . . . This community thing has become the way to promote yourself.[12]

Collective arrangements are labeled as "special projects" and "champion areas" that provide a "platinum service" to their clients. Such arrangements allow companies to amalgamate pockets of clients to create and consolidate "strongholds" and "dedicated areas." Their profitable nature is also linked to their catalytic effect: The creation of a collective arrangement in one area often instigates the establishment of another in a neighboring area due to crime displacement (Crawford 1996; McManus 1995), as a marketing manager emphasized:

> You see an area where they've got guards or a vehicle, and crime goes down. . . . But then it shoots up in another area, so then those residents want a guard or a vehicle. If you follow the crime stats, you literally see it moving down the hill . . . so each road keeps setting up their own community thing and we keep getting in on it.[13]

Collective arrangements are thus both the cause and result of purposeful marketing strategies implemented by companies. When combined with citizens' perceptions of (in)security and active encouragement by the state police, collective arrangements are portrayed as an upgrade of one's security subscription that will be effective in combating crime.

THE LOCAL SECURITY NETWORKS

With the creation of various collective arrangements, the types of local security networks have diversified enormously, and in this section, I analyze this diversity and subdivide these networks in two ways. The first distinction is between formal and informal local security networks. Formal local security networks are based on an official relationship, generally involving a contractual agreement between a client and a company. Informal local security networks, meanwhile, are based not on an official contractual agreement but on social networks and ad hoc interactions. The former always consist solely of clients, while the latter consist of both clients and nonpaying citizens.

Within this categorization, I make a second distinction that applies to both formal and informal local security networks. I argue that there are three types of local security networks: high maintenance, collaborative, and competitive. Due to the saturated nature of the market and the prevailing mentality that the client is always right, clients generally have the upper hand in defining the nature of the local security networks: They are the "dominant actors." The aforementioned categories thus describe both the networks and the clients themselves. Therefore, the way an armed response officer views a client corresponds to how he defines the interactions that make up the security network.

High-maintenance local security networks are those where the dominant role of clients is unmistakable, and thus the clients are experienced by armed response officers and companies as demanding and "high maintenance." Collaborative networks consist of interactions where the dominant position of citizens is less pronounced; this provides room for citizens and armed response officers to work together to combat crime. Competitive networks refer to networks marked by power struggles, in which actors compete with one another for the status of the "dominant" and the "dominated."

These two categorizations allow me to analyze the plurality and diversity of local security networks that prepare the ground for twilight policing. I argue that each type of network—high maintenance, collaborative, and competitive—heightens competition between companies and encourages reaction officers (and their employers) to perform additional tasks that draw them (i.e. officers) into the public domain.

Formal Local Security Networks

There are three types of formal local security networks: individual clients, sponsorship, and collective clients.

Individual Clients

An individual client is someone who subscribes to an armed response company as a single unit, either residential or commercial. Although this is the most common type of formal local security network, it can assume numerous forms and this diversity is too enormous to discuss. Yet there is one adjective that is assigned to almost all clients, namely high maintenance, which suggests that provision of security to that person requires a lot of effort. Armed response officers repeatedly mentioned that their main concern is to "keep clients happy." Yet they also experienced this task as "impossible," because clients often expected supplementary, unrealistic, or contrasting services. Officers complained greatly about clients' demands, claiming that they were treated like "slaves" or "dogs."

There are certain clients who are notorious for being high maintenance, such as the female client whom Brian described as "a bit of a pain." Each company has specific clients who are the "daily headaches," those who "push our guys to the limits."[14] Although clients never define themselves as "high maintenance," many exhibit a strong sense of entitlement when it comes to making demands of their service providers. Due to the large amount of armed response companies, clients are aware that they possess a great deal of purchasing power. This was evident when I interviewed clients about their subscription and how they perceived their position vis-à-vis their security provider, as shown in the following two statements:

> We pay these companies good money, so if they don't respond on time or escort me home, I'll complain and threaten to go elsewhere.[15]

> I pay them for a particular service, so they must provide that service well, and if they don't, I'll complain. It's like any other service delivery really. And with security, lives are at stake.[16]

Many private security employees feel that clients abuse their purchasing power and claim that this has intensified over the years, with clients increasingly wanting "more for their money."[17]

Using a geographical lens, residential areas in Durban have particular reputations and degrees of popularity within the armed response sector, based on the attitude of clients and citizens in general. Areas regarded as "more difficult" tend to be affluent suburbs populated by citizens who are less hesitant to express racist sentiments. One particular part of Durban, which I refer to here simply as area A, is highly affluent and has a predominantly white population. Eight companies work in this area, and the employers of *all* of these firms described it as the most arduous to operate in, both at the management and operations level. Armed response officers dreaded working in area A, claiming that the clients are more suspicious of them, are quicker to complain about response times, and demand more from them (such as jumping over gates and walls) than clients in other areas.

In November 2008, I accompanied Gayle on a day shift in area A, during which he discussed his disdain for working there. He stated that, although he felt that armed response officers were treated poorly by most people in society, "it is here where you really feel it." In the course of the day he pointed out an array of negative factors that characterized this area, such as the gestures of citizens and the way clients treated him when we came to their premises. I slowly started to understand what he meant. Just as it was difficult for Gayle to explain this atmosphere to me, it is hard for me to convey exactly what it entails. It is perhaps best described as a heightened sense of hostility, contempt, and suspicion. Most armed response officers working in area A (for different companies) echoed Gayle's sentiments, noting that the place had "something different to it." They also provided examples of citizens displaying their contempt overtly, such as by refusing to get out of the way during an emergency or by readily notifying company managers when one of their vehicles was driving too fast. Regardless of whether this perceived behavior and attitude were intentional on the part of the inhabitants of area A, they were experienced as such by armed response officers, which affected their daily performance. For them, area A was high maintenance.

There are also individual clients who are regarded as collaborative. This refers to individuals who assist armed response officers in their tasks, such as by opening a gate rather than expecting him to climb over it or by moving out of the way if his emergency lights are on. It also refers to a kinder and friendlier approach toward reaction officers. Gayle and I visited one such collaborative client in August 2010. Although he had just experienced a break-in and was visibly distressed, he was extremely kind to us, offered us a drink, took the time to clarify exactly what had happened, and offered us his assistance. As we left his premises, Gayle smiled and said, "I wish all clients were like him." Similarly, certain geographical areas have a more "collaborative" reputation, and unsurprisingly, armed response officers prefer working in these areas.

Sponsorship

The second type of formal local security network is a sponsorship, which refers to an official agreement in which a company provides financial assistance to a citizen-based partner organization in exchange for free advertising. One example was the relationship between a large company and an individual who designed an anticrime SMS-alert system to update subscribers about suspicious activity, recent crime, and safety tips. The system works as followed: All (paying) members are linked to a system-wide network and are sent notifications via SMS about their specific residential area; thus, when a crime-related incident occurs, such as a break-in, or if someone sees something suspicious, an SMS is circulated among all members in that area who subscribe to the system. In 2009, the system had approximately 1,600 members who each paid R 25 per month.[18]

This SMS-alert system was sponsored by one of the biggest private security companies of South Africa; it paid for the system's phone bill, which was approximately R 9,000 per month in 2009.[19] In return, the company enjoyed free advertising on the website, and each notification featured the company's logo and slogan. This arrangement provided the firm with advertising that spanned the entire city and conjured an image that it "looks out for the community." It was thus a mutually beneficial partnership for both parties—a collaborative local security network. Other company employees working in the area, however, blamed the sponsoring company for excluding them and experienced this arrangement as direct competition.

A second example of sponsorship was a community-based armed response company that sponsored an anticrime citizen organization in its area. In return, the organization featured the company's signage on its vehicle and actively promoted the firm in its newsletters. Although the founder of the organization and employees of the armed response company did not reveal any specific details about the nature of the sponsorship,[20] it is well known that the company has seen its client base grow exponentially through this partnership. For other companies, this sponsorship has been a "nightmare."[21] They have lost many clients in the area, and several claim that the citizen-based organization was paid to badmouth them.

These two examples of sponsorship show how companies align themselves with citizen-led crime initiatives without signing them up as a client, as a means to acquire new clients. For the parties involved, sponsorship is a collaborative security network. Yet for other companies, it can be a source of increased competition.

Collective Clients

November 2008

I was living in an apartment complex with three housemates on a street off Florida Road, one of Durban's nightlife hot spots. Over a period of approximately four weeks, several break-ins occurred within the apartment house, prompting the realty management company to organize a meeting with all the residents to discuss the security problem. On a Monday evening, approximately twenty-five of us gathered by the communal braai-area.[22] The meeting began with the "victims" sharing their personal accounts of the break-ins: how the criminals had entered, what had been taken, and how the residents thought they had been victimized. The victims were questioned about their own role in the events: Had they taken the necessary precautions, or had they been slack in maintaining a secure environment? Interestingly enough, the break-in that received the most attention had occurred in the only apartment with black occupants. Suspicions were raised about their ability to afford the rent in this prime location and the trustworthiness of their visitors. After the residents were questioned, a watchful eye was directed toward frequent visitors to the complex, such as domestic workers, to eliminate the possibility of an inside job.

Discussion then turned to the kinds of precautions that people needed to take to prevent future break-ins. Based on their own views on how to prevent crime, each resident proceeded to offer instructions on how to be more security conscious. To assist us in taking these precautions, the security system of the complex itself would be updated, with a new and improved security fence, new remote controls for the gate, and, most pressingly, the establishment of a new security contract with a better private security company.

The meeting ended with a well-intended message from the head of the management company: "We are like a family, a community. It is important that we all stick together and pay close attention to each other in order to know what's going on in our building and who is coming in and when." Many residents responded with approving nods and remarks, evidently concurring with the familial metaphor. This came as a surprise to me, however; many residents did not know the names of their neighbors, and ongoing tensions were apparent throughout the meeting. It seemed bizarre to regard the residents of this apartment complex as a united group of individuals, let alone a community or family.

. . .

This apartment complex eventually became a collective client, the most prominent form of collective arrangement, whereby several individuals (in this case, residents) establish a contractual agreement with an armed response company to collectively purchase its services. The creation of a collective client is a process whereby residents "club together" to

TABLE 4   RESIDENTIAL COLLECTIVE CLIENTS OF ARMED RESPONSE

Letter	Inception year	Number of participants	Membership cost (per month)
A	2007	3,000 homes	R 57 (flat) R 114 (house)
B	1997	270 homes (out of 358, 75%)	R 265
C	2007	125 people (out of 420 homes, 29%)	R 400–900[a]
D	2006	7 homes	R 4,000

SOURCE: Data collected and compiled by the author.

[a] This community organization has several options for residents, hence the price range. Some pay for a dedicated vehicle and some only for guarding. Each individual has a different arrangement with the company despite being part of the same collective client.

collectively benefit from security by establishing "contractual communities" (Crawford 2006: 121) of security.

Table 4 presents basic information on four residential collective clients for the period 2008–10.[23] The collectives are arranged according to size and assigned a single letter for anonymity purposes. Each of the four collectives paid for a dedicated armed response vehicle. Table 4 shows that the size of a collective client can vary greatly, with the largest consisting of three thousand members and the smallest of just seven. Three of the collectives were established between 2006 and 2007, which highlights that such arrangements are a recent trend. Each collective was steered by an individual or a few prominent members. Companies refer to these persons as "road captains" or "psych drivers."

The implementation of a contractual community is based on the shared use of particular spaces. Some of those I encountered, such as collectives A and B, were built on existing community-policing initiatives that served the "community," while others, such as collectives C and D, profiled themselves as an "initiative" or "association." The rules governing a collective are not straightforward, as is discussed later, but geographical demarcations generally determine membership.

Collective clients are not only perceived to be more efficient in combating crime but they also provide financial benefits to their members. In my apartment complex, for example, residents were offered a discounted fee if they all subscribed to the same company. Table 4 shows that collective A paid far less than the average monthly premium for armed response of R 240 (see Chapter 3), while collective B paid slightly more. This means that, for approximately the same amount of money, the members of collectives A and B enjoy a "better service" with a "dedicated" armed response vehicle. Due to their membership size, collectives C and D paid above the average monthly premium. In fact, collective D paid far above average and was thus unusual in the armed response sector. Yet in exchange, it enjoyed a "special status" with its security company.

Collective clients are regarded as the most high-maintenance clients. Because of the lucrative nature of such arrangements, armed response officers are instructed to be at clients' beck and call. For many individuals, establishing a collective is a means of increasing their control over the provision of security. Operating as a collective rather than being one of the many provides clients with an increased sense of ownership and entitlement, as a white female member of collective C emphasized:

> We did this whole thing to have more control over our security. We decided amongst ourselves what we want, and we are paying the company to do that. We expect them to meet our demands; if they don't, we'll find a company that does. We are in control here, as a community, and the armed response officers must meet our needs and demands. . . . So if my neighbor asks him [the armed response officer] to do an escort outside the area, he does it. And if I ask him to check the suspicious *oak* walking down my road, he does it. And if I want the *oak* to leave, he must make sure that he's gone. It's that simple. And I couldn't make these demands before, when I was just one of the many.[24]

This feeling of ownership is also reflected in the type of payment, namely through collective payment. The collective client gathers the monthly premiums from all its members and then pays the company a single sum through its own administrative system, rather than each individual paying his or her own fee to the private security company directly. Collective clients feel that the collective payment arrangement provides them with more power because it enables them to control all of the finances. A female member of the executive committee of collective B elaborated on this:

> If you are just one client, then the company can come up with long stories and excuses about why they didn't do this, why they took so long to respond. . . . They don't want to lose you, but at the end of the day, you're just one client. But if you are 10, or 100, and you all complain, together, then they need to answer. This financial control gives you power, because losing all of us would make them suffer—they'll feel it. It gives us the opportunity to de-

mand good service, to make sure that they do as they're told and that they answer to us.[25]

The high-maintenance nature of collective clients is also evident in—and consolidated by—the various forms of surveillance employed by certain collectives. For example, collective C demanded that armed response officers undergo polygraph testing every six months. It also installed its own tracking system to monitor the movement of response vehicles, and officers were required to use a Magtouch system to record their whereabouts.[26] Collective D stipulated that its allotted armed response vehicle was never allowed to leave the area and implemented a strict daily schedule that specified where the vehicle should be at different times (e.g., it must park outside certain houses when a client leaves or enters, it cannot move too far up or down the street, it has to be parked in a certain way, and so on). The head of collective D kept track of this movement and reported any deviation from procedure to the company manager.[27] Therefore, in addition to the discipline and surveillance measures implemented by companies (see Chapter 3), armed response officers endure further surveillance by clients, particularly collective clients, which exacerbates their feelings of always being watched.

Although collectives are generally defined as high maintenance, they may also be regarded as competitive and collaborative, as was the case for collective A. This collective paid for a dedicated armed response vehicle, yet it also operated and staffed three of its own vehicles to provide additional "security." Furthermore, the company also operated another vehicle to serve clients who lived in the area, but were not members of the collective. There were thus five vehicles operating in the area: Three had the signage of the collective and two of the armed response company. Residents in this area therefore had several options when it came to private security: to be a (paying) member of the collective, to subscribe to the private security company, to do both for a reduced fee, to subscribe to neither, or to subscribe to another armed response company.

The relationships between the five different vehicles were generally collaborative. I witnessed numerous incidents where they responded to alarms and chased and arrested suspects together. However, there were also instances that resulted in hostility. One such incident occurred at the end of 2008, when one armed response officer from the company and another from the collective arrested a suspect together and both provided a statement to the police. Shortly afterward, the armed response officer from the company claimed that he had been "forced" to lie in his statement by the officer from the collective.[28] When this information surfaced, a range of accusations emerged from both sides about previous incidents of illegal activity and misconduct. This caused an uproar between the collective client and the company and almost resulted in the termination of the partnership. The issue was eventually settled, but tensions and animosity lingered.[29]

In this local security network, there were two types of armed reaction officers operating in the same area—those working directly for the collective and those working for the armed response company—yet all of whom owed their salaries to the residents. Different operational styles, different rules, and different salaries between the partners produced friction and competition. Therefore, although these two actors shared a common objective—to fight crime—they did not always agree on how to do this, which incited tension. They also competed with each other for new clients. This highlights how fine the line is between a community-based organization and a private security company when they provide similar services, and especially when they are "partners." In such contexts, it becomes difficult to see where and when the community and the private constituents begin and end.

Other companies operating in the area saw the provision of security by collective A as a direct form of competition. Not only was collective A in a partnership with one of their competitors but also it was conducting its own policing operations, as the manager of an armed response company explained:

> That whole thing going on in [area name] is wrong on so many levels. There's some community organization acting like a private security company, arming their own guys who simply stand on top of the hill, watch the cars of other companies, and steal your clients. They call themselves a community thing, but they private, they do what we do! And then they're running around with [company name]—one of our biggest competitors. It's cleaned us out there; our clients have all left us.[30]

Informal Local Security Networks

These three types of formal local security networks—individual clients, sponsorship, and collective clients—are the most common arrangements between citizens and the armed response sector. But there are also *informal* local security networks between members of the public and armed response companies that consist of systematic encounters. Though these citizens may also be clients, this section is primarily concerned with informal interactions that occur independently of their role as clients. In what follows, I examine informal local security networks between "active policers" and neighborhood watches.[31]

Active Policers

Active policers are nonclients who have an active relationship with armed response officers, such as the man who knocked on Brian's window during one of our night shifts. These are individuals (mainly male) who play several policing roles, such as police reservists, founders of neighborhood watches, and participants in community policing forums (CPF).

Many active policers are police reservists, but engage in other policing duties while off duty.[32] One example of an active policer was a white male in his forties who was a police reservist, conducted regular patrols in his community in his spare time, ran a company that did "private security-related work," and was on the provincial board of the CPF.[33] Most active policers have a military or policing background and describe their willingness to contribute their skills as being born of a need to "play their part" and "give back to the community."[34] Although many active policers subscribe to armed response companies, it is not their role as a client that defines this local security network. Rather, it is their "active" role in policing that shapes their informal interactions with armed response officers. Another example of an active policer is Vikayiphi Ngcoco, who received considerable media attention at the beginning of 2009 for his active patrols and the arrests that he made.[35] The community applauded him for his hard work, and armed reaction officers in the area also expressed appreciation for his efforts.[36]

Sometimes active policers work closely with a specific company, particularly community-based companies. I knew of several cases of reaction officers and active policers patrolling together and sharing crime information. In June 2010 I patrolled with the operations manager of a small community-based company who conducted night patrols in his residential area. On some shifts, several friends who described themselves as "dedicated individuals" accompanied him. These friends were not trained or licensed individuals, but patrolled with their personal firearms and were actively engaged in policing efforts, such as making arrests.

Armed response officers generally view active policers as collaborators, since the latter are also in the "policing game," understand the nature of armed response work, and share a passion for fighting crime.

The following statement from Brian reflects this widely held view of active policers:

> These are guys who understand and know what's going on, how to act, how to be. . . . They've seen the shit, been there and done that. They don't hassle us, ask too many questions, give us shit for driving too fast—they get out of the way, ask us if they can help us with anything, that sort of stuff. They let us know what's up, what's going on. But, they're a pain in the ass if we fuck up; then they act like they know what's better and come and tell us what to do, but even that keeps up fresh and sharp. They work with us. We're in it together.

Because active policers do not act as clients, armed response officers do not approach them with the mentality that "the client is always right." Thus, the relationship is based not on economic gain but on sharing crime information and working together. This eliminates competition and leads to collaborative efforts.

Neighborhood Watches

Some areas are home to numerous active policers, very often in the form of a neighborhood watch. Although the various individuals who comprise a neighborhood watch are also sometimes clients, they do not have a collective contractual agreement with a company and are therefore not defined here as a collective client. This section analyzes two contrasting informal local security networks made up of neighborhood watches and armed response companies.

The first example is a neighborhood watch that worked closely with a large armed response company, primarily because many members of the watch were also clients of the company. In addition to sharing information and using a communal radio, they frequently patrolled together. I spoke with Keith, a reaction officer who had been stationed in this particular area for a long period of time. He felt that his company's collaboration with the neighborhood watch was a major reason for the high number of arrests they made, and he repeatedly conveyed how he loved working in the area and felt appreciated and respected by the community members:

> These guys are good to work with and they know what they're doing. And they let me in, let me be part of it. And the people here, whether they're part of the whole patrolling thing or not, they know that we work together, they see us as a part of the team, so they're just nicer, friendlier, like greet you on the street and ask how you're doing and all that. They're more involved, this

whole community, because of these patrols, and it matters. It makes this area nice to work in.[37]

Although this area was a stronghold for the company Keith worked for, armed response officers from other companies shared his sentiments.

The second example is a neighborhood watch that had a rather hostile relationship with several companies. The watch consisted of approximately fifty members who each paid a monthly fee of R 150 for administrative costs. The founder and several other members conducted regular patrols in the area. However, unlike the previous example discussed, this neighborhood watch did not work closely with an armed response company. In fact, when I interviewed the founder, he expressed an acute disdain for the industry at large and said that he refused to patrol alongside them.[38] He felt that the neighborhood watch was a "community form of armed response" and a much more efficient one at that. He himself was not a client of private security and actively encouraged other residents to revoke their subscriptions.

The founder's perception of private security translated into competition between the members of this watch (particularly the founder) and the armed response officers working in the area. Information was not shared, encounters were often hostile, and companies lost clients. Dirk, an armed response officer who had worked in this area for a long time, respected what the neighborhood watch was doing, but he also resented how they treated him. He felt that they monitored him excessively and interfered in his work. He also claimed that several clients who were not members of the watch had complained to him that the watch was encouraging them to terminate their contracts. Dirk felt that he repeatedly had to "fight" the initiative to maintain his company's clients.[39]

CREATING AND MAINTAINING "COMMUNITIES OF SECURITY"

To summarize, high-maintenance local security networks are those in which the client is clearly the "dominant actor" and steers the constituent interactions. Armed response officers find working with these clients to be very difficult. Collaborative local security networks, meanwhile, are effectively partnerships in which clients and armed response officers work together toward a common goal. However, these networks can also be experienced as competitive when the actors involved compete over the provision of security. This is particularly common when citizens provide similar services that compete with those of armed response companies, as was the case with collective A and the second neighborhood watch.

Despite their obvious differences, I argue that all three of these local security networks place constant pressure on companies and reaction officers to "up their game" and outshine their competitors. To acquire new clients, companies provide extra services and increasingly profile themselves as "community orientated." Doing so entails an expansion into public spaces. Thus, their work is no longer limited to servicing individual clients in private spaces; armed response officers are increasingly working for collective entities, both formal and informal, in public spaces.

I do not claim that these local security networks *directly* instigate twilight policing. Rather, they cultivate a competitive mentality within the armed response sector that encourages companies and officers to police public spaces. These local security networks, particularly collective arrangements, provide a blueprint for the twilight zone. In this section, I analyze how this competitive mentality engenders various social processes that define twilight policing as exclusionary and unpredictable.

A Community?

Collective arrangements project social cohesion, particularly when they claim to represent a community, such as with collectives A and B. In fact, both of these collectives started as community organizations and only later made contractual arrangements with private security companies.

As discussed, creating a collective and operating as a community are perceived to instill social order and combat crime. The word "community" connotes a sense of cohesion and togetherness, and it has great "emotional resonance" (Amit and Rapport 2002: 14). The participants in many collective arrangements are described as "family members" or "close neighbors", as was the case for my apartment complex. Slogans for such arrangements—such as "A united community is a strong community," "Together we stand," and "Watching each other's back"—are geared toward creating and consolidating this community feeling.

While the use of the word "community" may evoke an image of a united group of individuals, intra-communal conflicts surrounding representation, legitimacy, membership, and participation are commonplace. Like Brown and Lippert (2007), I found that several collectives functioned more as sequences of individual subscribers who happened to share a particular space, rather than as community initiatives that equally served all members. In several cases, it was the arrangement with the armed response company that created the collective: Members were bound solely by their security contract. Other collectives, such as collective B, contained a large majority of their self-defined community and were therefore regarded as more representative of the community. However, collectives that consist of a minority of the community, such as collective C with a 29 percent membership, are more common. Thus, collective arrangements rarely act for all of the residents living in an area, and many nonmembers expressed that they did not feel represented, as shown by the following statement from a nonmember living in an area with a large collective client:

> Those people that run all these meetings and patrol the streets here, they don't stand for me. I haven't really given them my permission, or should I say, my consent, to do that. I know they don't need it, but they don't work on behalf of me, they don't stand for what I want; it's not a democratic thing or anything like that. That's why I don't pay them.[40]

Several nonparticipants were "named and shamed" for not participating, as one white female nonmember complained:

> I don't agree with what they're doing, so I don't want to pay for it. But if they want to do it, fine, just don't ask me to get involved, and I let them, but they don't leave me alone. They send out newsletters with the lists of people who aren't involved, so that everyone knows, or put flyers into my post box, trying to convince me to join. Now I am the bad one . . . you should see the way some of them look at me, like I'm the criminal.[41]

Members of collective arrangements view nonmembers as apathetic, lazy, and irresponsible. They are seen as "free-riders," "free-loaders," and "piggy-backers" and are ostracized by others, as one member of the executive committee of a citizen-based initiative claimed:

> This initiative is meant for all of us, so that we can all be safe. It's done so that we can all walk without being scared on the street. . . . So we pay and do it. But they don't, because they say they don't agree. But they are benefitting from it, they are profiting from our money. They don't work with the community, but against us.[42]

Benefiting from the security provision of a collective client without paying for it is a constant source of communal conflict. For example, collective D consisted of just seven houses on one street, yet other nonpaying residents on that street also benefited from this arrangement, which agitated the paying members. To eliminate this potential benefit for nonmembers, most collectives put a clause in their agreement with their armed response provider stipulating that the allocated vehicle is only permitted to respond to calls made by members of the collective. Armed response officers must then refuse requested assistance from nonmembers.

In some cases, particular individuals are refused membership, mainly by "road captains," who generally determine the membership rules. In one neighborhood watch, more than half of the members were "kicked out" for misbehaving by not adhering to the rules set out by the organization. Membership rules are tightened if members are found to be engaging in criminal activity. Since security initiatives are intended to combat crime, crime conducted by members undermines the purpose of the initiative and destroys the perception that crime always come from "outside" (Crawford 1996). I encountered three separate cases where members of a citizen-based initiative were engaged in criminal activity. In some cases, potential members then have to "prove their innocence," as the founder of another collective explained:

> We didn't invite everybody and don't allow just anybody to join, because you don't know where the criminal element may be—not everyone means well, you know? A criminal can easily pretend, he can give a good cover-up, and then know our secrets. You have to be careful and be certain. You can't let crime manage you—you have to manage crime.[43]

The creation of collective arrangements, and thus the materialization of security as a "club good" (Crawford 2006), involves a distinction between insiders and outsiders. Yet these rules are continuously contested, and perceptions of free-riders, measures of naming and shaming, and the denial of membership are continuous points of friction. Therefore, although the notion of "communities of security" may connote a united group of individuals, such arrangements are very often marked by intra-communal conflicts.

These intra-communal conflicts also cultivate an additional element of uncertainty and a heightened need for armed response officers to be on their best behavior. Pleasing the client, which is the main objective for companies, is arduous when it is unclear who exactly the client is, where the power balance lies among the constituent members, and which of several opposing demands to attend to. Thus, armed response officers are often required to negotiate between the divergent expectations of different members.

Borders and "Gatekeepers"

While defining membership of collective arrangements is invariably contentious, the recognition of the common external threat (i.e., the "criminal," the "deviant," and the "dangerous Other") unifies individuals and consolidates social cohesion. Crime and disorder are generally seen as external forces, as illustrated by the following statement from a member of one collective: "Communities are being violated by people from outside the community."[44]

Blaming and scapegoating in regard to a collective fear of crime enhance social control and loyalty (Douglas 1986), increase feelings of belonging and exclusion (Bourke 2005; Reguillo 2002), and maintain social borders (Sparks, Girling, and Loader 2001). They create boundaries between insiders and outsiders, with the latter excluded through both symbolic and literal means. Many collectives put up signs at the entry points of their area to announce the presence of a private security company, as shown in Figure 7.

Such signage gives the impression of a unified community that has eyes and ears that are on the lookout for trespassers (Berg 2010; Brown and Lippert 2007; Lemanski 2006; Singh 2008). The use of the message "Be Warned, Criminals Will Not Be Tolerated" is a key part of the process of creating communities of security that are marked by social and physical boundaries. The literal ways in which armed response officers keep people out are through "chasing them out," asking (or commanding) people to leave, and arresting them—behaviors discussed in Chapter 7.

On a larger scale, such exclusionary messages and practices create an array of local security networks (both formal and informal) that do not necessarily join up to create a larger security network. For example, three neighboring areas in Durban each had a collective arrangement with a different armed response company and these companies did not interact. With another collective client, choosing the company caused a split among the residents and led to the creation of two separate collective clients, with one half of the residents subscribing to one company and the other half to another. This split was not made along geographical lines, which meant that two companies were providing overlapping services in the same area. Therefore, rather than "reshuffling the decks of cards,"[45] each suit is consolidated by different client-steered mandates and implemented by different companies.

FIGURE 7. Signage of BLUE Security by a collective client. Photo taken by the author.

The "motley patchwork of self-defence" (Steinberg 2008: 176) is constructed by clients and preserved by armed response companies. The borders between insiders and outsiders are defined by clients, but are enforced and policed by armed response officers. Through the creation of local security networks, clients assign armed response officers authority and legitimacy to control access to the collective; they are the gatekeepers. And as people are denied access to or expelled from certain areas, there is an inherent "*immediate violence potential*" (Franzén 2001: 214, italics in original). This prompts a punitive policing style.

To consolidate this gatekeeper role, each collective arrangement often demands that the most experienced armed response officer work in its area permanently so he can build up local knowledge of the clients' specific needs and the hot spots of criminal activity. Clients and armed response officers often establish personal relationships. In many cases, clients become fond of the stationed armed response officer and complain if he is reassigned elsewhere. For example, collective B had three permanent armed response officers for several years, and these individuals were widely regarded as "an integral part of our community."[46]

However, armed response officers are also potential outsiders. When an incident of crime occurs, citizens generally believe that the armed response officer has failed to prevent a breach of the collective's security. He is very often the first to be suspected and is treated with the same suspicion afforded to other outsiders who repeatedly enter the collective, such as criminals. The various surveillance measures enforced by many collectives strengthen the perceived need to control the activities and movements of armed response officers. Since social boundaries are unceasingly reconfigured and redesigned through community interaction and social change (Amit 2002; Barth 1969), the locus of the armed response officers is fragile and continuously in flux.

Social boundaries are therefore based on what is "shared" within the community and how this differs from nonmembers, that is, outsiders (Crawford 1996). An armed response officer can thus fill both shoes: He is defined as an insider by working with the community and sharing the same goal of combating crime, yet he is reclassified as an outsider when suspected of foul play. Thus, while armed response officers may be given the gatekeeper role, maintaining this position is a continuous struggle. Furthermore, the boundaries that distinguish insiders from outsiders transcend established notions of public and private space. Generally speaking, public spaces are sites that are accessible and available to all citizens, while private spaces are sites where citizens, based on ownership, can exercise their right to "privacy" and prevent others from entering. In the early days of the industry, armed response officers served and protected private spaces and responded to alerts (such as alarms and panic buttons) that originated therefrom. Although this is still a part of their mandate, reaction officers are increasingly moving into public spaces, and this movement is largely due to the growth of collective arrangements. With collective arrangements, armed response officers are instructed to police the spaces *between* residences, such as the streets and parks—in other words, public spaces.

It is precisely this movement into the public realm that clients and citizens are now demanding from security providers. For the general public, the control over public spaces provides a heightened sense of reassurance and peace of mind, as the secretary of collective C explained:

> I used to live in fear. . . . I didn't even dare to enter my own garden at night, always scared someone was hiding behind the bushes. But now, it's gone. I walk freely and I sit in my garden at night. I know that when I go out at night and leave my kids at home, I don't need to worry about them, I can relax, because I know that everything will be okay. Somebody is taking care of my house and my street.[47]

Thus, private security is no longer simply about security for "my house," but is increasingly about securing and defending "my street." Public spaces are increasingly experienced and defined by feelings of ownership, which is evident in the prevalence of phrases such as "my road," "our area," and "our streets." Collective arrangements increasingly create "privately controlled public spaces" (Crawford 2006: 132) that are experienced as "club realms" (Webster 2001, quoted in Crawford 2006: 131) rather than "public realms."

The establishment of collective arrangements emerges from a perceived need and entitlement to control public spaces, and armed response officers are invariably the ones assigned the legitimacy and authority to exert this control. Their movement into the public realm is a purposeful one, which highlights how citizens, particularly clients, play a central role in pushing armed response officers into public spaces through various local security networks.

CONCLUDING REMARKS

In this chapter, I analyzed the different types of local security networks comprising armed response officers (and companies) and citizens, of which the majority are clients (i.e., paying citizens). I examined various forms of formal and informal local security networks that I further categorized as high-maintenance, collaborative, and competitive networks. In so doing, I demonstrated the multitude of ways in which clients create an environment conducive to twilight policing.

This chapter revealed how citizens employ *private* agents, yet increasingly encourage them to operate in *public* spaces. High-maintenance networks reaffirm the dependence of companies on clients (and potential clients) for income, collaborative networks consist of and enhance partnerships between citizens and armed response officers, and competitive networks are marked by power struggles. Despite their differences, each type augments the competitive nature of the sector (and industry), which encourages armed response companies and officers to provide and do more. This "more" entails that armed response officers increasingly act like the state police by operating in public spaces. Furthermore, due to the growth of collective arrangements, communities of security—in which borders are created that distinguish between insiders and outsiders—are flourishing, which exacerbates the exclusionary nature of twilight policing. Clients define these borders, but armed response officers are contracted to police them: They are the gatekeepers.

These different local security networks have also brought together two types of policing that are frequently distinguished in the literature:

citizen/community policing and private policing. This chapter illustrated that these two types of policing do not always operate as two separate fields, but increasingly work in unison and even come to resemble one another. Although it is possible to distinguish between their respective members, such as the armed response officer whose uniform exudes his "private" nature, the policing practices of armed response officers are increasingly shaped and penetrated by citizens. And due to the saturated nature of the industry, clients have a great deal of steering power: They play a leading role in determining how armed response officers police the streets. Thus, we can only understand the performance of twilight policing by analyzing the behind-the-scenes role of clients and citizens.

CHAPTER 7

Performances of Twilight Policing

Public Authority, Coercion, and Moral Ordering

This chapter analyzes twilight policing through a performative framework that defines policing as a performance in which participants interact with each other on a specific stage for a particular audience. Using a performative framework permits one to investigate the expressive process by which human beings, in their relationships and interactions with others, construct and give meaning to their social realities.

This chapter has three aims. The first is to stress that twilight policing is a *joint performance*. This entails that the full meaning of twilight policing is located in the coming together of different factors and local security networks. I illustrate this by analyzing three performances of twilight policing: a car chase, the arrest of two suspects, and "disciplining." For each performance, I show how various participants, through their interactions with armed response officers, shape twilight policing practices. My second aim is to show that twilight policing consists of practices that contain both public and private elements, are based on the ability to use force (punitive), aim to create a social and moral order (disciplinary), and serve a particular group of "insiders" and "outsiders" (exclusionary).

Because armed response officers are the main subjects of this research, they are the initial point of reference in this chapter, positioned as the lead players interacting with other actors who function as both audience members and other actors on stage. This does not imply that armed response officers are the dominant or decisive players: It merely means that their perspectives and experiences are granted more attention. Given this focus, the third aim of this chapter, which expands on the analysis presented in the previous chapter, is to show how armed response officers are assigned two roles in the performance of twilight policing: They are the "gatekeepers" of the imagined communities created by citizens/clients and the "negotiators" between citizens' expectations and the (perceived) shortcomings of the state.

This chapter approaches these three aims in the following order. After a brief conceptual introduction to the performative framework, which builds on the work of Goffman (1959), the first and largest section of this chapter presents three ethnographic performances that show the punitive, disciplinary, and exclusionary nature of twilight policing. The second section explores the racial and social construction of the dangerous criminal "Other," which defines the outsiders and subjects of policing. This section on race does not intend to imply that issues of race are an inherent part of twilight policing, but it aims to show how the South African context gives meaning to social constructions of race that exacerbate the punitive, disciplinary, and exclusionary nature of twilight policing. An analysis of race is also relevant for understanding the third section of this chapter, which examines the emotional experience of working as an armed response officer—the key performers of twilight policing. This chapter ends with a microanalysis of twilight policing that focuses on the ambiguity and liminality of such performances.

PERFORMANCES OF TWILIGHT POLICING

This chapter does not refer to theater anthropology, the structure of rituals, cultural performances, or the more aesthetic and imaginative activities associated with the word "performance."[1] Rather, it draws on Goffman's dramaturgical approach to analyze the expressive process by which human beings, in their relationships and interactions with others, construct and give meaning to their social realities. Performance is defined here as "all the activity of an individual which occurs during a period marked by his continuous presence before a particular set of observers and which has some influence on the observers" (Goffman 1959: 32).

Goffman's dramaturgical approach to understanding ordinary social situations centers on three key parties: the main player, other participants, and the audience. Every performance consists of two main regions: a front and a back. The performance is carried out in the front region and consists of a *setting* (context and geographical location) and a *personal front*. The latter includes one's *appearance*—the fixed and changeable expressive items that are identified with the performer, such as clothing, race, age, and facial expressions—and one's *manner*: "those stimuli which function at the time to warn us of the interaction role the performer will expect to play in the oncoming situation" (Goffman 1959: 35).

For armed response officers, the setting of the front region was originally the private domain (i.e., residences and businesses), but in recent years it has enlarged to include public spaces. In terms of appearance, armed response officers are generally non-white males between the ages of twenty and forty who wear a company uniform, carry a radio and a firearm, and drive a company vehicle. Their manner largely depends on their personal characteristics. Taken together, these attributes (i.e., appearance and manner) shape people's expectations of what an armed response officer can and will do. Although other actors, such as clients and police officers, recognize the differences among companies and armed response officers, there is a collective understanding of their role: The front region can be regarded as a "collective representation" (Goffman 1959: 37).

While the front region tends to consist of respectable (socially) behavior, the back region (also referred to as the backstage) includes more "informal" behavior and suppressed activities. The back region is where performers assume that audience members will not intrude, where performances are contrived, and where flaws in the personal front can be adjusted. It can therefore contradict the appearance and manner cultivated in the front region. This chapter highlights the importance of this back region among armed response officers. In fact, armed response officers depend on the back region; it is a space where they can dismantle the façade that they have to uphold for other actors (such as company managers and clients) and where they can reveal attitudes more aligned with their actual experience. This difference between the front and back regions, and the need for the back region, further highlight the fluid nature of twilight policing and the arduousness of performing.

In every performance, each participant possesses preconceived notions and expectations of other participants based on existing routines of interaction and established social relationships. For example, armed response officers can regard a call-out as a routine, and when performed for the same client on numerous occasions, a social relationship is established between the two parties. An armed response officer has expectations of how a client will behave, and vice versa. However, as Schieffelin (1998: 205) argues, relationships are shaped as the performance is carried out. Thus, performances are not pre-programmed, guided by a fixed and unchangeable set of rules; rather, as this chapter shows, they are flexible and very often shaped by improvisation.

Scholars have criticized Goffman's approach for presenting performances as "bounded acts that take place within a performance space (the 'front region') and therefore retain discernible temporal and spatial boundaries" (Jeffrey 2013: 29). Although I concur that Goffman's method poses a rather rigid situation, I choose to employ it here because it enables us to understand how a social reality is created and maintained. It is a framework that allows us to discern the different parts of a performance. In my analysis, however, I emphasize how performances are shaped through a complex recursive relationship between social structures and individual agency that are not bound to a particular time and space. I analyze the "stage" not as a fixed entity within a distinct phase or space, but rather as part of an "ongoing social process" (Turner 1987: 24) that is continuously reconfigured. This framework ties into the performative dimension of twilight policing, which entails that policing practices are performed repeatedly, are continually changing, and (re)produce a series of effects (Butler 1997).

I therefore focus on the collective nature of performance, which moves beyond an individual analysis (Jeffrey 2013). It is for this reason that I analyze twilight policing as a joint performance between actors located in a variety of social and historical contexts. Within a (joint) performance, there are a division of labor and an "interactional modus vivendi" (Goffman 1959: 21), which refers to the different roles ascribed to various participants, the necessary information each possesses, and their contribution to creating an encompassing definition of the situation. When armed response officers police the streets of Durban, what sort of "working consensus" (Goffman 1959: 21) is established and how is it achieved? If the primary aim of performers is to maintain a particular consensus in order to give meaning to their realities, then what reality is sustained in a joint performance? The remainder of this section addresses these questions.

198 | Chapter 7

Performance 1: The Car Chase

November 2008

It's been a long day; no real positives, but an exhausting day neverthe-less. The heat of the midday sun has taken its toll on Gayle and me, and our usually lively conversations have been reduced to a few terse com-ments punctuating a deep silence. Just as we think that we're done for the day, we receive a call-out: An alarm at a nearby residence has gone off close by. Gayle immediately speeds off in the direction of the client's residence, but a few seconds later we hear that Tim has already attended and that it was a false alarm. Gayle sighs deeply. We turn around and slowly drive back from Durban North toward Morningside.

Just as we come off a bridge, I spot a short, bald white man standing at the side of the road by a gas station, screaming and waving his arms frantically at us to stop. We're caught by surprise, and Gayle breaks sharply and pulls up next to him.

"Open your window; let's see what this guy wants," Gayle instructs me. Wracked with panic, the man tells us that a woman has just been robbed not far from here and that the suspects are in a vehicle close by. It's extremely difficult to make out what he's saying, but it emerges that he has the suspects' license plate number written on the palm of his hand.

"Get in the back; come on," Gayle tells the man. I'm shocked. I know this is against the rules: Armed response officers aren't allowed to take other people in their vehicles, especially nonclients. I look at Gayle, try-ing to make eye contact with him in order to understand why he's doing this, but he doesn't look back at me; he just slams on the gas and races off. The man sits in the back of the car and continues to yell, "Oh my god, I just had them. The fucking assholes, I almost had them!"

Shortly afterward, the man points to a car driving on the other side of the road. "It's them; that's the car," he exclaims. "You see, those two Col-ored guys and that fucking *kaffir*, that's them. Go after them!" Gayle squeezes in front of the other cars, makes an abrupt U-turn, and chases after the vehicle. The suspects in the car look back at us and, spotting that the bald man is with us, start to accelerate. The vehicle is now in front of us, but there are two other cars in between. We're back on the bridge, but Gayle can't get right behind the car because other cars won't let us pass them. The man continues to scream at Gayle: "Fucking hell, can't you just pass this car? Fucking *coolie*,[2] do you even know how to drive prop-erly? Drive faster, fucking drive faster! Get these assholes! Put on your sirens, get them!" As we approach a set of traffic lights, we see that the suspects' vehicle has just gone through them. We're forced to stop at the lights, and then it dawns on us that this is an intersection: The car could have headed in any direction, and we've lost them. "Fuck! I can't believe they just left!" screams the bald man from the back seat. "Why didn't you just drive through the traffic light? We should have driven faster; you should have hooted [honked] at that car in front of you. . . . Fuck, fuck. . . ." He continues like this for a while longer, yelling and swearing at Gayle and blaming him for letting the suspects get away.

We drive around the area for a while, taking different routes to see where the car could have headed, but it's clear that we've lost them. The man is still screaming at Gayle, at himself, and at the suspects in the vehicle. I'm extremely irritated by him and finding it difficult to stop myself from shouting back at him. I try to make eye contact with Gayle, but he's practically ignoring me and appears to be extremely calm, his eyes focused on the road. When the man finally calms down a little bit, Gayle asks, "So what exactly happened?" And then the story comes.

The man was working in his office when he heard a woman scream. He and a colleague went outside to see what was going on and found a woman in tears. She explained that, while she was walking down the road, a black male had pointed a gun at her head, grabbed her handbag, and then ran across the street to a waiting vehicle and sped off. Out of anger and frustration, the bald man and his colleague had decided to chase after the vehicle, but they lost it. They then drove to the gas station because they had often seen police vans parked there, but when they arrived there were no police officers around. His colleague decided to phone the police while he went to the side of the road in the hope that a police van would pass by. And then he saw us.

Only at the end of his story does the man finally acknowledge my presence and inquire, somewhat curtly, "Who the fuck are you?" I explain to him that I'm doing research, but I keep it brief. I'm annoyed with his attitude, and I don't feel like explaining myself. I ask him why he stopped us and he answers, "Well, that's what you're here for, to catch criminals. I mean, you guys got a gun, you can do more than I can, you know? You're practically the police."

Gayle drops the man off at his workplace, near where the robbery took place. When we get there, several people are standing outside. We join the crowd, and the bald man explains to them what happened. He describes how he personally chased the vehicle with the suspects. Everybody, with concern, tells him that he shouldn't act like that again, which is seconded by Gayle: "You shouldn't be chasing guys like this—they could have had a gun. What would you have done?" The man replies, "Man, so many of my friends have been robbed and shot, I'm sick of this shit, I really am. I can't just sit around and do nothing anymore. . . . People need to step up!"

We find out that the woman who was robbed is sitting inside her office and that the police are on their way. Gayle provides his contact details in case the police want to contact him for further information, and then we get back into the car and drive off. Gayle finally looks at me and starts laughing. We then have the following conversation:

Me: What is it? What's so funny?

Gayle: You know that guy, I know him. I've had to take him out of a bar about three times because he was drunk and getting into a fight.

Me: Is it? Where?

Gayle: Thunderroad, that place on Florida Road. He got all racist and aggressive on me, calling me a *coolie*, refusing to leave, that kinda shit. And now he doesn't even fucking recognize me. And now here I am helping the racist drunk out. [Starts chuckling] You okay Tess?

Me: Yeah, I was just a bit irritated. I know he was upset, but he had no right to scream at you like that. And you were so calm; I almost flipped out at him.

Gayle: You see, that's how it goes. I have to put up with his stupid shit. If I get aggressive at him, he's gonna phone the head office and I'm gonna have to explain myself. And I'm gonna give the company a bad name. Like I've said before, the client is always right . . . and the client always needs or wants something and we must listen and follow, do as they say. We deal with this shit everyday; you've seen it, how people treat us like shit, like we're stupid dogs that are trained to protect them, like their own private little police. It comes with the job. It's the nasty part of this job. Now you see, if we would have got that vehicle, now that would have been nice. Then people realize we actually do do something. That we don't just spend our time driving around, being useless all day . . . that we actually do have a purpose. . . . Ag, next time man, next time.

. . .

The preceding vignette describes an incident in which a citizen (i.e., a nonpaying client) seeks assistance from a private agent in the public domain, because the public agent (i.e., the police) has failed to meet his expectations. The citizen also describes the private agent as being "practically the police."

The private security industry's expansion into the public realm has become a common feature of policing worldwide. Yet, although the armed response sector emerged in the 1980s with one-man shows that patrolled the streets, armed response had traditionally been a private affair. Yet as the last four chapters showed, in contemporary South Africa, "the power of private security in public spaces is beginning to equal the power it holds in private spaces (albeit symbolic rather than legal power)" (Berg 2010: 288).

It is thus not uncommon to witness armed response officers engaged in the management of car accidents, parking issues, and funeral processions or to see private security companies provide security at public events, such as local fairs, fundraisers, and sporting functions. All of the company representatives I interviewed stressed that their companies were engaged in "more than just response." They repeatedly asserted that their armed response officers were proactive rather than reactive, which is evident in some of their statements: "We are a proactive company and we do more than just respond," and "We don't just prevent crime, we do something about it."

The encroachment of armed response into the public domain began with the expansion of services that were closely related to armed response. The first step was offering an escort service, whereby clients request a vehicle to escort them on the road when they need extra protection. Escort services entail providing security to clients outside the private domain of their homes. Patrolling has played an even bigger role in pushing private security into public spaces. Patrolling is a mandatory part of the daily routine of armed response officers as they respond to call-outs in their vehicles. Although there are companies that discourage patrolling (primarily for financial reasons), armed response officers are generally encouraged to make their presence known and to be constantly "on the look out for anything suspicious." Patrolling is seen as a way for companies to increase their visibility and gather crime intelligence. Various companies, especially those that work closely with the public police, conduct regular crime analyses and instruct armed response officers to patrol areas found to have higher levels of criminal activity. Additionally, certain clients, particularly collective ones, demand that armed response officers are very conspicuous and on patrol at all times.

An increase in patrolling results in a more perceptible presence in the public domain, thereby expanding the setting (stage) of the performance.

And as the stage becomes larger, the number of participants increases; the stage becomes more accessible to others—such as nonclients—to enter and shape the performance, either as participants or as additional members of the audience. In the case of the car chase, patrolling took place in the front region of Gayle's performance, and an audience member became a participant. If Gayle had stood down at a particular place, we would not have encountered this citizen's request for assistance. And if Gayle had not been encouraged by his company managers to assist nonclients, he probably would not have stopped in any case. The moment that Gayle allowed the citizen to enter his car, the latter became an active participant in the performance.

Armed response officers are increasingly providing assistance to nonclients. All of the companies I researched interacted with nonclients and assisted them if they could. One small company placed the statement, "We will render assistance to anyone that calls us for help," on the front page of its promotional pamphlet and website. Engagement with nonclients tends to occur more among community-based companies, because they have closer ties with the citizens of a given area. I witnessed numerous incidents where armed response officers assisted acquaintances and colleagues' family members. One community-based company received an average of 12,000 calls from nonclients per month in 2009, compared to 3,000 calls from clients and 4,900 signals from alarms and panic buttons.[3] For this company, therefore, nonclients were more frequent recipients of security services than paying customers.

Assisting nonclients is not restricted to community companies, however. Larger companies may receive fewer calls from nonclients, but they are not adverse to helping them. Indeed, Gayle works for a large firm. Armed response officers also engage more with nonclients if they are part of a collective client or neighborhood watch. Because of the lucrative nature of collective clients, companies prioritize them and clearly instruct their armed response officers to be on "top form" when working in these areas. Although collective clients generally inhabit a protected geographical area, there are numerous problems in defining and maintaining the "collective." Because armed response officers are often unaware of which individuals make up a particular collective, they therefore tend to treat everybody residing in that area as a part of it, even though some may not be paying customers. Even when armed response officers are aware who the nonmembers are, they may assist such persons in order to encourage them to join the collective; that is, to win them over as potential clients. All inhabitants are thus regarded as audience members.

What we find, therefore, is that the setting and the audience are both expanding, which constantly creates new forms of engagement. Performances are based on larger scripts with new public expectations in which a new working consensus is continuously constructed. With the car chase, for example, the citizen demanded that Gayle assist him under the supposition that he was entitled to such assistance. The citizen regarded Gayle's help as a public service available to all and thereby assigned a new role to him. And although he was not a client, he was treated as one. However, as Goffman (1959) argues, new tasks are always based on existing social interactions and performances. The expanding role of armed response officers is an extension into the domain of the state police.

In the case of the car chase, the police were what Goffman refers to as "outsiders": participants who are not intended to witness the performance. However, although the police may have been physically absent, the participants felt their presence. Like Goldstein (2012), who coined the term "phantom state," I argue that the physical absence of a state does not mean that it is absent from one's experiences and perceptions. In the car chase incident, the citizen was initially seeking the police, but he found us instead. The police thus clearly influenced the performance. In fact, such acts may have the intention to "catch the eye of an inattentive state and to perform for it visually and unmistakably the consequences of its own inaction" (Goldstein 2004: 182). This performance shows how twilight policing simultaneously contains public and private dimensions and refers not only to a private agent operating in the public domain; it also concerns the appropriation of activities and behavior associated with the state police. It is an example of how armed response officers simultaneously mimic and undermine the state police.

Performance 2: Arresting Suspects

May 2010

It's Friday morning, and a bunch of us are standing outside the office having a cigarette break. When a call comes in about the presence of two suspects in someone's yard, the guys throw down their cigarettes, start screaming at each other to hurry up, and rush over to their vehicle. I quickly grab my vest and hop into the front seat of the car that Chris, an Indian armed response officer in his late thirties, is driving.

On our way to the premises in question, we hear over the radio that the suspects have been apprehended. When we reach the site, I am asked to stay in the car, but I can see that a group of eight armed response officers are standing around two suspects lying face down on the ground with their hands cuffed. For the next few minutes, they repeatedly hit the suspects with their batons and kick them while the suspects howl with pain. A large crowd of members of the community begins to gather. The armed response officers continue going at it hard; they thump the suspects, rebuke them, and accuse them of stealing from innocent people. I feel extremely uncomfortable to be sitting in the car—almost as if I am hiding—especially after I realize that several of the bystanders are looking at me. I feel somehow responsible, as if I am partaking in this violent act.

The armed response officers then pick up the suspects, and I finally get a full view of them: The two men are bleeding from various parts of their bodies, and their clothes are torn. The officers dump each suspect into the back of a pick-up truck, including the one I am sitting in. The beatings continue in the rear of the vehicle, which rocks from side to side with each blow. The sound of the suspect's screams and grunts are ear piercing. Chris then gets into the front seat and asks me whether I am all right. When I say, rather hesitantly and unconvincingly, "yes," he replies, "Ach, all that violence . . . ," interrupted by a smirk, "but I told you we were tough and know how to hit."

Everyone then gets back into the vehicles, and we drive approximately one hundred meters farther up the road. The suspects are taken out of the trucks and thrown onto the ground. I am told that I can get out of the vehicle. For the next twenty minutes or so, the armed response officers continue to interrogate the suspects, knocking them about in a playful manner. Two officers cock their firearms, point them at the suspects, and then threaten to shoot them, which is met with laughter from the other officers. The armed response officers tease and provoke one another, some using this as an opportunity to show off their fighting skills. At one point, one suspect makes eye contact with me, and I instantly look away, unable to cope with his pained expression. And then it dawns on me: Here I am, standing on the side of the road, watching a group of armed men in uniform berating and beating two unarmed suspects. And they seem to enjoy it. I am absolutely disgusted by what I see. I long for them to stop. Everything inside me is screaming, yet I do not make the slightest sound.

To cope with the situation, I purposely focus on other events happening around me. I start questioning community members about their feelings and opinions, but few seem to share my feelings of disapproval and disgust. One elderly man, who has been at the scene since the beginning, explains how often the local residences have been burgled. He points to several houses that have been robbed over the last few months and to a spot (where the suspects were apprehended) where two carjackings took place in the last year. He then says, "The guys deserve it—it's good that they're hitting them; they deserve it." Other community members voice similar statements, such as "We need these guys to stop the animals from killing us" and "We're constantly under attack; these men need to teach them a lesson, to stop them from destroying our communities." At one point, two bystanders even ask to join in with the interrogation, but the armed response officers do not allow this.

When the police arrive, my first thought is that they will condemn the actions of the armed response officers, particularly their use of violence, and arrest some or all of them. However, nothing of the sort happens: The two police officers—an Indian male and a black female—make a few cursory inquiries and then simply place the two suspects in the back of their vehicle and prepare to head back to the police station. The two armed response officers who first apprehended the suspects are asked to come to the station to make a statement, but no further action is taken.

A week or so later, I run into the male police officer and ask him about this incident. Rather than condemning what the armed response officers did, particularly their treatment of the suspects, he actually praises it. He recognizes that "such cases can be problematic," but he maintains that there is a "need for it."

. . .

In this performance, armed response officers used violence in the public streets and in broad daylight as a "team," a team being "any set of individuals who cooperate in staging a single routine" (Goffman 1959: 85). As a team, they overtly projected violence in their front region. Chapters 3 and 4 discussed how bodily and force capital are cultivated in the armed response sector through the use of violence and coercion by armed response officers, how the continuous presence of danger and risk affects their occupation, and how their moral frameworks are shaped with regard to the use of violence. Armed response officers' exposure to violence and crime leads to a degree of moral cynicism, so that they regard everyone as potentially threatening, and certain armed response officers do not shy away from using coercion and violence.

Armed response officers use coercion and violence to apprehend, intimidate, and search suspects. During their training, security officers are taught how to search individuals without the use of force, yet in practice, they use more coercive methods to apprehend suspects, such that they are increasingly employing a "detection and punishment mentality" (Berg 2010: 295). In addition to physical violence, I witnessed various other forms of coercion, such as the use of pepper spray and making suspects sit or stand in very uncomfortable positions. Swearing at suspects, calling them names, and making threats were also common. Armed response officers frequently made statements such as "If you don't stop, we'll come back next time" and "Next time I won't be so polite." They regularly lectured suspects as a form of "moral disciplining," admonishing them at great length for their immorality and wrongdoings.

However, to assume that all of the armed response officers involved in the earlier case of arresting the suspects were trigger happy and prone to violence would be too simple. Although some appeared to derive enjoyment from the performance, we must recognize that their use of violence was also steered by other factors and participants. For a team to operate as one, its members must work together to create a coherent impression; otherwise, the entire performance will be disrupted. Operating as a team, rather than as individuals, is often regarded as more powerful and convincing for the audience. One owner cited this as a key strategy:

> When we hear something has happened, I want as many of our vehicles as possible to go there. This is for safety reasons, so that the guys can help each other out, but it's also to show force to the community: we come as a group, a force to be reckoned with.[4]

In addition to the way in which team members influence and encourage each other, the audience also plays a crucial role in armed response officers' usage of force. In the performance described earlier, the audience members (i.e., the bystanders) tolerated, encouraged, and even praised the use of physical violence and thereby configured the joint performance. In this case (and numerous others), physical violence was accepted and legitimized by the audience members as well as by the police officers who appeared later. The latter were initially outsiders, but became insiders by approving of the situation. In the following example, Performance 3, we see how a client signed up with a company based on its reputation for fighting and disciplining "wrongdoers." Echoing the findings of Sharp and Wilson (2000: 125), clients sometimes view the criminal past of company employees as a "positive advantage." Many companies are well aware of this and emphasize their violent capabilities accordingly.

Armed response officers often displayed conscious knowledge of when violence was "appropriate." Its appropriateness depended not only on the context and severity of a crime but also on who was the client and how the audience would react. Michael explained this as follows:

> If I had the choice, I would whack every guy that I thought was suspicious, but I can't go and do that. You see, at night, you can do more: less people around, less witnesses . . . I mean, I'm not going to hit a guy, bleeding and all, in the middle of the CBD [central business district] on a Monday morning. . . . And I know that certain clients are alright; they like the way we do our work, they expect it from us, so we have to show them something to keep them, to show that we're worth their money, but there are others . . . they are a bit more difficult. You have to act more professional in front of them; screaming is good, and a few smacks, but no excessive hitting.[5]

When various teams come together, they form a *performing team*, one that directs and controls the setting, sets the pace of the performance, allocates roles in the performance, readjusts any possible disruption, and restores order when others do not act correctly. In the case described earlier, the armed response officers were assigned the authority to be the performing team. Their use of violence was a crucial means of obtaining and maintaining legitimacy and authority; they used it to display power and to underscore their leading role. Violence is thus very often a demonstration of power, particularly when performed in public spaces (Goldstein 2004; Hall et al. 1978).

The expanding role of armed response officers is also reflected in an increasing use of punitive behavior. Twilight policing does not necessarily imply the use of coercion and physical violence, but it does imply the ability to use violence that is confidently placed in the front region. Although this ability is inherent to all forms of policing, twilight policing is unique in that it occurs in an ambiguous fashion. Furthermore, punitive behavior cannot be reduced to the armed response officers being trigger-happy, but must instead be understood in relation to the roles played by other participants in either encouraging or tolerating the use of violence. The performance of violence is therefore part of an emerging working consensus.

Performance 3: Disciplining

May 2010

We're in the middle of a staff meeting when we hear about an alarm notification at an important client's residence. David is ordered to respond and asks me to come with him. When we get to the premises, an Indian male is standing outside. We initially assume that nothing is wrong, but then he waves at us to come inside the house. When we enter the residence, David and the client address each other by their first names, shake hands, and engage in some banter. It is clear that they know each other. When we move into the living room, I see the client's wife holding a young boy of about two years of age and then notice a young black girl sitting on the couch, looking down at the ground. There is an eerie vibe, and I'm confused about what is going on. The clients tell us that the girl is a maid who been working for them for the past two weeks. Last week, there had been two occasions when the wife had suspected the maid of stealing between R 20–50, but she wasn't sure. She discussed her suspicions with her husband, and they decided to set a trap using four R 20 notes as bait. Now the money was gone, and they were confident the maid was to blame.

The client then looks at us and says, "We asked you to come here because we want to show her [the maid] how quick you guys come here, what will happen next time. It's not about the money—it's about the trust. I want her to know what will happen next time she does this." He then nods at David to signify that he can take over. David approaches the girl and starts talking to her in a stern tone of voice, asking her what she did. The girl's gaze is fixed on the ground, but she is clearly afraid of David. David raises his voice and commands her to look at him and explain herself. The girl says she needed the money to buy bread for her family; she admits to stealing R 10, then admits to stealing R 20, and then denies the theft altogether. David grows increasingly frustrated. I stand in the corner of the room, trying to remain as inconspicuous as possible, but the girl repeatedly looks at me, probably wondering who I am and what I'm doing here.

The clients then reiterate to the girl why they called the company, and David intervenes to support their claim. "Do you know what will happen next time they call us?" he asks. "You'll arrest me," replies the maid. Then David smirks and says, "No, we're not the police. We won't arrest you—we'll beat you. I don't care how old or young you are, male or female—if you steal, you must be taught a lesson." The client nods and supports David's threat by saying, "You know [name of the company]? Do you know what they do? They're not the police; they'll hurt you if you do this again." Still staring at the floor, the maid murmurs that she understands.

The clients, David, and I leave the living room to discuss the matter outside. The clients question whether they should give her a second chance. David strongly advises against this: "You can't trust her. She will steal again. Better you get an older lady; they are more reliable. These young ones . . . they are out to steal. Next thing you know, she'll get her friends and they'll come and steal everything." David provides numerous examples of maids who have worked alongside criminals, including one who orchestrated an armed robbery and watched as the suspect raped the woman of the house. Nevertheless, the clients say that they want to give the maid another chance, so we return to the living room and David orders the girl to return the money she took.

The wife and I head into the kitchen for a glass of water. She repeatedly emphasizes how disappointed she is, because she treats the maid with dignity and wants to help her. I ask her why she phoned the company and not the police. She explains to me to that they've been clients of the company for years; they respond quickly, she tells me, and—she stresses this—she likes "their way of operating." She then asserts, "I don't want the girl arrested; I want her to know that what she did was wrong. Going to jail won't teach her anything; it will just make it worse. She needs to be disciplined, and the police won't do that for you." I find this situation incredibly sad, and I sympathize with the maid. I somehow feel that she is not the wrongdoer, and I am appalled by the clients' and David's attempts to impart moral discipline.

On our way back to the office, David explains how these clients' problem was not uncommon: Maids, gardeners, and other black employees often steal from their employers. When I ask him what will happen if the maid steals again, he says, "We will eat her." He repeats this several times. I ask him what he means exactly. "We'll beat her," he replies, "give her a good hiding . . . she needs to be taught a lesson. Only like that will she learn. Going to prison isn't a punishment at all." David appears to notice my disapproval. "People like you," he says, "from overseas, you think it isn't right, that it's inhumane, but they [the criminals] are the inhumane ones; they're the ones who don't care and they must be punished."

. . .

This performance depicts a particular role that is expected of armed response officers in the private domain, whereby clients legally entitle security officers to execute their policing needs. Armed response officers are increasingly providing all sorts of help in the private sphere that far exceeds a basic "response," such as providing medical and technical assistance. They are often viewed as negotiators and mediators, being called on to diffuse tense situations or to intervene between different parties, and intimidation is inherent in these roles. In the case of the errant maid, David was called on to insert his symbolic authority and bodily capital in the front region of his performance. The threat of force was used to deter further acts of crime, protect the interests of the clients, and instill morality. Armed response officers refer to this as "disciplining."

I was initially surprised at the frequency with which armed response officers responded to domestic disputes between siblings, neighbors, tenants, and housemates, because I assumed that these incidents were in the domain of the public police. Armed response officers and company managers described domestic disturbances as the most annoying and least rewarding call-outs. They were also regarded as the most risky and difficult: Although armed response officers want to help clients and provide "maximum service," they also feel constrained in addressing such disturbances and are concerned about the potential problems they may cause. Many armed response officers have had their attempts to solve cases of domestic violence backfire on them, with the person (very often a woman) they intended to protect ending up pressing charges against them.

When called to a domestic dispute, armed response officers, because they operate with a client mandate, will usually side with their clients to protect their interests without investigating the situation. This was evident in a neighborly quarrel that occurred in May 2010 while I was on the day shift with Ryan, an Indian armed response officer in his mid-twenties. We had been called out to a site to address a "domestic"; when we arrived, we saw an Indian man (the client) sitting behind his gate and exchanging insults with an Indian woman standing on the road. The man explained to us that she was swearing at him, calling him all sorts of things, while the woman accused him of entering her house without permission and spreading rumors about her in the neighborhood. Ryan intervened and told the woman that there was nothing the company could do and that she must go to the police to resolve the dispute. He kept highlighting that she was disturbing the peace in what was a quiet residential area. When we got back into the car, Ryan told me that he actually sympathized with the woman and thought that she was probably right, because he had heard stories of this man acting up before. When I asked him why he defended the man, he said, "He's our client and that's all that matters. It's not my job to choose sides, but to protect our clients, not just everybody."

In cases such as this, clients and armed response officers operate as co-actors, reading from the same script and pursuing the same goal, perhaps even functioning as a team. In the earlier episode involving the maid, for instance, the clients and David worked as a team to maintain a particular working consensus that identified the maid as the target of the performance due to her deviant behavior. David and the clients displayed the same mentality, and David gladly acted in a front region in a way that suited the clients' needs. However, this team performance may be a façade, because armed response officers may actually feel differently from their clients, something that they conceal in the back region. This is exemplified by the dispute between neighbors that Ryan responded to, in which he acted as a team member to maintain the particular working consensus despite its clashing with his actual interpretation of the situation, as he later admitted.

These domestic disputes also highlight how armed response officers are employed to impose and maintain a certain moral order. In the case of the maid, stealing from clients was considered a crime, and using physical means to "punish" her was regarded as necessary. Although David did not use physical force on this occasion, I witnessed other cases where armed response officers were expected to use force to convey moral teachings.

The state police are often referred to as the "thin blue line" that serves as a moral buffer between social order and chaos. Violence perpetuated by criminals is regarded as "bad violence," while violence that counteracts this criminal activity is regarded as "good violence" because it is intended to create and maintain a "good" social order. Defining, and preserving, this distinction is increasingly the role of the private police; they have come to be involved in "moral social ordering" (Berg 2010: 297). This is primarily due to the growing consensus that public institutions are failing to "punish" and "discipline" those committing "bad violence." By defining what is permitted (and what is not) and assuming the role of the "punisher," the conduct of armed response officers is increasingly resembling vigilante behavior (Jensen 2007; Johnston 1996). Because moral communities must be protected and order must be maintained, violence is often seen as "a necessary and justified form of discipline, as a legitimate way to restate and internalize the core moral values of the community" (Buur 2005: 193).

These three performances show that twilight policing entails a physical and symbolic expansion into the public realm, that it rests on the armed response officers' ability to use violence, and that it produces and maintains a particular social and moral order. The next section focuses on how the exclusionary nature of twilight policing is framed by racial hierarchies.

RACIALIZED CONSTRUCTIONS
OF THE DANGEROUS "OTHER"

In this section, I address how race shapes understandings of crime in South Africa, how "the criminal" is invariably associated with the young black male, and how armed response officers are used to police this socially constructed threat. Similar to Hall et al.'s (1978) study on mugging, I show that crime and security in South Africa have an underlying racial element.

Fear of crime is a powerful emotion that is felt both individually and collectively and creates boundaries within social groups, making distinctions between "us" and "them"—with risk, evil, and the dangerous "Other" located outside the social group. Such a categorization creates order, structure, and "cleanliness" in an otherwise disordered, dirty environment (Douglas 2002). To consolidate cohesion and solidarity, an external threat is required. Although the concept of crime is vague and abstract, the "criminal" is much easier to pinpoint: "When fear has a face, it can be faced" (Reguillo 2002: 199). The criminal is, in essence, the personification of crime. Caldeira analyzes the "talk of crime" (2000) that leads certain "others" to be labeled as dangerous and immoral, thereby determining who belongs and who does not. Douglas (2002: 44) argues that each society has its own "systematic ordering and classification of matter" that rejects elements regarded as dirty. Criminals are often regarded as untrustworthy, deceitful, and immoral; they are the "dirt" that originates from marginal places (Caldeira 2000; Douglas 2002; Goldstein 2004, 2012; Hall et al. 1978). In South Africa, this description and association of the "criminal" remain highly racialized (Clarno and Murray 2013; Samara 2010).

The "Bravo Mike Syndrome"

November 2008

During one of my first days on duty with Nick, we received word over the radio that we should be on the lookout for a "suspicious individual" who was wearing a "woollen jacket with red stripes." I had not yet mastered the language used in the radio communication, so I did not quite understand what had been said. What follows is an excerpt from our conversation.

Me: What exactly did he say?

Nick: There is a suspect we need to look out for: a black male wearing a woollen jacket with red stripes.

I became confused and started to question what I thought I had heard.

Me: Was that in the original message?

Nick: No, control didn't say black male, I added that on, for you.

Me: Why?

Nick: To make it clearer.

Me: But why didn't control mention that?

Nick: Because he doesn't have to, it's already clear. When I hear about a suspect or suspicious person, I assume it's a black male. Sometimes control will mention it specifically, and say, "suspicious Bravo Mike," but many times, it's left out. But I know what he means—we all do.

Me: And what about a suspicious Whiskey Mike [white male]?

Nick: [laughs] If that's the case, he'll mention it. But I haven't heard that said in years, maybe never. In this line of work, a suspicious Whiskey Mike doesn't exist. It's almost always a Bravo Mike, maybe sometimes an India Mike [Indian male], but that's only in certain areas. A suspicious man is a Bravo Mike. And we all understand it like that.

. . .

In the course of my fieldwork, Nick's claim that "we all understand it like that" was repeatedly borne out. On countless occasions, I witnessed the identification and apprehension of "suspicious individuals" who were defined as "Bravo Mikes" (i.e., black men) and for whom armed response officers were always on the lookout. When I asked my informants what "suspicious behavior" meant, I received various answers that mainly referred to someone's behavior; for example, someone who is walking quickly and continuously looking behind might be suspected of running away from a crime scene.

Yet when I probed further, it became evident that the description of a suspicious person was not only linked to behavior, but primarily to *who* was doing it. Suspicious individuals are generally described as poor and "unwashed." However, the context in which such a person is identified is very significant, and I refer to it as *class matching*. For example, if an apparently poor person were seen walking in an affluent area, it would be regarded as suspicious, yet if the same person were spotted in a township there would be no reason to be wary of that individual. Detecting suspicious individuals is about identifying contradictions between their appearance and manner with the context; in other words, it is about deciding whether an actor is entitled to be on that particular stage. It is about identifying "matter out of place" (Douglas 2002).

In many parts of the world, certain ethnic minorities are more likely to be labeled as suspicious, and thus stopped and searched, than others (Hall et al. 1978; Rowe 2004; Weber and Bowling 2011). A common explanation for this racial profiling is that certain ethnic communities are more likely to live in areas with higher crime rates and are thus statistically more likely to be engaged in criminal activity. However, my research does not focus on men who are suspected, stopped, and searched in their own areas of residence, but on those who are regarded as suspicious outside their own neighborhoods. I am concerned with the areas where they are not supposed to be, where they are "matter out of place." As my conversation with Nick suggests, race plays a major role in defining "matter out of place" in South Africa.

During my time on duty, clients and armed response officers used a range of descriptions that cut across racial lines, yet the terms "white female" and "white male" were conspicuous by their absence. Rather, their calls always concerned suspicious black males or suspicious Indian males. I term this the "Bravo Mike Syndrome," which refers to the framing of the criminal as the immoral and dangerous black male and to the consequent policing practices of armed response officers. In describing the importance of color in constructing fear in South Africa, Hansen makes the following claim:

> The enemy of the post-apartheid society is conceptualized as the ordinary, under-educated and impatient young man of colour, emerging from an anomic and morally distorted township culture, armed with lethal weapons and imagined to be aligned with crime syndicates. This popular and official view of "the criminal" as a morally inferior person, beyond redemption and reform, only amenable to punishment and incarceration, seemed to be in tune with a broader global trend . . . (2006: 284).

During apartheid, race was a political and social grouping that defined moral categories. Racial segregation aimed to prevent mixing and to protect "racial purity" (Posel 2001b: 52). The apartheid state created racial categories to reject and keep out the "dirt," the non-Whites, from the pure and clean: the Whites. Swanson (1977, cited in Steinberg 2011: 354) shows how "the notion of contagion," which framed Blacks as "bearers of disease" who would bring disorder, was used to instill and maintain segregation. The depiction of Blacks as "dirt" was thus used during apartheid and served as a powerful metaphor; current racial framing shows that this classification is still present in South Africa.

State policing maintained racial segregation during apartheid. Although crossing geographical borders was permitted for economic reasons, such movement was heavily policed and non-Whites were regularly subjected to checking of their *dom passes* (i.e., to ascertain where they were permitted to be). When apartheid was dismantled and the policing of the "new South Africa" was designed and implemented, geographical borders no longer determined policing strategies. Many policing agents found it difficult to adjust to this transformation. Johnny, a white armed response officer who had been working in the industry for more than twenty years, shared some of his experiences with me:

> Back in the 80s and 90s, being a good security officer meant checking the Blacks—questioning them about what they're doing, making sure they've got their papers. . . . And then, with the new government, all of that changed; we were now told we couldn't do that anymore. And you know, it was difficult. If you're used to something—it was how we were taught to think and do— it's difficult to turn it off. But we did it. . . . But now, with crime being so high and people in South Africa, we're fed up, we've had enough. So we're going back again, because now I am questioning Blacks again and clients are phoning in about these suspicious black men. . . . I sometimes wonder what it all changed for? Or did it change?[6]

Racist Policers?

One explanation of the Bravo Mike Syndrome centers on the dominant presence of racist attitudes and perceptions among armed response officers. Racist remarks, jokes, and comments were common among the staff of all of the companies I researched. When racist comments were made to colleagues, they were done in a joking manner, whereas when directed at suspects, they tended to be more serious. I clearly recall a day shift with Michael in May 2010, during which he pointed to a group of black children standing outside a school and said, "What a waste of money of even educating them. It's a tragedy. They're just going to grow up to hijack or kill innocent people." Similarly, one afternoon in February 2009, Gayle and I were talking about apartheid. The conversation started with him condemning it, but he then proceeded to say, "But eventually, you can't mix a bunch of barbarians and criminals with civilized people. It's like putting lions loose with cats. It just doesn't go."

Such views highlight how Blacks are characterized as untrustworthy barbarians in much the same way as criminals are. In my research, armed response officers and citizens often described criminals as deceitful, inhumane, and bloodthirsty individuals who lacked morality and were guided by hate and a "desire for revenge": They were "animals," "hungry beasts," "soulless killers," and "individuals that need to be punished." For example, in Performance 2, the suspects were described as "animals," while in Performance 3, the maid was said to be "out to steal." The newsletters of community organizations also highlight these viewpoints, with criminals portrayed as "the scum,"[7] yet also as clever and deceitful individuals who "do not hesitate to shoot to kill if need be."[8] Although these descriptions are not necessarily racialized, they are never directed toward Whites and contain implicit racial categorizations.

As with the issue of "moral cynicism," encountering crime on a daily basis for years and seeing Blacks as forming the majority of suspects and criminals have shaped many of these racialized perceptions on part of armed response officers. Gayle was very astute about this phenomenon:

> You see, when I was in CIT,[9] I saw a lot of fucked-up shit. I stopped it, because I was becoming a racist. I started to think that every black man was going to shoot me. But you know, black men do kill more. They don't give a shit—they will pull the fucking trigger and end your life. Without a doubt. You see, we might have trouble sleeping at night, but these guys . . . they just fucking do it. Just like that. And the next day they'll do it again.[10]

Such racist sentiments not only constitute the Bravo Mike Syndrome but they also influence how black citizens are treated. For example, after the car chase (Performance 1), I asked Gayle about the circumstances in which he would provide assistance to nonclients and he explained how he based his decision to aid them on whether "they look like they needed help." When I probed further, it became clear that appearance, particularly skin color, largely influenced Gayle's decision-making process. Another example concerns the incident described at the beginning of Chapter 5, in which a black man requested assistance from an armed response company. The man was sent back and forth between the company and the police and was eventually turned away by both. When I asked the armed response officers afterward why they did not help him, they claimed that he was drunk and did not have a good case. However, one of them also said, "He's probably a criminal himself anyways." When I inquired further, it became evident that they were referring to his race. And then one of them openly stated, "If he would have been Indian or White, I would have helped. But this Blackie? Hell no!"

Company owners and managers often voiced similar opinions. One Indian owner explained how his company had a strict policy of offering assistance to anyone in need, yet when I asked whether this also applied to the neighboring black townships, he bluntly said "no." The owner initially cited safety reasons, but awhile later he said, "We wouldn't be welcome there, even if somebody called us. . . . It's not safe, but they also deal with things differently, and chances are, that they're involved in crime themselves, so who are we protecting?"[11] Perceptions of crime are thus very often racially framed.

This racial framing is even more evident when intra-racial interactions occur. Although they form a minority of clients, there are, of course, also black South Africans who purchase private security (Burton et al. 2004, cited in Kempa and Singh 2008: 346). Black clients hold very similar views of criminals to those outlined earlier, but their understanding differs through its incorporation of poverty and class as defining factors, which differentiate the client from the criminal. The criminals are those who have not "made it out of the townships" and improved their economic standing since the political transformation. Here, the notion of "economic outsiders" (Kempa and Singh 2008: 345) is significant. The criminals are the "Other" because of their economic position; they are judged by "the moral measure of success in capitalist markets" (Kempa and Singh 2008: 347). This notion highlights the link between racist security policies and broader political economies. Generally speaking, black clients of private security in former white areas are not categorized as "Bravo Mikes." Although they may not be considered full and worthy members of the "us," they are also not identified as the dangerous and dirty "Other." Rather, the "dirt" refers to individuals who reside in certain "marginal spaces" that are seen as dangerous, chaotic, and the source of disorder (Caldeira 2000; Douglas 2002; Goldstein 2004; Hall et al. 1978). In South Africa, townships continue to be perceived as "breeding grounds of brutality" (Comaroff and Comaroff 2006b: 216).

"Carrying the Indian Torch"

Of the four companies that I selected for in-depth analysis, one was an Indian-owned company operating in a former Indian township. Although I chose this company for several reasons, I mainly wanted to see whether private policing was different in a racially homogeneous neighborhood that prided itself on being "Indian." However, it did not take long to identify the existence of racialized policing strategies and the pervasive Bravo Mike Syndrome.

On a sunny afternoon in 2010, one of the ward councilors from the area took me for a drive to show me around the neighborhood, and we started talking about crime and policing. He shared with me the history of the area:

> You see, after 1994, two things happened. The first was the free movement of Blacks. Before, Blacks that were walking on the road were stopped and checked—checked for their permits, their *dom passes*, controlled about what they were doing here, if they were allowed to be in the area, because they weren't. This area was 100 percent Indian. After 1994, this changed: Blacks could come in the area, buy from the same shops, go to the same schools. . . . At the same time, crime started to increase drastically, especially theft. We never had any real problems with crime beforehand; we used to walk freely down the street. . . . Now, imagine what this does for perception: many people see that when Blacks started coming into the area, so did the crime. So in their minds, there is a link, and for many, all Blacks are criminals. Although they'll employ them as gardeners or maids or whatever, they fear them. It is almost impossible to find an Indian living here that will trust his life with a black person, no matter what they tell you. And what you see now is that the style of policing under apartheid is coming back. . . . If a group of black males, or even just one of them, is walking on the street late at night, or even during the day, he'll be questioned by the police and the private security companies about what he's doing here, back to the apartheid ways. So these companies that are working here, they are carrying the Indian torch, protecting the Indians from the Blacks coming in all around us.[12]

In addition to identifying crime with Blacks, the ward councilor also noted that this predominantly Indian community preferred to work with Indian companies because they were "carrying the Indian torch." This comment highlights a certain racial solidarity between community members and policing agents. Hansen (2006) makes a similar observation in his study on Chatsworth, another former Indian township in Durban, where the presence of the Indian police provided a sense of racial solidarity during apartheid. The Indian armed response officers whom I encountered during my research, particularly those working in this community, took pride in their work and similarly regarded themselves as "local warriors defending the community against attack, literally defending what they see as the border between the Indian and the African world" (Hansen 2006: 290).

This former Indian township was not exceptional: Several geographical and/or socially defined areas—particularly racially homogeneous ones—are known for having particular "racial" preferences with regard to policing bodies. Furthermore, certain companies recruit armed response officers based on their race. This is primarily based on clients' demands: Some clients prefer a company with a particular racial majority among its armed response officers, while others openly state that they want armed reaction officers of a particular race. I discussed these racial preferences with a community leader from an affluent, predominantly white area who had been involved in an array of anticrime initiatives since the late 1980s. He concurred that his neighborhood had a "racist" reputation and claimed that it was due to the large amount of elderly residents, many of whom still had an apartheid mentality, according to which the *swart gevaar*[13] is ever present and non-white policing agents are not to be trusted. He also noted that this racially homogeneous community was surrounded by several black townships, which made people feel isolated and constantly under threat. He described it as "a safe island surrounded by nearby outsiders."[14]

During the Armed Reaction Man Competition in August 2010, one of the owners told me that he only employed white armed response officers because of client demands. He explained that the community "wouldn't tolerate a non-white to enter their house and protect their streets." During a shift in February 2009, I was talking to Anthony, a white armed response officer who had been stationed in an area with a majority of Muslim inhabitants. Anthony mentioned that he had been hugely popular in the area and numerous clients had complained when he was transferred to another area. When I inquired about the source of his popularity, he first emphasized that he was simply a "good" armed response officer who did his work exceptionally well, before casually adding, "And well, because I'm white." When I probed further, he simply shrugged, looked at me like I was asking something stupid, and said, "Well, people trust me. They know I'm not corrupt. They know I'm honest and legal. They don't think that of the other guys."[15]

In his excellent research on the South African state police, Steinberg discusses the idea that Whites are less corrupt—a "White is right" mentality. He gives the example of a police officer who made the following comment to him: "There is a perception that it is better to deal with a white policeman than a black one. . . . The white one will not be corrupt; he is just a professional" (2008: 112). A black company owner whom I encountered during my research echoed this claim: "When it comes to policing, I would trust a white guy over a black guy, any day. Not with everything, but with security, you just know a white guy's gonna do the job, and with Blacks, many questions can be asked."[16] Thus, racial constructions of criminals not only portray the black male as the "dangerous other" but also depict the white male as the incorruptible, professional policing agent.

In South Africa, dichotomies of dangerous versus safe and corrupt versus honest thus are racially framed. I am not claiming that all armed response officers are racist and always engaged in racial profiling, or that it is simply about institutionalized racism or particular "rotten apples" in the private security industry. Rather, it is about the prevalence of race in constructing and reproducing certain social realities and the role that race plays in South African society more generally. Performances are not single acts or deeds; rather, they are part of a larger social process. They highlight particular social values, and as policing cultures very often emerge from social structures and norms (Hall et al. 1978; Loyens 2009; Reiner 2000; Rowe 2004), one must examine racism within society to understand racist policing practices.

And because policing practices are performative, I argue that the Bravo Mike Syndrome reifies and consolidates particular exclusionary practices. As Kempa and Singh argue, "disciplinary and exclusionary policing practices such as those engaged by many streams of the private security industry (in South Africa and probably elsewhere) freeze essentialist conceptions of 'race'" (2008: 336). The urban architecture of South Africa shows how communities physically separate themselves through physical and imagined borders, and this separation is highly racialized.

Race is not a distinctive element of twilight policing. Policing everywhere is often defined as exclusionary and, in particular contexts, as racist. However, the issue of race shows how twilight policing acquires meaning in the South African context and shapes the disciplinary and exclusionary nature of the phenomenon. I therefore concur with Samara (2010: 640), who notes that "the governance of security can function as a form of racial governance." We need to understand how public spaces are racialized in a context where "every physical space remains historically marked and defined by a single racial category—rarely two or more" (Hansen 2012: 7). Thus, while racism is not specific to twilight policing, it is an important dimension and consequence of it due to the complexity of South Africa's racial legacies. Furthermore, it plays a crucial role in the emotional and liminal experiences of the performers of twilight policing, as I show in the following section.

"IT'S NEVER GOOD ENOUGH": EXPERIENCING THE TWILIGHT

In this section, I conduct a microanalysis of the individual experiences of armed response officers in which they feel that their work is "never good enough." This analysis shows how armed response officers experience their occupation and emphasizes their position as "dominated actors" within local security networks.

Working as a policing agent, whether public and private, has been characterized as "a (not so) rewarding job" (Loyens 2009: 466). Although this can be attributed to poor wages, boredom, and risk, the main factor is the poor treatment that policing agents endure on the job. This treatment is arguably even poorer for private security officers, given their limited legal powers and the additional burden of not being "good enough" for the public police (Loyens 2009; Rigakos 2002). Private security officers suffer from having "too many masters" (Button 2007: 135), including company management, clients, colleagues of higher rank, and state policemen. Each of these parties has its own interests and agendas, and private security officers struggle to please them all.

In addition to the occupational hazards discussed in Chapter 4, armed response officers' main complaints about their work concern their inability to please clients, the constant feeling of "gambling" in their interactions with clients and police officers, and the sense of never being "good enough." Nick once said to me, "It's like we are always walking on eggshells; you always have to be careful. It can make you go crazy, really."[17] Armed response officers are also often asked to do "ridiculous" things. For example, on one occasion in June 2010, David was expected to dispose of a dead cat that a client had placed in a box outside her house, and in February 2009, Sanjeev was asked to transport food from one client to another. Armed response officers loathe such requests and feel belittled by them.

Every armed response officer is continuously engaged in a process of "audience segregation," which means that he must ensure "that those before whom he plays one of his parts will not be the same individual before whom he plays a different part in another setting" (Goffman 1959: 56). Clients and police officers both exhibit diverse expectations from and approaches toward armed response officers. The demands of clients are strongly linked to the perception of a failing state police force. It is as if their lack of confidence in and frustration toward the public police are channeled in their attitudes toward and treatment of armed response officers, precisely because private security is essentially a private good. Indeed, clients feel that they can switch easily between private security companies; if one does not meet their demands, they will simply find another. This feeling of entitlement and consumer power is crucial in understanding how armed response officers are treated. The working consensus of a performance thus differs between audiences, and armed response officers must know which performance is legitimate for which audience.

Contrary to popular belief, assaults, abuse, and verbal threats against security officers are common, so common that they are regarded as a large part of the job (Button 2007; Lister et al. 2000; Loyens 2009; Rigakos 2002). For armed response officers, verbal assault and ill treatment are seen as something that comes with the territory, as Gayle clearly expressed after the car chase described earlier. However, these experiences and the officers' dislike for clients and police officers must remain in the back stage, as clearly illustrated by Performance 1: In the presence of the citizen, Gayle was calm and polite, but as soon as we were alone together, he expressed his disdain. Reaction officers are rarely able to express their disagreement with clients. During the car chase, for example, Gayle initially conveyed a willingness to support the nonclient's plea for assistance, though he later disagreed with the behavior by saying, "You shouldn't be chasing guys like this." If such opinions are pushed to the front region, armed response officers may be punished or dismissed.

The car chase also highlights the contradictory attitudes toward and expectations of armed response officers. They are regarded as having a certain degree of public authority and sometimes are even equated with the public police. Yet, because armed response officers do not possess the same powers and tools as the police, these expectations can never be met. During the car chase, the citizen expected Gayle to run red lights, and he swore at Gayle profusely throughout the entire episode. I often wonder what he would have demanded from Gayle if we had succeeded in apprehending the suspects. The work of armed response officers is marked by a conflicting combination of high expectations and contempt. Themba once described it as a constant balancing act: "Some clients want A, others want B; you never know until you get there. People pull and push, thinking that we can do everything, but we can't."[18] The reality is that most citizens are not aware of the legal limitations of armed response officers. This means that their initial expectations of the latter's performance are undefined, providing space for conflicting interpretations and further complicating the art of audience segregation.

Armed response officers also feel that clients frequently "test" them, such as by needlessly pressing panic buttons to test their response time. Some companies encourage their clients to test their alarm systems regularly to check that they are still functioning. However, this is also likely intended as a way to directly test the capability of armed response officers. During a day shift with Themba in November 2008, we responded to an alarm activation at a client's house. The client was not at home, as is commonly the case, so Themba climbed over the gate and conducted a perimeter check. He saw no sign of any criminal activity, so he left a call slip behind and we proceeded to the next alarm activation. A few hours later, the control room informed us that the client had called the company to complain that his gate was broken. Themba explained to the control room that this was not his doing, but the client insisted that he return to the property. On the drive over, Themba seemed rather anxious. I asked him why the client wanted us to come back, to which he replied,

> I think there is a problem with the gate. You see, there is always a problem. If you climb over the gate, then clients are angry that you come inside, they get suspicious. . . . But if you don't climb over the gate, then they ask: why am I paying all this money if he doesn't even come inside? Always a problem. And I, no we, are always doing something wrong.

When we arrived at the client's house, we saw that the gate's motor and several of the railings were indeed broken. The client immediately demanded an explanation, and Themba became very defensive, repeatedly saying that he had not done anything. Themba used me as a witness, and I readily concurred that the gate had been fine when we left, which was the truth. The client remained agitated, but he eventually let us go to respond to another call-out.

Private security officers are the first to be suspected if something is out of place or if a crime occurs at a client's premises. This can be emotionally grueling for security officers, especially if they have been stationed in a particular area for awhile and have established personal relationships with some of their clients. Frank told me about a period of shock and depression he had experienced after one of his long-term clients from a collective client was robbed and accused him of colluding with the criminals. The client made Frank take two polygraph tests, one conducted by the company and another by a personal contact. Frank passed them both, but the episode changed his mentality:

> I felt betrayed, completely. I loved working in this area and put my heart into it. I really felt like these people appreciate me, they trust me, it's worth taking the risk for, you know? But when this happened, *eish* . . . everything changed. I mean, I still enjoy working here, but it made me realize: I will never be one of them, and they will always see me as this [he points to himself], this uniform. And they will always suspect me. . . . Even if I work here for another twenty years.[19]

In cases like Frank's, the breakdown of trust is almost always irreparable and thus is carried toward the back regions of armed response officers' performances. When suspicions arise or accusations are made in such contexts, it implies that the members of the audience are not convinced that the performance is true (Goffman 1959: 59–66). There is concern about the authority of the performer, but not over the performance itself. In the incident involving the damaged gate, the client was not necessarily worried about the gate per se, but rather about Themba's honesty in carrying out the task and function as his security provider. The suspicion directed at armed response officers thus revolves around questions of their power and authority to react to "moral transgressions perceived to threaten the community" (Jensen 2007: 49). Similar to what Çankaya (2015) has identified with ethnic minority police officers in the Netherlands, armed response officers act as both "insiders and outsiders" (11), and endure an ongoing negotiation about whether they belong to the moral community.

Being the "Bravo Mike"

This ambiguity is intrinsically linked to the Bravo Mike Syndrome, since the majority of armed response officers are not white (see Chapter 3). There is an inevitable friction in this: A Bravo Mike is both a source of fear and safety. Armed response officers are believed to come from the same marginal spaces as criminals and thus to have the same potential to "pollute." Many black armed response officers I spoke to felt that clients made direct associations between them and criminals. Sipho, a black officer in his early thirties with a military background, expressed this view clearly:

> You see, many clients are very suspicious. They don't say that directly, but you can feel it, the way they look at you. It's so sad, really so sad. One time, I had a call-out. . . . When I got to the premises, the suspect had just climbed over the fence and left. The client was screaming at me: "Chase him, shoot him, there goes your brother, shoot your brother!" He was calling the suspect my brother, like I know him or something, just because we're both black. And it hurts to hear this, you know. It made me angry, so so angry. . . . But also just very, very sad.[20]

For many armed response officers, the Bravo Mike Syndrome is an emotional and conflict-ridden affliction, as Sipho elaborated:

> It's a very big problem. Many times, the males are just walking down the street and then I have to ask them what they are doing. It feels very uncomfortable; I feel guilty, because it's none of my business to ask them what they are doing. And I would hate somebody to ask me that. . . . But it's my job. It makes me very sad, but I have to do it, I just have to.[21]

Many armed response officers define the Bravo Mike Syndrome as "white paranoia" and sympathize with the black men whom they are obliged to observe and question. They are put in situations where "the performer is forced to take a line which is deeply contrary to his inward feelings" (Goffman 1959: 184). On a day shift in November 2008, Gayle and I conducted a "Bravo Mike" check at the bequest of a white client who had just moved to a new neighborhood, only to discover that the suspicious black male in question had in fact been working as a gardener in the area for the last ten years. Afterward, Gayle expressed his frustration:

> So this new guy just doesn't know his neighbors, he doesn't take the time to think and actually know what's going on his area, so we must do it. I must ask a poor black man, who has been working here for ten years, why he is walking on the street, all because of some lazy fuck [the client]? Their laziness, their stupidity, their ignorance . . . and so the black guy must be a criminal? And I must question him? Yes, that is exactly it. And it's fucked up, I can tell you that.[22]

Liminal Persons

Armed response officers function as both anomalous and ambiguous persons: They are anomalous for not fitting neatly within a given category and ambiguous for being able to fit into two different categories (i.e., the protector and the potential criminal) at the same time (Douglas 2002: 47). It is therefore unclear where to place them; their "status is indefinable" (118). Policing is about creating "a separation between the 'good' community and the evil outsiders" (Jensen 2007: 65), and armed response officers are recruited to police this boundary. Yet members of the public, particularly clients, continuously call this role into question. Armed response officers are "neither there nor here" (Turner 1967: 97); they are not fully accepted as insiders, yet nor are they equivalent to the "dangerous" Other. They are somewhere in the middle and are both at the same time: They exist within a liminal phase, defined by its "betwixt-and-between condition" (Turner 1987: 101).

I argue that twilight policing is performed in a liminal phase that has both temporal and spatial dimensions: It refers to the moment of performance and the spaces in which performances occur. More specifically, twilight policing is a type of public liminality that is accessible to many participants. Performances in a public liminal phase have a temporal structure, contain both constant and variable features, and function as spaces for spontaneity and improvisation (Turner 1987: 25–26). Armed response officers are governed by a set of rules and regulations created by the industry, the police, and clients, yet there is also the potential for alteration, and improvisation is repeatedly used to adapt to particular situations. When armed response officers receive a call-out or alarm notification, their work is structured by certain procedures and expectations, yet what will happen when they arrive on the scene is unpredictable. Thus, a set of rules and symbols may be in place, but their framework is continually being negotiated, resulting in a constant process of creating and redefining rules and relationships (i.e., the working consensus). Performances are thus not fixed, but rather are constantly reconfigured. And this is why there is so much discomfort and anxiety felt by the key performers, namely the armed response officers. Although these elements of unpredictability and rule bending may be hallmarks of policing more generally, this *constant* level of uncertainty defines twilight policing.

Armed response officers operate in a space of "ambiguity and paradox, a confusion of all the customary categories" (Turner 1967: 97). The presence of "too many masters," the disciplinary codes imposed by companies, the "gambling" sensation experienced when working with police officers, and the various demands made by clients all result in a constant experience of uncertainty and unpredictability. And although their shifts consist of mundane routines, there is always the potential for violence and risk, which carries an extra element of anxiety and stress. These feelings, which are compounded by a lack of knowledge about where their boundaries lie and what they are permitted and expected to do, create profound uncertainty for armed response officers. If one adds to this the occupational hazards discussed in Chapter 4, such as the feeling of being unable to provide security for their own families, their morally rigid views of crime, their moral cynicism, domestic issues related to "taking the work home," and the prevalence of violence surrounding them, one can only conclude that being the performer of twilight policing is a strained experience. It involves a constant movement from front to backstage performances, taking on and off certain characteristics.

CONCLUDING REMARKS

This chapter sought to show that twilight policing is a joint performance that involves the coming together of various actors, each of whom is influential in his or her own way. With reference to three performances, I demonstrated how twilight policing is not possible if one or more of the actors are absent, and this does not refer to a physical absence. For example, the performances discussed in this chapter occurred without the physical presence of the police, but this did not mean that the state was "absent." Citizens' perceptions that the state police are failing to provide security shape the performance. If such perceptions did not exist, then armed response officers would not police the public domain and engage in twilight policing. The state is thus very much present, albeit primarily in one's perceptions and experiences.

The second aim of this chapter was to show that twilight policing consists of practices that encroach on the public domain. The armed response sector has expanded into the public domain through its increasing presence in public spaces and the acquisition and designation of additional roles and tasks that resemble those of the state police. Twilight policing is occurring on a larger stage with more participants, which requires a constant process of reestablishing a working consensus in which clients and police officers generally have the upper hand. Due to the saturation of and competition in the private security industry, clients are able to pick and choose between companies, placing pressure on armed response officers to act according to their clients' interests alone. Furthermore, police officers, backed by the legal powers of the state apparatus, have the authority to decide whether to approve or disapprove of armed response officers' actions.

In addition, I analyzed the punitive, disciplinary, and exclusionary nature of twilight policing—implied not by the direct use of physical violence by armed response officers, but rather their ability to wield force to assert power and make claims to certain rights. Furthermore, twilight policing confers a moral order on public and private life by imposing boundaries between insiders and outsiders. Although this classification is context dependent, it is primarily directed against the dangerous, violent criminal: the poor "Bravo Mike."

My third aim was to show that armed response officers have two main roles as the key performers of twilight policing. First, they act as gatekeepers of the (imagined) boundaries between insiders and outsiders, a position that is innately problematic and contradictory, because the locus of armed response officers along these borders is continuously in flux. This process of negotiation not only highlights the problematic process of setting the boundaries but also defines the emotional experience of twilight policing. It is for this reason that the term "twilight" is highly pertinent, since it expresses a sense of capriciousness and uncertainty. Although social relationships between clients, police officers, and armed response officers may dictate certain routines, there is always a sense of the "unknown" when armed response officers respond to a call-out, and the sequence and nature of the joint performance may always change.

This unpredictability is connected to the second role of armed response officers: They are negotiators between citizens' demands and the perceived shortcomings of the state. Twilight policing is a way to "call attention to the predicament of insecurity in which the actors currently find themselves, as well as to criticize the failure of the democratic state and its claim to a rule of law" (Goldstein 2004: 182). Armed response officers (and perhaps private security personnel in general) are regarded as "better" than the public police by many because they provide services that the police cannot and clients can wield some form of control over the proceedings, thereby gaining a sense of ownership. However, because of their limited legal powers and poor reputation, armed response officers are also looked down on for not being the "real police." This yields friction and ambiguity, which are evident in the persistent lack of trust and the suspicion felt toward private security officers. The ambiguity and suspicion are not only due to the nature of the policing practices but also to the social structures in which these are performed. Twilight policing is therefore about operating in a twilight zone that is "neither here nor there."

Epilogue

Expanding the Twilight

This ethnography examined the complex relationships between violence, (in)security, and policing through an analysis of the daily policing practices of armed response officers in Durban, South Africa. The global proliferation of nonstate policing has been extensively studied across academic disciplines. Although this vast body of literature contains divergent approaches and epistemological stances, there has been an overall recognition that policing is not the sole prerogative of the state. This has resulted in a pluralized approach to security that acknowledges how numerous actors, both state and nonstate, are engaged in policing practices. One of the dominant and recurring claims in this approach is that the contemporary security landscape is marked by weak, failing, or absent states that are unable to provide security for their citizens. The general rationale is that state weakness or absence provides room for other actors to obtain authority and thereby threaten and undermine the legitimacy of the state. In this view, nonstate policing is an indication, result, and consolidation of state failure.

This book entered this debate by questioning whether the proliferation of nonstate policing worldwide can be explained through such a "state-failure" perspective. In so doing, it engaged with current developments in criminology that examine how different policing bodies interact, overlap, compete, and collaborate. This criminological debate has occurred alongside a growth of anthropological studies on sovereignty, which analyze it as a socially constructed source of power that is reproduced through daily practices and repeated public performances. This anthropological approach to sovereignty provides a conceptual framework through which to understand how diverse forms of authority are claimed in different contexts. In this book, I drew ideas from both academic fields to understand the numerous ways in which different policing bodies are interrelated. Specifically, I examined the policing practices of armed response officers—one type of private security officer—and their interactions with other actors through local security networks in Durban, South Africa.

The main argument of this book is that armed response officers are engaged in twilight policing: performances comprising policing practices that emerge through the interconnections between state and nonstate policing. Engaging with an anthropological conceptualization of sovereignty, I argue that twilight policing is the performance of sovereign power; in other words, in their daily practices and interactions with others, armed response officers claim authority through both the ability to use and the actual use of violence. I contend that twilight policing is needed as both a descriptive concept and a conceptual framework to make sense of what I encountered in the field, thereby contributing to debates on policing, violence, (in)security, and authority.

In the course of this book, I examined the different processes, policies, and practices that make up twilight policing and generate an environment in which such performances occur. To this end, I analyzed the historical background of and contemporary trends in violence and policing in South Africa (Chapter 2); the various components that constitute the armed response sector (Chapter 3); the experiences and perceptions of armed response officers (Chapter 4); the interactions between armed response officers and police officers (Chapter 5); the interactions between armed response officers and citizens, particularly clients (Chapter 6); and the coming together of these various elements in the form of twilight policing performances, which consist of punitive, disciplinary, and exclusionary policing practices (Chapter 7).

In this epilogue, I discuss three main threads that bind this ethnography together. In so doing, I reaffirm what twilight policing is and highlight its relevance. The first thread concerns the interconnections between public and private policing as armed response officers increasingly operate in the public domain by acting like the state and performing in public spaces. The second thread is the punitive and exclusionary nature of twilight policing; that is, the use of violence to claim authority and create a social order. The third thread concerns the "dominated" position of armed response officers and their experiences of being the performer under the panoptic gaze of "many masters." As I discuss each thread, I reassert how twilight policing is a joint performance, one that is shaped by the coming together of practices conducted by various actors and their subsequent interactions. I end this epilogue with a brief critical appraisal of the state-failure argument. I first conclude that armed response officers (re)produce statist policing practices and thereby reaffirm ideas and representations of the state. I then identify the state as the "arbiter"— the sovereign power that determines which claims to sovereignty are upheld and legitimized.

INTERCONNECTIONS BETWEEN PUBLIC AND PRIVATE POLICING

The first and most prominent thread of this book addresses how twilight policing consists of practices that emerge through the interconnections between state and nonstate policing. In this book I showed how armed response officers are simultaneously performing "state" and "nonstate" practices, thereby engaging in "unstately stateliness" (Lund 2006: 677). I expanded on this notion by demonstrating that armed response officers are private agents who work in a profit-making system with a client-steered mandate, yet who increasingly operate in public spaces, assist "non-clients," mimic the state police, and appropriate "languages of stateness" (Hansen and Stepputat 2001: 5).

In South Africa, state and nonstate policing have been interrelated for much of its history. During apartheid, the state repressively policed the non-white areas through numerous proxies and established an alliance with the private security industry to protect white privilege. Through various forms of legislation, such as the National Key Points Act (NKPA) of 1980 and the Security Officers Act (SOA) of 1987, collaboration between the state and the industry emerged, primarily as a means to control the latter's (predominantly black) labor force. This alliance gave rise to an "old boys' network"—a group of white men from the state armed forces and the security industry—that further consolidated the political, social, and economic ties between the two. By the time of the political transition in 1994, there were thus numerous links between state and nonstate policing bodies.

The post-apartheid state aimed to transform the former militarized state police into a force dedicated to democratic policing practices by focusing on community policing structures and outlining a "multi-agency approach" (Singh 2008: 14), in which the state would work alongside other actors, such as the private security industry, to combat crime. Under this new system, state bodies would lead policing initiatives, and other actors would take on a "junior" role to assist the state. The post-apartheid state therefore retained policies that outsourced particular policing functions and promoted partnerships with other policing bodies within the legal parameters of the state. Such policies demonstrate how the state actively shapes the policing practices of other actors. Thus, the prevalence of nonstate policing in South Africa does not imply a weakness or absence of the South African state. Rather, this book shows that the South African state has created a climate that encourages an increased involvement from nonstate actors, often alongside state representatives.

This encouragement is evident in the local security networks between state police officers and armed response officers. Similar to studies in criminology that have identified a dual-sided relationship between state and nonstate policing actors, I showed that armed response officers both undermine and support the state police through competitive and collaborative practices. Yet I developed this claim further by arguing that these competitive and collaborative practices often occur simultaneously and are not always distinct. This ambiguity and blurring of the lines is further complicated by practices whereby police officers transgress the public-private policing divide, with moonlighting as the prime example.

Twilight policing practices are thus often encouraged by the state police, particularly through their own engagement in private policing practices. This shows that, while private and public policing bodies may be physically distinguishable, their actions are often determined by motives that do not match this distinction. A police officer may represent the state, but his or her actions can be determined by profit-making motives or acts of reciprocity within a social relationship with private security members. Armed response officers may be private agents, but they are often managed by former police officers and work regularly with police officers to support state police actions. All of these practices point toward an immense diversity of entanglements between public and private policing bodies.

In addition to state encouragement, the occupational culture of the armed response sector cultivates an environment that is conducive to twilight policing practices. Although I concur with several studies on the occupational culture of private security that the industry bears many similarities to the state police, I argue that this resemblance differs between industry sectors. I demonstrated that the parallels are more prevalent in the armed response sector, which closely resembles the state police, both symbolically and operationally. This resemblance is first due to the nature of the occupation: Armed response work involves armed men who patrol communities, possess a firearm, and operate in vehicles and uniforms that resemble those of the state police. Their policing practices are therefore very different from those of, say, security officers who guard shopping malls. Second, the sector emerged largely from "one-man shows" that were run by former state police officers who exercised state policing practices. The sector thus began with a state policing mentality. Third, armed response officers regard themselves as "semi-policemen" and strongly differentiate themselves from other private security officers. This predominant "wanna-be policemen" mentality further attests to their eagerness to act like state police officers and to work alongside them.

I also examined how clients, and increasingly citizens, encourage armed response officers to operate in the public realm. Although existing studies on private policing emphasize that companies operate with a client-steered mandate, there are only a handful that closely examine how clients and other citizens interact with security officers and influence their policing practices. In this book, I identified three types of local security networks: high maintenance, collaborative, and competitive. High-maintenance networks feature demanding clients who clearly have the upper hand; collaborative networks are characterized by practices in which citizens and armed response officers work together to provide a policing service; and competitive networks are marked by power struggles between citizens and armed response officers. Despite their differences, these three types of networks all augment competition in the sector and encourage armed response companies and officers to provide and do "more," which entails a movement into the public realm. This is especially true for collective arrangements, which create "communities of security": public spaces that armed response officers are mandated to police.

We can only understand these demands for "more" by connecting them to citizens' perceptions of the state police. Armed response officers act as "negotiators" between citizens' expectations and the (perceived) shortcomings of the state. Despite the popularity of private security, it is experienced as a "grudge purchase," one that is regarded as necessary but unwelcome. Citizens channel their frustration with the state police into their interactions with armed response officers. This is evident in citizens' expectations and requests: Active patrols, quick response, and personal service are services that citizens perceive the state police are failing to provide. We can therefore only adequately understand why private security officers do what they do by analyzing what clients, and increasingly citizens, demand and expect of them.

This book therefore shows how historical processes, state policies and representatives, the organizational structures of the armed response sector, and citizens each contribute to creating an environment that encourages, and sometimes even forces, armed response officers to increasingly perform in the public realm. It further highlights how twilight policing is a joint performance shaped by the policies, perceptions, and practices of various actors. Armed response officers may be the *performers*, but they are not solely responsible for the practices that make up the *performance*. My analysis of twilight policing as a joint performance underlines the multidimensional relationships between state and nonstate policing. However, I also want to emphasize that I do not propose that we abandon the public-private policing dichotomy. Instead, I argue that we should regard "public" and "private" as useful reference points for describing what occurs "in between," rather than as definite states of being.

VIOLENCE AND EXCLUSION

The second thread of this book concerns the punitive and exclusionary nature of twilight policing. The anthropological literature on sovereignty has different perspectives on the role of violence in claiming sovereign power. This book is aligned with studies that define violence—the ability to kill and inflict pain—as the source of sovereign power. Yet I also demonstrated through numerous case studies that the *ability* to use violence is equally important. Therefore, both the possibility and reality of violence are means to create a particular social order and to define who belongs to it.

Although there is diversity among companies, officers, and contexts, the occupational culture of the sector at large centers on violence and the prospect of using it. Due to their limited legal powers, armed response officers rely often on other means—primarily by cultivating bodily and force capital—to obtain authority and secure compliance. Companies employ strategic branding and compel armed response officers to adhere to a particular "look" that projects force and bodily capital. The sector also (re)produces masculinization processes that profile it as a collective of masculinities: a "man's world." These processes incite reaction officers to overtly display certain masculine attributes, such as being "tough" and even aggressive. Although there are trigger-happy response officers who eagerly seek out violence, the punitive nature of twilight policing is apparent throughout the entire sector.

This punitive nature must, however, be analyzed with reference to broader social processes and perspectives on violence. Many studies conducted elsewhere, particularly in Latin America, have identified the growing public support for punitive responses to crime, which is reflected in mounting demands for more coercive policing practices. I also found this phenomenon in South Africa: Although the post-apartheid state has focused on democratic and community policing as means to eliminate the repressive nature of apartheid policing, recent developments highlight a return to militarized policing tactics. South African policing is "at a crossroads" (Marks and Wood 2010) due to divergent attitudes on how to police the streets, which I framed as a dispute between "old school" policing and that of the "new South Africa." The former refers to apartheid policing, which was repressive and racist, while the latter refers to post-apartheid policing, which is founded on democratic principles. The distinction between old school policing and the policing of the new South Africa has a temporal dimension, but it also connotes differences in policing practices and the role of violence therein. Twilight policing practices are thus not only punitive but are also influenced by contesting ideas about the appropriate use of violence.

These conflicting ideas are also apparent in clients' demands. I showed how private security companies are increasingly branding and marketing themselves as "community policing groups" to present a friendlier and less militaristic face to prospective clients. Yet I also analyzed numerous cases in which citizens encouraged or condoned the use of violence by armed response officers. For some people, in fact, a willingness to use violence is a prerequisite when choosing a security provider. Citizens thus view and prioritize the use of violence by armed response officers differently.

By subscribing to armed response, clients grant reaction officers the authority and legitimacy to police the streets and maintain a certain social order. Clients determine who belongs to this order—the "insiders" and "outsiders"—and armed response officers are mandated to police these borders; they are the "gatekeepers." In South Africa, these borders are demarcated by axes of race and class. The dangerous, criminal "Other"—the "matter out of place" (Douglas 2002)—is habitually defined as the poor black male: the "Bravo Mike." Armed response officers are employed to keep out this socially constructed threat. I refer to this social construction and its attendant policing practices as the "Bravo Mike Syndrome." The growth of collective arrangements between communities and the private security industry creates more borders, both imagined and real. This process results in differentiated clusters of security that point toward not only a manifestation and consolidation of social inequalities but also the diversity of views on how to maintain social order, particularly concerning violence and its rightful place in policing.

For armed response officers, violence therefore plays a crucial role in the acquisition of authority. It is precisely the centrality of violence that distinguishes sovereign power from other types of authority. Anthropological studies on violence are particularly pertinent in relation to the state-failure argument, which claims that the state has lost its presumed monopoly of violence. If, as I argued, twilight policing emerges through the interconnections between public and private policing, then violence, which is inherent to these practices, is also shaped by these interconnections. This implies that the state is implicated in the use of violence and is therefore not failing, let alone absent. Similar to Goldstein's (2012) analysis of the "phantom state," this book argues that the state (re)produces insecurity and thereby affects the performance of violence.

PERFORMING UNDER THE PANOPTIC GAZE(S)

The third thread of this ethnographic study concerns the "dominated" position of armed response officers and the uncertainty that they experience when policing the streets of Durban. Studies on private security officers generally overlook or underreport the individual experience of policing. I was able to include this dimension in my study thanks largely to my ethnographic approach.

In this section, I show how armed response officers have "many masters" (Button 2007: 135). Like Rigakos (2002), who draws on Foucault's (1977) idea of the Panopticon, I argue that armed response officers perform under a panoptic gaze. Armed response officers feel that they are always being watched, which fosters a constant sense of uncertainty. This feeling of ambiguity is not simply a part of their policing practices: It is what defines it. Twilight policing is defined by insecurity, unpredictability, and capriciousness, reflecting an understanding of "twilight" itself as a state of uncertainty and obscurity.

Summarizing his idea of an "uncertain anthropology," Goldstein (2012) emphasizes that studying security inherently means studying "insecurity." The twilight zone is an ill-defined area that contains features of distinct and often opposing conditions, including public versus private, legal versus illegal, and formal versus informal. Yet armed response officers themselves are in between: They are insiders who are aligned with communities of security and protect citizens from potential sources of danger, yet they are also potential outsiders who belong to the defined threat. Primarily because of their poor employment conditions, armed response officers are habitually suspected of corruption and/or working with the other side. And because most armed response officers are Bravo Mikes, they are routinely associated with the same physical, social, and economic spheres as criminals. They are "neither there nor here" (Turner 1967: 97)—not fully accepted as insiders, yet not equivalent to the dangerous Other. This creates a twilight sensation of belonging and exclusion, which is evident in the uncertainty experienced by armed response officers in the line of duty. Although there are rules and routines to guide them, there are always elements of unpredictability and a sense of the unknown about what they will encounter during their patrols, how citizens and clients will treat them, and how police officers will judge their actions. This uncertainty can leave officers feeling on edge and thus affects how they police the streets. But more importantly, armed response officers feel they are always being watched and must be on their best behavior: They perform under the panoptic gaze of their many masters.

Their first master is their company, which enforces a range of disciplinary and surveillance measures to exert constant control. Companies use numerous strategies to guarantee armed response officers are "good" and "do as they're told." They instill discipline by constantly monitoring and controlling their bodies without employing force. At the level of management, these measures are perceived as a necessary "part of the policing game." Reaction officers, however, experience them as oppressive and controlling. This creates a divide between management and operations, which is exacerbated by the racial differences that continue to define the industry, as summarized by the maxim, "Whites at the top and Blacks at the bottom."

Armed response officers' second masters are clients. Clients, and increasingly nonpaying citizens, impose an additional level of surveillance. Due to the saturated nature of the industry, all citizens are regarded as potential clients, and this exerts additional pressure on armed response officers to be in top form. Because the industry operates with a mentality that the "the client is always right," clients possess a great deal of purchasing and steering power and exercise it regularly. Clients often feel entitled to watch and test armed response officers, and with the growth of collective arrangements, this power is increasingly exercised collectively. This tendency is exacerbated by contrasting expectations of the capabilities of armed response officers in comparison to the state police. On the one hand, they are regarded as "better" than the public police because they provide services in a way that the latter cannot. However, due to their legal limitations and poor reputation, they are also scrutinized and mocked for not being the "real deal." Such contradictions result in armed response officers feeling that whatever they do "is never good enough."

The third master is the state police. The "gambling" sensation experienced by armed response officers in their interactions with police officers is a direct manifestation of the twilight sensation of insecurity and unpredictability. During every incident, armed response officers are hesitant about involving the state police because they are uncertain how the latter will react to their practices and whether or not they will enforce state law. Complex social ties between the two policing bodies, which are evident in the old boys' network, old boys' feud, and moonlighting, complicate this decision-making process.

The framework of twilight policing therefore includes the personal experiences of policing, of being the "performer." This dimension is often neglected in studies on private security, and I hope to have convinced others that individual experiences of policing influence how armed response officers conduct their work. And as is suggested by the term "twilight," these experiences are marked by uncertainty, ambiguity, and feelings of being watched.

THE STATE AS THE ARBITER

This ethnography shows that armed response officers are engaged in twilight policing performances, which consist of practices that emerge through the numerous interconnections between state and nonstate policing, that are punitive and exclusionary, and that are characterized by uncertainty and unpredictability. I now return to the state-failure argument, which I criticize here for two main reasons.

In the course of this book, I showed how armed response officers frequently withhold crime intelligence from the state police, engage in activities that occur without police supervision or interference, provide services that the state police do not, and often do so through violence.

Armed response officers are often preferred to the state police or even equated with the police. This could be interpreted as a sign of a failing or absent state that has been overpowered and undermined by nonstate policing actors. However, I argue that, in performing these practices, armed response officers act like the state police; they (re)produce state practices and reaffirm what the state is.

Anthropological studies of the state have emphasized that the state consists not only of state institutions and practices but also of representations and understandings. Throughout this book I show how armed response officers reproduce "state effects" (Mitchell 2006): They mimic the state police, both symbolically and operationally, and borrow symbolic authority from the state. Furthermore, they rely on state representations to obtain authority and legitimacy and to ensure compliance. Their claims to sovereignty are therefore based on the ideas and practices of the state, which reaffirm what the state is. Although state bodies are not the only actors to employ these practices and ideas, statist practices are (re)produced and maintained nonetheless. This can only lead us to conclude that the state is not absent. Rather, state power is continuously reconfigured through multiple claims to sovereignty.

The reproduction of statist practices and representations by nonstate actors has been analyzed in numerous anthropological studies. This book shows how this reproduction occurs among armed response officers in Durban, South Africa. However, I also identified a more specific role for state representatives in my research, namely that of "the final arbiters" (Rigi 2007: 41). This role entails that state representatives determine the course and nature of local security networks with private security personnel. This "arbiter" role is also applied to the use of violence by armed response officers: State police officers often condone, encourage, or outsourced such acts of violence, because doing so prevents them from "getting their hands dirty." Furthermore, armed response officers regularly use violence without state police involvement or interference, but this is not "hidden" from the state police because of the numerous economic and social ties between the two bodies. Rather, state police officers very often choose their level of involvement and degree of law enforcement.

However, this decision-making process is not straightforward, because the interactions between state representatives and private security members are both competitive and collaborative. The role of the arbiter is not uniform: Which practices are permitted or punished as transgression and when varies greatly and is more often determined by individual preferences, social connections, and economic gain than by "the law." Furthermore, the role of the arbiter is not fixed. Because sovereign power is precarious, claims to sovereignty must be constantly rearticulated. State representatives do not permanently possess or embody this arbiter role therefore, but must habitually reclaim it through their daily practices. One of the ways in which they do so is through their interactions with armed response officers. When the latter support the state police or take on a subordinate role, they reify the state's dominant position. And when they challenge or undermine the state police, they push state representatives to reclaim and reassert this position. The arbiter role is therefore acquired through diverse interactions between police officers and armed response officers, further highlighting how policing bodies influence each other in numerous ways.

Other authors conducting research on sovereign bodies in South Africa, such as Buur (2005, 2006) and Jensen (2008), have not identified this "arbiter" role of the state police. This entails that there is a specific relationship between the private security industry and the state in South Africa, whereby the former functions as the latter's ally in the fight against crime at both the national and local levels. One reason for the emergence of this relationship is state regulation of the industry. PSIRA may be flawed and subject to frequent criticism, but it does legally outline how the industry must operate and thereby offers the state a certain degree of control and oversight. State regulation defines private security companies as "permissible sovereign bodies" that operate within the legal parameters of the state. They therefore differ from gangs and vigilante organizations, which are often exempt from government control and are generally not regarded as potential allies in the state-envisioned strategy of "partnership policing." A second reason is that police officers and armed response share numerous traits and thereby often have the same objective and policing mentality; this congruence is consolidated by their numerous social and economic ties.

A third reason concerns socioeconomic factors that differentiate the private security industry from other sovereign bodies in South Africa. Although I conducted research in former townships, my conclusions are based primarily on policing practices performed in affluent or middle-class areas. There are unquestionably differences between my research location and those of Buur (2005, 2006) and Jensen (2008), both of whom worked in less economically privileged areas. In such places, issues, such as higher crime rates, social exclusion, poor access to goods and services, and unemployment, result in different socioeconomic contexts that give rise to different policing practices, particularly in relation to the state police. To therefore claim that the role of the state as the "arbiter" can be used to describe the relationships between the state and other sovereigns in South Africa would be to ignore the diversity of the dynamics and interactions between sovereignties.

I therefore propose that we move beyond the recognition that there are numerous sovereign bodies that claim authority to create a particular social order through violence. Although the anthropological literature on sovereignty has provided extensive insight into the complex relationships between violence, (in)security, policing, and authority, we need to take a step further by examining how different sovereignties contest and supplement each other, how these divergent processes lead to complex and imbricated policing practices, and which factors are most decisive in shaping this complexity. I have identified the state as the arbiter, but I also assume that the interactions between sovereign bodies across the globe are shaped by myriad forms of relationships, such as alliances, power struggles, and structures of domination. If we regard the sovereign landscape as a spider's web comprising numerous bodies and connected threads, we need to investigate further which claims to sovereignty are decisive in determining how and why the web is spun in a particular way.

This book addressed some of these issues by analyzing the policing practices of armed response officers and how these are influenced by their interactions with others. I introduced the concept of "twilight policing" to describe the types of practices that I encountered in the field and to provide a framework through which to analyze the multiple ways in which state and nonstate policing are entangled. My findings are based on performances of sovereignty in Durban, South Africa, yet this framework can also be used to examine how interconnections between different policing bodies in other contexts engender policing practices that are neither one nor the other, but something combined and in between, something "twilight."

. . .

In August 2010 I was finishing up my fieldwork and spent my last afternoon with Gayle. We were having lunch while sitting on the hood of his vehicle on a cliff overlooking the Indian Ocean in the south of Durban. I surprised myself by suddenly asking, "So what do you actually do? What is this world of armed response?" He laughed, looked at me, and said, "You should know that by now, after all these years. But yeah, we respond, we patrol, we're on the lookout. We do what clients ask us to;

we try to help out the police." He turned his face toward the ocean, stared out onto the crashing waves, and said, "I just try to help people, but it's not easy. All this crime, this violence. It's pretty damn dark, and there's not a lot of light to guide us. We do what the police do, but we're not them. We're somewhere halfway."

Notes

CHAPTER 1

1. Armed response companies use the NATO phonetic alphabet code for communication. Bravo thus stands for B and Mike for M. More specifically, "Bravo Mike" refers to "Black Male;" this issue of nomenclature is discussed further in Chapter 7.

2. Using an exchange rate of 11.3 South African Rand (ZAR) to the euro, this amounts to 8.5 euros. This exchange rate is used throughout this book.

3. Armed response is also referred to as armed reaction. These terms are used interchangeably throughout this book.

4. A common distinction is made between private military companies and private security companies. Although they are not always distinct, private military companies provide military services, whereas private security companies provide more police-like activities, such as guarding and access control (Avant 2005; Gumedze 2007; Schreier and Caparini 2005; Singer 2003; Zedner 2009). This book focuses on private security companies operating in South Africa.

5. All annual reports created by the Private Security Industry Regulatory Authority are accessible online at http://www.psira.co.za. This figure only includes the "active" registered private security officers, which is to say security officers who are actively employed in the industry. PSIRA also maintains a database of "inactive" registered security officers: security officers who are registered with PSIRA, but are not currently employed in the industry. In 2014, there were 1,381,340 inactive security officers compared to 487,058 active security officers, amounting to a total of 1,868,398 registered security officers.

6. For an overview of private security figures worldwide, see Abrahamsen and Williams (2011), Johnston (1992), Jones and Newburn (2006), and de Waard (1999).

7. Although Durban Metropolitan Area (DMA) is the official name, the city is more commonly referred to as Durban. The isiZulu name of the city, eThekwini (or the eThekwini Metropolitan Municipality), is also frequently used.

8. See Ballard (2005), Bénit-Gbaffou (2008), Hentschel (2011), Marks (2005), Marks and Bonnin (2010), and Marks and Wood (2007, 2010).

9. A township refers to a geographical area that was designated for non-Whites during apartheid. All non-Whites lived in townships.

10. Online database of *The Mercury* newspaper, accessed September 23, 2009.

11. These concepts are founded on empirical studies conducted in Latin America that analyzed marginalized communities where policing is performed by agents who frequently use force, such as gangs (Jones and Rodgers 2009; Rodgers 2004; Savenije and van der Borgh 2004), death squads (Huggins 1991; Oude Breuil and Rozema 2009; Scheper-Hughes 2006), and vigilantes (Godoy 2004; Goldstein 2004, 2012).

12. See Carothers (2002), Mansfield and Snyder (2001), Osaghae (2004), and O'Donnell (1993).

13. The terms "private policing" and "nonstate policing" are often used interchangeably. The former often refers solely to private security companies, whereas the latter includes other actors, such as neighborhood watches. In specific reference to the private security industry, Singh (2005) and South (1988) prefer using the term "private security sector" to incorporate all activities surrounding security, such as alarm systems, and Loader (2000) uses the term "commercial policing" to highlight the profit-making element of private security and to exclude voluntary forms of policing.

14. For more information on the changing nature of spaces, see Jones and Newburn (1998), Kempa et al. (1999, 2004), Lemanski (2004, 2006), and Wakefield (2003).

15. For more policing definitions, see Baker (2008), Button (2002), Findlay and Zvekić (1993), Johnston (1999), Johnston and Shearing (2003), Jones and Newburn (1998), Loader (2000), and Rigakos (2002).

16. Although policing is an essential part of social control, it is not equated with social control, which also involves actors, such as teachers, and activities, such as religious education, that are beyond policing. Some authors, such as Garland (1996) and Singh (2008), prefer the term "crime control" to emphasize this focus. See Button (2002), Johnston (1999), and Jones and Newburn (1998, 2006) for further discussion on this distinction.

17. The following are some of the different approaches and concepts that have emerged from the anthropological focus on sovereignty: social sovereignty (Latham 2000; Rodgers 2006b), shadow sovereigns (Nordstrom 2000), graduated sovereignty (Ong 2000), sovereignty without territoriality (Appadurai 2003), supra-sovereignties (Sassen 1996), selective sovereignties (Moore 2005), fragmented sovereignty (Davis 2010), the chaotic form of sovereignty (Rigi 2012), wild sovereignty (Kapferer 2004), and corporate sovereignty (Kapferer 2005).

18. As will be discussed in Chapter 3, the overwhelming majority of armed response officers are male, hence the use of the masculine pronoun.

19. For further reading on vigilantism in South Africa and elsewhere, see Abrahams (1998), Buur (2005, 2006), Buur and Jensen (2004), Goldstein (2004,

2012), Harnischfeger (2003), Heald (2005), Kirsch and Grätz (2010), Oomen (2004), and Pratten and Sen (2007).

20. For further discussion, see Arias (2006), Bayart, Ellis, and Hibou (1999), Beek and Göpfert (2013), Caldeira (2002), Davis (2009), Heyman and Smart (1999), Jauregui (2013), Kapferer and Bertelsen (2012), and Rigi (2012).

21. Dupont (2004) analyzes three other types of security networks: institutional security networks, international security networks, and virtual/informational security networks. These networks are not directly applicable to my research and are therefore not discussed here.

22. In his analysis of security networks, Dupont (2004) also examines how networks consist of different types of capital, namely political, economic, cultural, social, and symbolic capital. In the rest of this book, I focus on the different elements and factors that make up local security networks. However, I do not categorize these factors as different types of capital, but regard them as resources and traits.

23. Existing research tends to focus on a specific site, such as a shopping mall or theme park (van Steden 2007; Wakefield 2003), a specific company (Rigakos 2002), or a certain type of security officer, such as bouncers (Hobbs et al. 2002; Monaghan 2002).

24. These twenty months were spread across three periods: October to December 2007, June 2008 to May 2009, and April 2010 to September 2010.

25. See for example Beek (2012), Beek and Göpfert (2013), Çankaya (2011), Fassin (2013), Garriot (2013), Göpfert (2012), Hornberger (2011), Jauregui (2013), and Kyed (2014).

26. In Chapter 3, I provide more information about the various levels of training for security officers.

CHAPTER 2

1. The 1923 Urban Areas Act entailed that Blacks could only reside in urban areas for labor and economic purposes, the 1950 Population Registration Act functioned as the official racial classification register, and the 1950 Group Areas Act determined the various residential areas designated for each race.

2. The Bantustans were created through the Bantu Authorities Act in 1951 and the Bantu Self-Government Act of 1959 (Beinart 2001; Terreblanche 2002).

3. The forty reports produced by the Goldstone Commission and the hearings from the Truth and Reconciliation Commission (TRC) yielded a great deal of information regarding state support for such vigilantes and the promotion of violence (Shaw 2002: 14).

4. My informants provided the following names of companies that existed during the 1970s: Durban Security, Induna Security, Safeguard Security, AA Security, Springbok Security, and Anderson Security.

5. For example, the security officers at a national key point site fell under government authority, and the Minister of Defence could decide which company would provide security for each particular site (Grant 1989: 107–8).

6. "Dom pas" (literally, dumb pass) was the name given to the passbooks implemented under the Pass Laws of 1923 to control the movement of

non-Whites. All non-Whites were compelled to carry their "dom pas" wherever they went.

7. The term "watchman" refers to a security officer. It is currently regarded as derogatory and is rarely used.

8. Interview: March 13, 2009.

9. Interview: June 30, 2010.

10. Interview: white former owner of an armed response company, June 30, 2010.

11. These individuals are also referred to as the *"bakkie brigade,"* because most of them operated from *bakkies,* a South African term for a pickup truck.

12. SASA still operates as one of the many security associations. Its core function is its monthly publication of *Security Focus,* a journal that is widely read by industry employees.

13. For more detailed information regarding the amalgamation of the armed forces, see Cawthra (2003) and Cock (2005).

14. Interview: April 3, 2009.

15. Interview: April 22, 2010.

16. Interview: June 30, 2010.

17. Furthermore, crime is no longer seen as a post-apartheid phenomenon. Crime was no less common during apartheid, but its prevalence was concealed for political ends, as Kynoch argues: "South Africa's endemic urban violence, in other words, is not a post-conflict affair, but rather a continuation of generations of violence" (2005: 495). Additionally, various crime studies have argued that crime rates post-1994 cannot be compared to crime rates during apartheid, because the latter excluded "black-on-black" crime on the basis that "blacks did not count" (Comaroff and Comaroff 2006b: 220).

18. These feelings were particularly evident during CPF meetings, when crime statistics were released to those in attendance. Citizens often felt that the statistics were inaccurate or wrongly categorized.

19. As highlighted in "A Note on Writing" I focus here on the crime trends at the time of fieldwork and do not include the most recent statistics.

20. Despite a general drop in murder rates since 1995, crime statistics show that murder rates have increased recently (2012–14).

21. The trio crime rates have been obtained from the data provided by the Institute for Security Studies (ISS), and can be found on the ISS website, www .issafrica.org.

22. In fact, recent crime statistics from 2013–14 show an increase in all trio crime rates: house robberies by 7.4 percent, business robberies by 13.7 percent, and carjackings by 12.3 percent (ISS website, http://www.issafrica.org/uploads/ISS -crime-statistics-factsheet-2013-2014.pdf). These statistics only confirm the crucial role that trio crimes play within the larger crime situation in South Africa.

23. Interview: May 12, 2010.

24. There is a lack of reliable data about the amount of private security providers before 1990, as formal regulation and registration only commenced in 1989 with the establishment of the Security Officers Act (SOA). Although data are available from 1990 onwards, the figures for 1989–2001 cannot be compared

to those for 2001–2009. This is because the SOA, which operated between 1989 and 2001, excluded in-house security and private security operating in the homelands, whereas the new database, which was established through PSIRA registration in 2001, does include these forms of security.

25. *Oak* is slang for male.

26. Interview: white former employee of the industry, currently managing an anticrime community organisation, September 10, 2008.

27. Interview: March 13, 2009.

CHAPTER 3

1. See Berg (2010), Button (2003, 2007), Hobbs et al. (2002), Lister et al. (2000), Livingstone and Hart (2003), Loyens (2009), Manzo (2006, 2009), Micucci (1998), Mopas and Stenning (2001), Rigakos (2002), Singh and Kempa (2007), Stenning (2000), van Steden (2007), and Wakefield (2003).

2. Interview: August 28, 2010.

3. Recent figures attest to this claim: between 2013–14, the armed reaction sector grew by 66.06 percent, in comparison to the guarding sector, which experienced a growth of 13.34 percent (PSIRA 2013–14).

4. Interview: SAIDSA administrator, August 18, 2010.

5. Interview: July 6, 2010.

6. Chubb operates throughout South Africa and is owned by United Technologies Fire and Security, which is part of United Technologies Corporation (see www.chubb.co.za and www.utcfireandsecurity.com). ADT operates throughout South Africa and is part of Tyco International, a company operating in fifty countries (see www.adt.co.za and www.tyco.com). BLUE Security is a South African-owned company that only operates in the Durban Metropolitan Area (see www .bluesecurity.co.za).

7. Interview: July 7, 2010.

8. Interview: July 2, 2010.

9. Interview: white marketing manager of a large company, July 7, 2010.

10. Lekker means good/delicious in Afrikaans.

11. Interview: operations manager, April 22, 2010.

12. Interview: September 1, 2010.

13. Interview: July 2, 2010.

14. Interview: owner of a guarding company, September 19, 2008.

15. Interview: February 20, 2009.

16. Interview: April 3, 2009.

17. Interview: March 31, 2009.

18. Interview: operations manager, December 9, 2008.

19. Interview: July 6, 2010.

20. See Button (2007), Micucci (1998), Rigakos (2002), South (1988), van Steden (2007), and Wakefield (2003).

21. Interview: November 5, 2008.

22. Interview: December 9, 2008.

23. Interview: April 22, 2010.

24. See Button (2007), Erickson, Albanese, and Drakulic (2000), Micucci (1998), Monaghan (2002), Rigakos (2002), Sanders (2005), van Steden (2007), and Wakefield (2003).

25. Interview: PSIRA employee, August 17, 2010.

26. Interview: September 29, 2009.

27. Interview: September 18, 2008.

28. Interview: September 1, 2010.

29. Interview: September 19, 2008.

30. Interview: September 18, 2008.

31. Interview: August 26, 2010.

CHAPTER 4

1. Black Label is a brand of beer in South Africa.

2. See Button (2007), Rigakos (2002), Thumala et al. (2011), van Steden (2007), and Wakefield (2003).

3. See for example Livingstone and Hart (2003), McLeod (2002); Michael (cited in Button 2007: 168), and Miccui (1998).

4. This classification thus excludes other security officers, such as bodyguards, bouncers, and private investigators, who are seen as separate because they undergo different types of security training.

5. Rejected applications can be appealed. In 2010–11, 1,348 appeals were made against PISRA's refusal to register or withdraw a security service provider, of which 851 were dismissed and 497 were upheld.

6. The term "inside job" refers to any criminal act that occurs with the assistance of someone on the "inside," such as a security officer or domestic worker.

7. Interview: November 20, 2008.

8. Interview: May 11, 2010.

9. Interview: July 22, 2010. This armed reaction officer also works voluntarily as a police reservist.

10. Interview: November 21, 2008.

11. Interview: November 19, 2008.

12. Elsewhere (Diphoorn 2014), I spelled this as *umantshingelani*. Because various informants provided different spellings of this work, I am unsure of this spelling.

13. Interview: white owner of an armed response and guarding company, September 1, 2010.

14. Interview: June 30, 2010.

15. Throughout my research period, the training standards, qualifications, and regulations were undergoing change. This section thus concerns the conditions from 2008–10 and excludes changes that were implemented after 2010.

16. Grade E was jettisoned in September 2010 as part of a new Sectorial Wage Determination Act. However, because Grade E existed when I underwent security training, it is included in this analysis.

17. Source: http://m.mywage.co.za/main/salary/minimum-wages/domestic-workers-wages.

18. This applies to employers with ten or fewer employees. See: http://www
.mywage.co.za/main/salary/minimum-wages/hospitality.

19. Interview: May 26, 2010.

20. Interview: March 9, 2009.

21. Interview: April 21, 2010.

22. In recent work on Johannesburg, Clarno and Murray (2013: 218) state
that armed response vehicles are increasingly staffed with two officers. However,
this was not the case during my research, and based on recent conversations with
informants, I have the impression that this has not yet been implemented in
Durban.

23. Interview: November 19, 2008. This reference to "old schoolers" once
again highlights how old school policing is associated with a particular time
period.

24. See Button (2007), Loyens (2009), Mopas and Stenning (2001), Stenning
(2000), and Thumala et al. (2011).

25. Interview: August 6, 2010.

26. Interview: May 15, 2010.

27. Although I have remained in touch with many informants, it is possible
that another death has occurred since December 2007 of which I am not aware.

28. Interview: February 3, 2009.

29. Interview: December 9, 2008.

30. *Eish* is a slang expression that conveys one's surprise or confusion. It is
similar to "gosh" or "oh my God."

31. Interview: May 28, 2010.

32. Interview: May 15, 2010.

33. Interview: May 16, 2010.

34. *Kaffir* derives from an Arabic term meaning "disbeliever." In South
Africa, it is a racist word used against Blacks.

35. The armed response officers' perceptions of the state police and the state
as a whole are discussed in more detail in Chapter 5. However, it should be noted
here that Goldstein's (1975) idea of "moral cynicism" also refers to a cynicism
and lack of confidence in state law and legal procedures. It is for this reason that
many scholars, such as Newburn (1999), have posited a link between this and
police corruption.

CHAPTER 5

1. In Durban, there are two public police forces: the Durban Metro City Police (commonly referred to as "metro") responsible for enforcing bylaws such
as parking-related issues, and the South African Police Service (SAPS). Although
there are differences between these two bodies, there is not sufficient space to
discuss these here. The majority of the incidents discussed in this chapter involved
SAPS officers. Furthermore, though armed response officers are aware of the differences between "metro" and "SAPS," they usually use the term "police" in a
generic manner.

2. Interview: owner of a company, April 6, 2009.

3. Interview: March 25, 2009.

4. Interview: March 25, 2009.

5. Interview: owner of a guarding company, March 13, 2009.

6. Interview: former member of PSIRA council, August 24, 2010.

7. Focus group discussion with armed response officers, February 10, 2009.

8. Searching for stolen vehicles and reporting them to the police are the most fundamental parts of the obligation, because many companies retrieve vehicles but do not inform the police (Interview: Operations Manager, KZN Tracker, July 1, 2010).

9. Interview: owner of a company involved in the initiative, July 30, 2010.

10. Interview: member of anticrime community organization, April 1, 2009.

11. These are also known as Extended Station Crime Combating Forum (ESCCF) meetings or Station Crime Combating Forum (SCCF) meetings.

12. Interview: April 3, 2009.

13. Interview: owner of a company, August 26, 2010.

14. Interview: May 8, 2010.

15. During a chat with the guard awhile later, without the police officers present, he told me that the rules are strict because there were criminals living in the apartment complex. He recalled an incident from the previous month in which stolen vehicles were recovered in the parking lot of the building and a resident was arrested.

16. Interview: police officer, April 21, 2010.

17. Interview: August 4, 2010.

18. Interview: March 15, 2009.

19. Interview: May 6, 2010. The term "active policers" refers to individuals who are involved in policing in various ways.

20. Interview: police superintendent, April 3, 2009.

21. "Location" was the term used for non-white urban areas until the 1960s, when "township" became more common. The two continue to be used synonymously.

22. Interview: January 29, 2009.

23. Interview: March 3, 2009.

24. See Ayling and Shearing (2008), Crawford and Lister (2006), Davis (2009), Grabosky (2004), and Reiss (1987).

25. Interview: April 21, 2010.

26. Interview: former police officer, April 26, 2010.

27. Taxi violence refers to violence between taxi owners over transport routes. In KwaZulu-Natal, taxi violence was closely linked to the political violence between the ANC and IFP (Beinart 2001).

28. Interview: security consultant, April 26, 2010.

29. Interview: police officer, April 30, 2010.

30. Interview: former police officer, August 16, 2010.

31. Interview: police reservist, May 6, 2010.

32. Interview: PSIRA employee, August 17, 2010.

33. Interview: police reservist, May 6, 2010.

34. Interview: police reservist, August 6, 2010.

35. Interview: joint interview with two owners of private security companies, April 22, 2010.

36. Interview: police reservist, August 31, 2010.

37. Interview: owner of private security company and ex-police officer, July 30, 2010.

38. Interview: former police officer, April 26, 2010.

39. Interview: security consultant, April 26, 2010.

40. Interview: owner of private security company and ex-police officer, July 30, 2010.

41. It is common to register the company in a family member's name. The income accrued from the company's profits can then be labeled as a "family gift."

42. Interview: April 30, 2010.

43. Interview: former PSIRA council member, August 26, 2008.

44. Interview: former PSIRA council member, May 25, 2010.

45. Interview: police officer, April 30, 2010. "Docket" refers to a police case/document.

46. Interview: owner of private security company, August 2, 2010.

47. Interview: police officer, April 30, 2010.

48. Interview: two owners of private security companies, April 22, 2010.

49. Interview: April 30, 2010.

50. Interview: co-owner of a private security company, August 6, 2010.

51. Interview: May 6, 2010.

52. This option also leaves the suspect's car unattended. At one point, David and Matthew consider having me drive the suspect's vehicle to the police station. However, I quickly make it clear I will not get involved.

53. Sharing a police radio is illegal, and the police officer was risking his job by permitting it.

54. Interview: operations manager, KZN Tracker, July 1, 2010.

55. Interview: white owner of an armed response company, September 1, 2010.

56. They were released the following night, having spent just over twenty-four hours in jail.

57. Interview: May 22, 2010.

58. Interview: May 25, 2010.

59. Interview: November 20, 2008.

CHAPTER 6

1. For literature on a wide range of forms of community policing in South Africa, see Bénit-Gbaffou (2008), Emmett and Butchart (2000), Marks and Bonnin (2010), Marks and Wood (2007), Schärf (1989), and Steinberg (2008).

2. Interview: November 27, 2008.

3. Interview: July 7, 2010.

4. Roberts (2010) further states that individuals who described feeling safe also expressed more trust in the state police, and correspondingly, those who described fearing for their safety expressed more distrust and lower levels of

confidence in the state police. However, although levels of distrust remained the same between 2000 and 2005, levels of trust in the state police rose from 41 to 45 percent.

5. The perception of the police force as corrupt is most likely influenced by recent corruption cases involving two former police chiefs, Jackie Selebi and Bheki Cele. Jackie Selebi was appointed police chief of South Africa in 2000 and was elected Interpol president in 2004. He resigned from both duties in 2008 due to allegations of corruption. Selebi was charged with accepting bribes worth of 1.2 million rand and having active links to organized crime. His prison term started in December 2011, but he was released from prison in July 2012 for health reasons. President Jacob Zuma appointed Bheki Cele as police chief in 2010, but in October of the following year Cele was charged with corruption and suspended from office. Cele's predecessor was Mangwashi Phiyega, South Africa's first female police chief.

6. Interview: December 1, 2008.

7. For further information on this issue, see Crawford and Lister (2006), McManus (1995), Noaks (2000), Sharp and Wilson (2000), and Wakefield (2007).

8. Interview: July 7, 2010.

9. Interview: marketing manager of a large company, July 2, 2010.

10. "Domestic watch" training refers to security training given to domestic workers.

11. Interview: marketing manager, July 7, 2010.

12. Interview: marketing manager of a large company, July 7, 2010.

13. Interview: July 7, 2010.

14. Interview: operations manager, December 9, 2008.

15. Interview: December 10, 2008.

16. Interview: May 19, 2010.

17. Interview: manager, July 19, 2010.

18. Interview: founder of the SMS initiative, February 2, 2009.

19. Interview: founder of the SMS initiative, February 2, 2009.

20. Interviews: April 1, 2009 and August 10, 2010.

21. Interview: manager, April 21, 2010.

22. *Braai* is a South African term for a barbecue. As these commonly occur, apartment complexes often have designated areas for them.

23. It is likely that these figures have changed since this time.

24. Interview: white female member of collective C, August 11, 2010.

25. Interview: member of executive committee of collective B, April 16, 2009.

26. Magtouch is an electronic system used to monitor the patrols of security officers. This system involves security officers, most commonly guards, using a patrol baton to "check in" on different locations during their patrol. For more information, see the website: http://www.mag-touch.com.

27. Interview: road captain of collective D, April 30, 2009.

28. The officer from the company stated that he was made to lie about finding the suspect exiting the house with the stolen goods, which he denied having witnessed.

29. The "truth" about this incident never surfaced. Not long after the event, both of the individuals involved were arrested for separate Schedule One offenses

and are currently imprisoned. Examples of Schedule One offences are murder, fraud, sabotage, rape, kidnapping, and extortion.

30. Interview: February 10, 2009.

31. I use the term "neighborhood watch" because this was how the organizations defined themselves.

32. A police reservist is a member of the community who volunteers his services to perform policing functions or activities for the South African Police Service without being remunerated for such service. Definition obtained from the South African Police Services (SAPS) website: http://www.saps.gov.za/comm _pol/reservists/reservist_index.htm.

33. Interview: May 6, 2010.

34. Interview: police reservist, May 6, 2010.

35. Vikayiphi worked closely with Miles Steenhuisen, whom he befriended after a lawnmower was stolen from Miles's garden and they retrieved it together. Interview: March 23, 2009.

36. During a brief return to the field in 2011, I heard that he was working as an armed response officer for a community-based company.

37. Interview: February 17, 2009.

38. Interview: April 10, 2009.

39. Interview: December 2, 2008.

40. Interview: September 4, 2008.

41. Interview: August 16, 2010.

42. Interview: September 23, 2008.

43. Interview: April 19, 2009.

44. Interview: February 27, 2009.

45. Interview: an active policer, February 23, 2009.

46. Source: minutes from Annual General Meeting (AGM) of collective B, March 18, 2009.

47. Interview: August 11, 2010.

CHAPTER 7

1. See Barba (1995), Beeman (1993), Kapferer (1986), and Schechner (1985).

2. "Coolie" is a derogative term for Indian South Africans.

3. Needless to say, the company did not respond to all 12,000 of these calls.

4. Interview: April 24, 2009.

5. Interview: May 11, 2010.

6. Interview: February 10, 2009.

7. Digital newsletter of an anticrime community organization: August 4, 2011.

8. Digital newsletter of an anticrime community organization: April 19, 2009.

9. CIT refers to the cash-in-transit sector.

10. Interview: May 28, 2010.

11. Interview: May 25, 2010.

12. Interview: May 11, 2010.

13. *Swart gevaar* is an Afrikaans term meaning "black threat."

14. Interview: February 27, 2009.

15. Interview: February 17, 2009.

16. Interview: August 26, 2010.
17. Interview: November 20, 2008.
18. Interview: November 22, 2008.
19. Interview: July 22, 2010.
20. Interview: December 4, 2008.
21. Interview: December 4, 2008.
22. Interview: November 28, 2008.

Glossary

BAKKIE Pickup truck.

BLACK LABEL Brand of South African beer.

COOLIE Derogatory term for Indian South Africans.

DOCKET Police case/document.

DOM PASSES Afrikaans for "dumb pass." Passbooks implemented under the Pass Laws of 1923 to control the movement of non-Whites.

EISH An expression to show one's surprise, confusion, anger, or other emotion (slang). Similar to "gosh" or "oh my God".

GRAPH Work (slang).

KAFFIR Derogatory word for black South Africans; derived from Arabic term for "unbeliever."

LOCATION Synonym for township.

MACHINJINGILANI isiZulu for "marching the line". Refers to security guards and is currently regarded as a derogatory term.

NECKLACING A form of lethal punishment, often described as lynching, whereby a rubber tire is filled with petrol, placed around a person's chest or arms, and set on fire.

OAK Male (slang).

SKOP, SKIET EN DONDER Afrikaans for "Kick, shoot, and thunder." Refers to the mentality of the state police during apartheid.

STEKKIE Woman (slang).

SWART GEVAAR Afrikaans for "black threat."

TOWNSHIP Area (residential) designated for non-Whites during apartheid. Also referred to as a "location."

Bibliography

Abrahams, Ray G. 1998. *Vigilant Citizens: Vigilantism and the State.* Malden, MA: Polity Press.

Abrahamsen, Rita, and Michael C. Williams. 2011. *Security beyond the State: Private Security in International Politics.* Cambridge: Cambridge University Press.

———. 2007. "Securing the City: Private Security Companies and Non-State Authority in Global Governance." *International Relations* 21 (2): 237–53.

Abrams, Philip. 2006. "Notes on the Difficulty of Studying the State." In *The Anthropology of the State: A Reader*, edited by Aradhana Sharma and Anal Gupta. Oxford: Blackwell Publishing, 112–30.

Agamben, Giorgio. 1998. *Homo Sacer: Sovereign Power and Bare Life.* Stanford: Stanford University Press.

———. 2005. *State of Exception.* Chicago: University of Chicago Press.

Albrecht, Peter, and Louise Wuiff Moe. 2015. "The Simultaneity of Authority in Hybrid Orders." *Peacebuilding* 3 (1): 1–16.

Altbeker, Antony. 2007. *A Country at War with Itself: South Africa's Crisis of Crime.* Jeppestown, South Africa: Jonathan Ball Publishers.

Amit, Vered. 2002. "Reconceptualizing Community." In *Realizing Community. Concepts, Social Relationships and Sentiments*, edited by Vered Amit. London: Routledge, 1–20.

Amit, Vered and Nigel Rapport. 2002. *The Trouble with Community: Anthropological Reflections on Movement, Identity and Collectivity.* London: Pluto Press.

Appadurai, Arjun. 2003. "Sovereignty without Territoriality: Notes for a Postnational Geography." In *The Anthropology of Space and Place: Locating Culture*, edited by Setha M. Low and Denise Lawrence-Zúñiga. Oxford: Blackwell Publishing, 337–49.

Arias, Enrique Desmond. 2006, "The Dynamics of Criminal Governance: Networks and Social Order in Rio de Janeiro." *Journal of Latin American Studies* 38 (2): 293–325.

Arias, Enrique Desmond and Daniel M. Goldstein, eds. 2010. *Violent Democracies in Latin America*. Durham: Duke University Press.

Ashforth, Adam. 2005. *Witchcraft, Violence, and Democracy in South Africa*. Chicago: University of Chicago Press.

Avant, Deborah D. 2005. *The Market for Force: The Consequences of Privatizing Security*. Cambridge: Cambridge University Press.

Ayling, Julie and Clifford Shearing. 2008. "Taking Care of Business: Public Police as Commercial Security Vendors." *Criminology and Criminal Justice* 8 (1): 27–50.

Baker, Bruce. 2010. *Security in Post-Conflict Africa: The Role of Nonstate Policing*. Boca Raton, FL: CRC Press.

———. 2008. *Multi-Choice Policing in Africa*. Uppsala: Nordiska Afrikainstitutet.

Ballard, Richard. 2005. "When in Rome: Claiming the Right to Define Neighbourhood Character in South Africa's Suburbs." *Transformation* 57: 64–87.

Barba, Eugenio. 1995. *The Paper Canoe: A Guide to Theatre Anthropology*. London: Routledge.

Barth, Fredrik. 1969. "Introduction." In *Ethnic Groups and Boundaries. The Social Organization of Cultural Difference*, edited by Fredrik Barth. Bergen: Universitets Forlaget, 9–38.

Bauman, Zygmunt. 2001. *Community: Seeking Safety in an Insecure World*. Cambridge, MA: Polity Press.

Bayart, Jean-François, Stephen Ellis, and Béatrice Hibou, eds. 1999. *The Criminalization of the State in Africa*. Oxford: James Currey.

Bayley, David H. and Clifford D. Shearing. 2001. *The New Structure of Policing: Description, Conceptualization, and Research Agenda*. Washington, DC: National Institute of Justice.

Beall, Jo, Owen Crankshaw, and Susan Parnell. 2002. *Uniting a Divided City: Governance and Social Exclusion in Johannesburg*. London: Earthscan Publications.

Beck, Ulrich. 1992. *Risk Society: Towards a New Modernity*. London: Sage Publications.

Beek, Jan. 2012. "'There Should Be No Open Doors in the Police': Criminal Investigations in Northern Ghana as Boundary Work." *Journal of Modern African Studies* 50 (4): 551–72.

Beek, Jan and Mirco Göpfert. 2013. "Police Violence in West Africa: Perpetrators' and Ethnographers' Dilemmas." *Ethnography* 14 (4): 477–500.

Beeman, William O. 1993. "The Anthropology of Theater and Spectacle." *Annual Review of Anthropology* 22: 369–93.

Beinart, William. 2001. *Twentieth-Century South Africa*. Oxford: Oxford University Press.

Benda-Beckmann, Keebet von and Fernanda Pirie, eds. 2007. *Order and Disorder: Anthropological Perspectives*. New York: Berghahn Books.

Bénit-Gbaffou, Claire. 2008. "Community Policing and Disputed Norms for Local Social Control in Post-Apartheid Johannesburg." *Journal of Southern African Studies* 34 (1): 93–109.

Berg, Julie. 2010. "Seeing like Private Security: Evolving Mentalities of Public Space Protection in South Africa." *Criminology and Criminal Justice* 10 (3): 287–301.

———. 2004a. "Challenges to a Formal Private Security Industry-SAPS Partnership: Lessons from the Western Cape." *Society in Transition* 35 (1): 105–24.

———. 2004b. "Private Policing in South Africa: The Cape Town City Improvement District—Pluralisation in Practice." *Society in Transition* 35 (2): 224–50.

———. 2003. "The Private Security Industry in South Africa: A Review of Applicable Legislation." *South African Journal of Criminal Justice* 16: 178–96.

Bertelsen, Bjørn Enge. 2009. "Multiple Sovereignties and Summary Justice in Mozambique: A Critique of Some Legal Anthropological Terms." *Social Analysis* 53 (3): 123–47.

Besteman, Caroline Lowe, ed. 2002. *Violence: A Reader.* New York: Palgrave MacMillan.

Boghosian, Heidi. 2005. "Applying Restraints to Private Police." *Modern Law Review* 70: 177–218.

Bourdieu, Pierre. 2002. *Language and Symbolic Power.* Cambridge: Polity Press.

Bourke, Joanna. 2005. *Fear: A Cultural History.* London: Virago Press.

Braun, Michael and David Lee. 1970/1971. "Private Police Forces: Legal Powers and Limitations." *University of Chicago Law Review* 38: 555–82.

Brewer, John D. 1994. *Black and Blue: Policing in South Africa.* New York: Clarendon Press.

Brodeur, Jean-Paul. 2010. *The Policing Web.* Oxford: Oxford University Press.

Brogden, Mike and Clifford Shearing. 1993. *Policing for a New South Africa.* London: Routledge.

Brookfield, H. C. and M. A. Tatham. 1957. "The Distribution of Racial Groups in Durban: The Background of Apartheid in a South African City." *Geographical Review* 47 (1): 44–65.

Brown, Jeffrey and Randy Lippert. 2007. "Private Security's Purchase: Imaginings of a Security Patrol in a Canadian Residential Neighbourhood." *Canadian Journal of Criminology and Criminal Justice* 49 (5): 587–616.

Brown, Jennifer. 2007. "From Cult of Masculinity to Smart Macho: Gender Perspectives on Police Occupational Culture." In *Police Occupational Culture: New Debates and Directions*, edited by Megan O'Neill, Monique Marks, and Anne-Marie Singh. Amsterdam: Elsevier, 205–26.

Bruce, David. 2011. "Beyond Section 49: Control of the Use of Lethal Force." *SA Crime Quarterly* 36: 3–12.

Burger, Johan, Chandre Gould, and Gareth Newham. 2011. "An Analysis of the SAPS Crime Statistics for 2009/10—Can We Rely on Them?" *Security Focus* 29 (1): 30–35.

Butler, Judith. 1997. *Excitable Speech: A Politics of the Performative.* New York: Routledge.

Button, Mark. 2007. *Security Officers and Policing: Powers, Culture and Control in the Governance of Private Space.* Aldershot: Ashgate Publishing.

———. 2003. "Private Security and the Policing of Quasi-Public Space." *International Journal of the Sociology of Law* 31 (3): 227–37.

———. 2002. *Private Policing.* Devon: Willan Publishing.

Buur, Lars. 2006. "Reordering Society: Vigilantism and Expressions of Sovereignty in Port Elizabeth's Townships." *Development and Change* 37 (4): 735–57.

———. 2005. "The Sovereign Outsourced: Local Justice and Violence in Port Elizabeth." In *Sovereign Bodies: Citizens, Migrants, and States in the Postcolonial World*, edited by Thomas Blom Hansen and Finn Stepputat. Princeton: Princeton University Press, 192–217.

Buur, Lars and Steffen Jensen. 2004. "Introduction: Vigilantism and the Policing of Everyday Life in South Africa." *African Studies* 63 (2): 139–52.

Buur, Lars, Steffen Jensen, and Finn Stepputat. 2007. "Introduction: The Security-Development Nexus." In *The Security-Development Nexus: Expressions of Sovereignty and Securitization in Southern Africa*, edited by Lars Buur, Steffen Jensen, and Finn Stepputat. Cape Town: HSRC Press, 9–33.

Buzan, Barry, Ole Wæver, and Jaap de Wilde. 1998. *Security: A New Framework for Analysis.* Boulder: Lynne Rienner Publishers.

Caldeira, Teresa P. R. 2002. "The Paradox of Police Violence in Democratic Brazil." *Ethnography* 3 (3): 235–63.

———. 2000. *City of Walls: Crime, Segregation, and Citizenship in Sao Paulo.* Berkeley: University of California Press.

Campbell, Rebecca. 2002. *Emotionally Involved: The Impact of Researching Rape.* New York: Routledge.

Çankaya, Sinan. 2015. "Professional Anomalies: Diversity Policies Policing Ethnic Minority Police Officers." *European Journal of Policing Studies* (forthcoming).

———. 2011. *Buiten veiliger dan binnen: in- en uitsluiting van etnische minderheden binnen de politieorganisatie.* Delft: Academische Uitgeverij Eburon.

Carlson, Marvin. 2004. "What Is Performance?" In *The Performance Studies Reader*, edited by Henry Bial. Second edition. London: Routledge, 70–75.

Carothers, Thomas. 2002. "The End of the Transition Paradigm." *Journal of Democracy* 13 (1): 5–21.

Cawthra, Gavin. 2003. "Security Transformation in Post-Apartheid South Africa." In *Governing Insecurity: Democratic Control of Military and Security Establishments in Transitional Democracies*, edited by Gavin Cawthra and Robin Luckham. London: Zed Books, 31–56.

Chan, Janet B. 2007. "Police Stress and Occupational Culture." In *Policing Occupational Culture: New Debates and Directions*, edited by Megan O'Neill, Monique Marks, and Anne-Marie Singh. Amsterdam: Elsevier, 129–52.

———. 1997. *Changing Police Culture: Policing in a Multicultural Society.* Cambridge: Cambridge University Press.

Chipkin, Ivor. 2007. *Do South Africans Exist? Nationalism, Democracy and the Identity of "the People."* Johannesburg: Wits University Press.

Chisholm, Amanda. 2014. "Marketing the Gurkha Security Package: Colonial Histories and Neoliberal Economies of Private Security." *Security Dialogue* 45 (4): 349–72.

Clarno, Andy and Martin J. Murray. 2013. "Policing in Johannesburg after Apartheid." *Social Dynamics: A Journal of African Studies* 39 (2): 210–27.

Cock, Jacklyn. 2005. " 'Guards and Guns': Towards Privatised Militarism in Post-Apartheid South Africa." *Journal of Southern African Studies* 31 (4): 791–803.

Cock, Jacklyn and Laurie Nathan, eds. 1989. *War and Society: The Militarisation of South Africa*. Cape Town: David Philip.

Cohen, Albert Kircidel. 1966. *Deviance and Control*. Englewood Cliffs, NJ: Prentice-Hall.

Comaroff, Jean and John L. Comaroff. 2006a. "Law and Disorder in the Postcolony: An Introduction." In *Law and Disorder in the Postcolony*, edited by Jean Comaroff and John L. Comaroff. Chicago: University of Chicago Press, 1–56.

———. 2006b. "Figuring Crime: Quantifacts and the Production of the Un/ Real." *Public Culture* 18 (1): 209–46.

Crawford, Adam. 2006. "Policing and Security as 'Club Goods': The New Enclosures?" In *Democracy, Society and the Governance of Security*, edited by Jennifer Wood and Benoît Dupont. Cambridge: Cambridge University Press, 111–38.

———. 1996. *The Local Governance of Crime: Appeals to Community and Partnerships*. Oxford: Clarendon Press.

Crawford, Adam and Stuart Lister. 2006. "Additional Security Patrols in Residential Areas: Notes from the Marketplace." *Policing and Society* 16 (2): 164–88.

Das, Veena and Deborah Poole. 2004. "State and Its Margins: Comparative Ethnographies." In *Anthropology in the Margins of the State*, edited by Veena Das and Deborah Poole. Santa Fe, NM: School of American Research Press, 3–33.

Das, Veena, Arthur Kleinman, Mamphela Ramphele, and Pamela Reynolds, eds. 2000. *Violence and Subjectivity*. Berkeley: University of California Press.

Davies, R. J. 1981. "The Spatial Formation of the South African City." *GeoJournal* 2: 59–72.

Davis, Diane E. 2010. "Irregular Armed Forces, Shifting Patterns of Commitment, and Fragmented Sovereignty in the Developing World." *Theory and Society* 39 (3–4): 397–413.

———. 2009. "Non-State Armed Actors, New Imagined Communities, and Shifting Patterns of Sovereignty and Insecurity in the Modern World." *Contemporary Security Policy* 30 (2): 221–45.

Denzin, Norman K. 1997. *Interpretive Ethnography: Ethnographic Practices for the 21st Century*. Thousand Oaks, CA: Sage Publications.

Derrida, Jacques. 1992. "Force of Law: The 'Mystical Foundations of Authority.' " In *Deconstruction and the Possibility of Justice*, edited by Drucilla Cornell, Michel Rosenfeld, and David Gray Carlson. New York: Routledge, 3–67.

De Waard, Jaap. 1999. "The Private Security Industry in International Perspective." *European Journal on Criminal Policy and Research* 7: 143–74.

DeWalt, Kathleen M. and Billie R. DeWalt. 2002. *Participant Observation: A Guide for Fieldworkers*. Walnut Creek, CA: AltaMira Press.

Diphoorn, Tessa. 2015. "'It's All about the Body': The Bodily Capital of Armed Response Officers in Durban, South Africa." *Medical Anthropology* 12: 1–17.

———. 2014. "The Private Security Industry in Urban Management." In *Urban Governance in Post-Apartheid Cities: Modes of Engagement in South Africa's Metropoles*, edited by Christoph Haferburg and Marie Huchzermeyer. Stuttgart: Schweizerbart, 197–209.

———. 2013. "The Emotionality of Participation: Various Modes of Participation in Ethnographic Fieldwork on Private Policing in Durban, South Africa." *Journal of Contemporary Ethnography* 42 (2): 201–25.

Diphoorn, Tessa and Julie Berg. 2014. "Typologies of Partnership Policing: Case Studies from Urban South Africa." *Policing and Society* 24 (4): 425–42.

Douglas, Mary. 2002. *Purity and Danger*. Second edition. New York: Routledge.

———. 1986. *Risk Acceptability According to the Social Sciences*. London: Routledge and Kegan Paul.

Dupont, Benoît. 2006. "Mapping Security Networks: From Metaphorical Concept to Empirical Model." In *Fighting Crime Together: The Challenges of Policing and Security Networks*, edited by Jenny Fleming and Jennifer Wood. Sydney: University of New South Wales Press, 35–59.

———. 2004. "Security in the Age of Networks." *Policing and Society* 14 (1): 76–91.

Ellis, Stephen. 1998. "The Historical Significance of South Africa's Third Force." *Journal of Southern African Studies* 24 (2): 261–99.

Emmett, Tony and Alex Butchart, eds. 2000. *Behind the Mask: Getting to Grips with Crime and Violence in South Africa*. Pretoria: HSRC Publishers.

Erickson, Bonnie H., Patricia Albanese, and Slobodan Drakulic. 2000. "Gender on a Jagged Edge: The Security Industry, Its Clients, and the Reproduction and Revision of Gender." *Work and Occupation* 27 (3): 294–318.

Ericson, Richard. 1994. "The Division of Expert Knowledge in Policing and Security." *British Journal of Sociology* 45 (2): 149–75.

Fassin, Didier. 2013. *Enforcing Order: An Ethnography of Urban Policing*. Cambridge: Polity Press.

Faull, Andrew. 2010. *Behind the Badge: The Untold Ttories of South Africa's Police Service Members*. Cape Town: Zebra Press.

Findlay, Mark and Uglješa Zvekić. 1993. *Alternative Policing Styles: Cross-Cultural Perspectives*. Deventer: Kluwer Law and Taxation Publishers.

Fine, Derrick. 1989. "Kitskonstabels: A Case Study in Black on Black Policing." *Acta Juridica* 44–85.

Foucault, Michel. 1977. *Discipline and Punish: The Birth of the Prison*. London: Penguin Books.

Franzén, Mats. 2001. "Urban Order and the Preventive Restructuring of Space: The Operation of Border Controls in Micro Space." *Sociological Review* 49 (2): 202–318.

Freeland-Hughes, Felicia. 1998. "Introduction." In *Ritual, Performance, Media*, edited by Felicia Freeland-Hughes. London: Routledge, 1–28.

Galtung, Johan. 1969. "Violence, Peace, and Peace Research." *Journal of Peace Research* 6 (3): 167–91.

Gans, Jeremy. 2000. "Privately Paid Public Policing: Law and Practice." *Policing and Society* 10 (2): 183–206.

Garland, David. 1996. "The Limits of the Sovereign State: Strategies of Crime Control in Contemporary Society." *British Journal of Criminology* 36 (4): 445–71.

Garriot, William, ed. 2013. *Policing and Contemporary Governance: The Anthropology of Police in Practice*. London: Palgrave MacMillan.

Ghassem-Fachandi, Parvis, ed. 2009. *Violence: Ethnographic Encounters*. Oxford: Berg.

Glaser, Clive. 2005. "Whistles and Sjamboks: Crime and Policing in Soweto, 1960–1976." *South African Historical Journal* 52 (1): 119–39.

———. 2000. *Bo-Tsotsi: The Youth Gangs of Soweto, 1935–1975*. Oxford: James Currey.

Godoy, Angelina Snodgrass. 2004. "When "Justice" Is Criminal: Lynchings in Contemporary Latin America." *Theory and Society* 33 (6): 621–51.

Goffman, Erving. 1959. *The Presentation of Self in Everyday Life*. London: Penguin.

Goldstein, Daniel M. 2012. *Outlawed: Between Security and Rights in a Bolivian City*. Durham: Duke University Press.

———. 2010. "Toward a Critical Anthropology of Security." *Current Anthropology* 51 (4): 487–517.

———. 2004. *The Spectacular City: Violence and Performance in Urban Bolivia*. Durham: Duke University Press.

Goldstein, Herman. 1975. *Police Corruption: A Perspective on Its Nature and Control*. Washington, DC: Police Foundation.

Goold, Benjamin, Ian Loader, and Angelica Thumala. 2010. "Consuming Security? Tools for a Sociology of Security Consumption." *Theoretical Criminology* 14 (1): 3–30.

Göpfert, Mirco. 2012. "Security in Niamey: An Anthropological Perspective on Policing and an Act of Terrorism in Niger." *Journal of Modern African Studies* 50 (1): 53–74.

Gordon, Diana. 2006. *Transformation and Trouble: Crime, Justice, and Participation in Democratic South Africa*. Ann Arbor: University of Michigan Press.

Grabosky, Peter. 2004. "Toward a Theory of Public/Private Interaction in Policing." In *Beyond Empiricism: Institutions and Intentions in the Study of Crime. Advances in Criminological Theory*, edited by Joan McCord. Piscataway, NJ: Transaction Books, 69–82.

Grant, Evadne. 1989. "Private Policing." *Acta Juridica* 92–117.

Grassiani, Erella. 2013. *Soldiering under Occupation: Processes of Numbing among Israeli Soldiers in the Al-Aqsa Intifada*. New York: Berghahn Books.

Gumedze, Sabelo, ed. 2007. *Private Security in Africa: Manifestation, Challenges and Regulation*. Pretoria: Institute for Security Studies (ISS).

Habib, Adam and Kristina Bentley, eds. 2008. *Racial Redress and Citizenship in South Africa*. Cape Town: HSRC Publishing.

Hall, Stuart, Chas Critcher, Tony Jefferson, John Clarke, and Brian Roberts. 1978. *Policing the Crisis: Mugging, the State, and Law and Order*. New York: Palgrave Macmillan.

Hansen, Thomas Blom. 2012. *Melancholia of Freedom: Social Life in an Indian Township in South Africa.* Princeton: Princeton University Press.

———. 2006. "Performers of Sovereignty: On the Privatisation of Security in Urban South Africa." *Critique of Anthropology* 26 (3): 279–95.

———. 2005. "Sovereigns beyond the State: On Legality and Authority in Urban India." In *Sovereign Bodies: Citizens, Migrants, and States in the Postcolonial World*, edited by Thomas Blom Hansen and Finn Stepputat. Princeton: Princeton University Press, 169–91.

Hansen, Thomas Blom and Finn Stepputat. 2006. "Sovereignty Revisited." *Annual Review of Anthropology* 35: 295–315.

———. 2005a. *Sovereign Bodies: Citizens, Migrants, and States in the Postcolonial World.* Princeton: Princeton University Press.

———. 2005b. "Introduction." In *Sovereign Bodies: Citizens, Migrants, and States in the Postcolonial World*, edited by Thomas Blom and Finn Stepputat. Princeton: Princeton University Press, 1–36.

———. 2001. "Introduction: States of Imagination." In *States of Imagination: Ethnographic Explorations of the Postcolonial State*, edited by Thomas Blom and Finn Stepputat. Princeton: Princeton University Press, 1–39.

Harnischfeger, Johannes. 2003. "The Bakassi Boys: Fighting Crime in Nigeria." *Journal of Modern African Studies* 41 (1): 23–49.

Hastrup, Kirsten. 1992. "Out of Anthropology: The Anthropologist as an Object of Dramatic Representation." *Cultural Anthropology* 7 (3): 327–45.

Heald, Suzette. 2005. "State, Law, and Vigilantism in Northern Tanzania." *African Affairs* 105 (419): 265–83.

Hentschel, Christine. 2011. "Outcharming Crime in (D)urban Space." *Social Dynamics* 37 (1): 148–64.

Heyman, Josiah McC. and Alan Smart, eds. 1999. *States and Illegal Practices.* Oxford: Berg.

Higate, Paul. 2012. "Drinking Vodka from the 'Butt-Crack': Men, Masculinities, and Fratriarchy in the Privatized Military Security Company." *International Feminist Journal of Politics* 14 (4): 450–69.

Hobbs, Dick, Philip Hadfield, Stuart Lister, and Simon Winlow. 2002. "'Door Lore': The Art and Economics of Intimidation." *British Journal of Criminology* 42: 352–70.

Hornberger, Julia. 2013. "From General to Commissioner to General—On the Popular State of Policing in South Africa." *Law & Social Inquiry* 38 (3): 598–614.

———. 2011. *Policing and Human Rights: The Meaning of Violence and Justice in the Everyday Policing of Johannesburg.* New York: Routledge.

Huggins, Martha D., ed. 1991. *Vigilantism and the State in Modern Latin America: Essays on Extralegal Violence.* New York: Praeger.

Huggins, Martha and Marie-Louise Glebbeek, eds. 2009. *Women Fielding Danger: Negotiating Ethnographic Identities in Field Research.* Plymouth, UK: Rowman & Littlefield.

Hummer, Don and Mahesh Nalla. 2003. "Modeling Future Relations between the Private and Public Sectors of Law Enforcement." *Criminal Justice Studies* 16 (2): 87–96.

Humphrey, Caroline. 2007. "Sovereignty." In *A Companion to the Anthropology of Politics*, edited by David Nugent and Joan Vincent. Oxford: Blackwell Publishing, 418–36.

Irish, Jenny. 2000. "The Business of Private Policing in South Africa: Sentry Security and the Armed Response Sector." In *The Public Accountability of Private Police: Lessons from New York, Johannesburg and Mexico City.* New York: Vera Institute of Justice, 21–33.

———. 1999. *Policing for Profit: The Future of South Africa's Private Security Industry.* Pretoria: ISS.

Jackson, Jonathan. 2004. "Experience and Expression: Social and Cultural Significance in the Fear of Crime." *British Journal of Criminology* 44 (6): 946–66.

Jaffe, Rivke. 2013. "The Hybrid State: Crime and Citizenship in Urban Jamaica." *American Ethnologist* 40 (4): 734–48.

Jauregui, Beatrice. 2013. "Beatings, Beacons, and Big Men: Police Disempowerment and Delegitimation in India." *Law and Social Inquiry* 38 (3): 643–69.

Jeffrey, Alex. 2013. *The Improvised State: Sovereignty, Performance and Agency in Dayton Bosnia.* Malden, MA: Wiley-Blackwell.

Jensen, Steffen. 2014. "Conflicting Logics of Exceptionality: New Beginnings and the Problem of Police Violence in Post-Apartheid South Africa." *Development and Change* 45 (3): 458–78.

———. 2008. *Gangs, Politics and Dignity in Cape Town.* Oxford: James Currey.

———. 2007. "Policing Nkomazi: Crime, Masculinity and Generational Conflicts." In *Global Vigilantes*, edited by David Pratten and Atreyee Sen. London: Hurst Publishers, 47–68.

———. 2005. "The South African Transition: From Development to Security?" *Development and Change* 36 (3): 551–70.

Joachim, Jutta and Andrea Schneiker. 2012. "Of 'True Professionals' and 'Ethical Hero Warriors': A Gender-Discourse Analysis of Private Military and Security Companies." *Security Dialogue* 43 (6): 495–512.

Joh, Elizabeth E. 2005. "Conceptualizing the Private Police." *Utah Law Review* 573–617.

Johnston, Les. 2003. "From 'Pluralisation' to 'the Police Extended Family': Discourses on the Governance of Community Policing in Britain." *International Journal of the Sociology of Law* 31 (3): 185–204.

———. 1996. "What is Vigilantism?" *British Journal of Criminology* 36 (2): 220–36.

———. 1992. *The Rebirth of Private Policing.* London: Routledge.

Johnston, Les and Clifford D. Shearing. 2003. *Governing Security: Explorations in Policing and Justice.* London: Routledge.

Jones, Gareth A. and Dennis Rodgers, eds. 2009. *Youth Violence in Latin America: Gangs and Juvenile Justice in Perspective.* New York: Palgrave Macmillan.

Jones, Trevor and Tim Newburn, eds. 2006. *Plural Policing: A Comparative Perspective.* London: Routledge.

———. 1998. *Private Security and Public Policing.* Oxford: Clarendon Press.

Kapferer, Bruce. 2005. "New Formations of Power, the Oligarchic-Corporate State, and Anthropological Ideological Discourse." *Anthropological Theory* 5 (3): 285–99.

———. 2004. "Democracy, Wild Sovereignties and the New Leviathan." *Bulletin of the Royal Institute for Inter-Faith Studies* 6 (2): 23–38.

———. 1986. "Performance and the Structuring of Meaning and Experience." In *The Anthropology of Experience*, edited by Victor W. Turner and Edward M. Bruner. Urbana: University of Illinois Press, 188–206.

Kapferer, Bruce and Bjørn Enge Bertelsen. 2012. "Introduction: The Crisis of Power and Reformations of the State in Globalizing Realities." In *Crisis of the State: War and Social Upheaval*, edited by Bruce Kapferer and Bjørn Enge Bertelsen. New York: Berghahn Books, 1–26.

Kempa, Michael, Ryan Carrier, Jennifer Wood, and Clifford Shearing. 1999. "Reflections on the Evolving Concept of 'Private Policing.'" *European Journal on Criminal Policy and Research* 7: 197–223.

Kempa, Michael and Anne-Marie Singh. 2008. "Private Security, Political Economy and the Policing of Race: Probing Global Hypotheses through the Case of South Africa." *Theoretical Criminology* 12 (3): 333–54.

Kempa, Michael, Philip Stenning, and Jennifer Wood. 2004. "Policing Communal Spaces. A Reconfiguration of the 'Mass Private Property' Hypothesis." *British Journal of Criminology* 44 (4): 562–81.

Kirsch, Thomas G. and Tilo Grätz, eds. 2010. *Domesticating Vigilantism in Africa*. Rochester: James Currey.

Koonings, Kees and Dirk Kruijt, eds. 2007. *Fractured Cities: Social Exclusion, Urban Violence and Contested Spaces in Latin America*. London: Zed Books.

———, eds. 1999. *Societies of Fear: The Legacy of Civil War, Violence and Terror in Latin America*. London: Zed Books.

Kosmatopoulos, Nikolas. 2011. "Toward an Anthropology of 'State Failure': Lebanon's Leviathan and Peace Expertise." *Social Analysis* 55 (3): 115–42.

Krohn-Hansen, Christian and Knut G. Nustad, eds. 2005. *State Formation: Anthropological Perspectives*. London: Pluto Press.

Kruijt, Dirk and Kees Koonings. 1999. "Introduction: Violence and Fear in Latin America." In *Societies of Fear: The Legacy of Civil War, Violence and Terror in Latin America*, edited by Kees Koonings and Dirk Kruijt. London: Zed Books, 1–30.

Kyed, Helene Maria. 2014. "State Policing and Invisible Forces in Mozambique." *Africa* 84 (3): 424–43.

Kynoch, Gary. 2005. "Crime, Conflict and Politics in Transition-Era South Africa." *African Affairs* 104 (416): 493–514.

———. 1999. "From the Ninevites to the Hard Living Gang: Township Gangsters and Urban Violence in Twentieth-Century South Africa." *African Studies* 58 (1): 55–85.

Landman, Todd. 2010. "Violence, Democracy, and Human Rights in Latin America." In *Violent Democracies in Latin America*, edited by Enrique Desmond Arias and Daniel M. Goldstein. Durham: Duke University Press, 226–41.

Latham, Robert. 2000. "Social Sovereignty." *Theory, Culture and Society* 17 (4): 1–18.

Lebone, Kerwin. 2012. "Crime and Security." In *South Africa Survey 2010/2011*. Johannesburg: South African Institute of Race Relations, 707–802.

Leeds, Elizabeth. 1996. "Cocaine and Parallel Politics in the Brazilian Urban Periphery: Constraints on Local-Level Democratization." *Latin American Research Review* 31 (3): 47–83.

Leggett, Ted. 2005. "Just Another Miracle: A Decade of Crime and Justice in Democratic South Africa." *Social Research* 72 (3): 581–604.

Lemanski, Charlotte. 2006. "Residential Responses to Fear (of Crime Plus) in Two Cape Town Suburbs: Implications for the Post-Apartheid City." *Journal of International Development* 18 (6): 787–802.

———. 2004. "A New Apartheid? The Spatial Implications of Fear of Crime in Cape Town, South Africa." *Environment and Urbanization* 16 (2): 101–11.

Lippert, Randy and Daniel O'Connor. 2006. "Security Intelligence Networks and the Transformation of Contract Private Security." *Policing and Society* 16 (1): 50–66.

Lister, Stuart, Dick Hobbs, Steve Hall and Simon Winlow. 2000. "Violence in the Night-Time Economy; Bouncers: The Reporting, Recording and Prosecution of Assaults." *Policing and Society* 10 (4): 383–402.

Livingstone, Ken and Jerry Hart. 2003. "The Wrong Arm of the Law? Public Images of Private Security." *Policing and Society* 13 (2): 159–70.

Loader, Ian. 2000. "Plural Policing and Democratic Governance." *Social Legal Studies* 9 (3): 323–45.

———. 1999. "Consumer Culture and the Commodification of Policing and Security." *Sociology* 33 (2): 373–92.

———. 1997a. "Policing and the Social: Questions of Symbolic Power." *British Journal of Sociology* 48 (1): 1–18.

———. 1997b. "Thinking Normatively about Private Security." *Journal of Law and Society* 24 (3): 377–94.

Loader, Ian and Neil Walker. 2007. *Civilizing Security*. Cambridge: Cambridge University Press.

———. 2006. "Necessary Virtues: The Legitimate Place of the State in the Production of Security." In *Democracy, Society and the Governance of Security*, edited by Jennifer Wood and Benoît Dupont. Cambridge: Cambridge University Press, 165–95.

———. 2004. "State of Denial? Rethinking the Governance of Security." *Punishment and Society* 6 (2): 221–28.

Louw, Antoinette. 2007. "Crime and Perceptions after a Decade of Democracy." *Social Indicators Research* 81 (2): 235–55.

Low, Setha. 2004. *Behind the Gates: Life, Security, and the Pursuit of Happiness in Fortress America*. London: Routledge.

Loyens, Kim. 2009. "Occupational Culture in Policing Reviewed: A Comparison of Values in the Public and Private Police." *International Journal of Public Administration* 32 (6): 461–90.

Lund, Christian. 2006. "Twilight Institutions: An Introduction." *Development and Change* 37 (4): 673–84.

MacDonald, Michael. 2006. *Why Race Matters in South Africa*. Scottsville: University of KwaZulu-Natal Press.

Mansfield, Edward D. and Jack Snyder. 2001. "Democratic Transitions and War: From Napoleon to the Millennium's End." In *Turbulent Peace. The Challenges of Managing International Conflict*, edited by Chester A. Crocker, Fen Osler Hampson, and Pamela Aall. Washington, DC: United States Institute of Peace, 113–26.

Manzo, John. 2009. "How Private Security Officers Perceive Themselves Relative to Police." *Security Journal* 23: 192–205.

———. 2006. "'You Can't Rent a Cop': Mall Security Officers' Management of a 'Stigmatized' Occupation." *Security Journal* 19: 196–210.

Marks, Monique. 2005. *Transforming the Robocops: Changing Police in South Africa*. Scottsville, South Africa: University of KwaZuluNatal Press.

———. 2004. "Researching Police Transformation. The Ethnographic Imperative." *British Journal of Criminology* 44 (6): 866–88.

Marks, Monique and Debby Bonnin. 2010. "Generating Safety from Below: Community Safety Groups and the Policing Nexus in Durban." *South African Review of Sociology* 41 (1): 56–77.

Marks, Monique and Jennifer Wood. 2010. "South African Policing at a Crossroads. The Case for a 'Minimal' and 'Minimalist' Public Police." *Theoretical Criminology* 14 (3): 311–29.

———. 2007. "The South African Policing 'Nexus': Charting the Policing Landscape in Durban." *South African Review of Sociology* 38 (2): 134–60.

Martin, James. 2013. "Informal Security Nodes and Force Capital." *Policing and Society* 23 (2): 145–63.

Marx, Colin and Sarah Charlton. 2003. *Urban Slums Reports: The Case of Durban, South Africa*. Understanding Slums: Case Studies for the Global Report on Human Settlements. London: University College London. http://www.ucl.ac.uk/dpu-projects/Global_Report/pdfs/Durban.pdf.

Mashike, Lephophotho. 2008. "Age of Despair: The Unintegrated Forces of South Africa." *African Affairs* 107 (428): 433–53.

Mathews, Harry. 1988. *20 Lines a Day*. Normal, IL: Dalkey Archive Press.

Mattes, Robert. 2006. "Good News and Bad: Public Perceptions of Crime, Corruption and Government." *SA Crime Quarterly* 18: 9–16.

McLeod, Ross. 2002. *Parapolice: A Revolution in the Business of Law Enforcement*. Toronto: Boheme Press.

McManus, Michael. 1995. *From Fate to Choice: Private Bobbies, Public Beats*. Aldershot: Avebury.

Meagher, Kate. 2012. "The Strength of Weak States? Non-State Security Forces and Hybrid Governance in Africa." *Development and Change* 43(5): 1073–1101.

Merry, Sally Engle. 1988. "Legal Pluralism." *Law and Society Review* 22 (5): 869–96.

———. 1981. *Urban Danger: Life in a Neighborhood of Strangers*. Philadelphia: Temple University Press.

Micucci, Anthony. 1998. "A Typology of Private Policing Operational Styles." *Journal of Criminal Justice* 26 (1): 41–51.

Minnaar, Anthony. 2005. "Private-Public Partnerships: Private Security, Crime Prevention and Policing in South Africa." *Acta Criminologica* 18 (1): 85–114.

———. 1992. *Squatters, Violence and the Future of Informal Settlements in the Greater Durban Region*. Pretoria: Human Sciences Research Council.

Minnaar, Anthony and P. Ngoveni. 2004. "The Relationship between the South African Police Service and the Private Security Industry: Any Role for Outsourcing in the Prevention of Crime?" *Acta Criminologica* 17 (1): 42–65.

Mitchell, Timothy. 2006. "Society, Economy, and the State Effect." In *Anthropology of the State: A Reader*, edited by Aradhana Sharma and Akhil Gupta. Oxford: Blackwell Publishing, 169–86.

Monaghan, Lee F. 2002. "Regulating 'Unruly' Bodies: Work Tasks, Conflict and Violence in Britain's Night-Time Economy." *British Journal of Sociology* 53 (3): 403–29.

Moore, Donald S. 2005. *Suffering for Territory: Race, Place, and Power in Zimbabwe*. Durham: Duke University Press.

Mopas, Michael S. and Philip C. Stenning. 2001. "Tools of the Trade: The Symbolic Power of Private Security—An Exploratory Study." *Policing and Society* 11 (1): 67–97.

Murray, Susan B. 2003. "A Spy, A Shill, a Go-Between, or a Sociologist: Unveiling the 'Observer' in Participant Observer." *Qualitative Research* 3 (3): 379–97.

Nalla, Mahesh K. and Eui-Gab Hwang. 2006. "Relations between Police and Private Security Officers in South Korea." *Policing: An International Journal of Police Strategies and Management* 29 (3): 482–97.

Newburn, Tim. 1999. *Understanding and Preventing Police Corruption: Lessons from the Literature*. Police Research Series Paper 110. London: Research Development Studies.

Noaks, Lesley. 2000. "Private Cops on the Block: A Review of the Role of Private Security in Residential Communities." *Policing and Society* 10 (2): 143–61.

Nordstrom, Carolyn. 2000. "Shadows and Sovereigns." *Theory, Culture and Society* 17 (4): 35–54.

O'Connor, Daniel, Randy Lippert, Dale Spencer, and Lisa Smylie. 2008. "Seeing Private Security like a State." *Criminology and Criminal Justice* 8 (2): 203–26.

O'Donnell, Guillermo. 1999. *Counterpoints: Selected Essays on Authoritarianism and Democratization*. Notre Dame, IN: University of Notre Dame Press.

———. 1993. "On the State, Democratization and Some Conceptual Problems: A Latin American View with Glances at Some Postcommunist Countries." *World Development* 21 (8): 1355–69.

O'Neill, Megan, Monique Marks, and Anne-Marie Singh, eds. 2007. *Police Occupational Culture: New Debates and Directions*. Oxford: JAI Press.

Ong, Aihwa. 2000. "Graduated Sovereignty in South-East Asia." *Theory, Culture and Society* 17 (4): 55–75.

Oomen, Barbara. 2004. "Vigilantism or Alternative Citizenship? The Rise of Mapogo a Mathamaga." *African Studies* 63 (2): 153–71.

Osaghae, Eghosa E. 2004. "Political Transitions and Ethnic Conflict in Africa." *Journal of Third World Studies* 21 (1): 221–40.

Oude Breuil, Brenda Carina, and Ralph Rozema. 2009. "Fatal Imaginations: Death Squads in Davao City and Medellín Compared." *Crime, Law and Social Change* 52: 405–24.

Owen, Olly and Sarah Jane Cooper-Knock. 2014. "Between Vigilantism and Bureaucracy: Improving our Understanding of Police Work in Nigeria and South Africa." *Theoretical Criminology*, online Nov. 2014: DOI: 10.1177/1362480614557306.

Pansters, Wil G. 2012. "Zones of State-Making: Violence, Coercion, and Hegemony in Twentieth-Century Mexico." In *Violence, Coercion, and State-Making in Twentieth-Century Mexico*, edited by Wil G. Pansters. Stanford: Stanford University Press, 3–39.

Philip, Kate. 1989. "The Private Sector and the Security Establishment." In *War and Society: The Militarisation of South Africa*, edited by Jacklyn Cock and Laurie Nathan. Cape Town: David Philip, 202–16.

Podgórecki, Adam 1987. "Polish Society: A Sociological Analysis." *PRAXIS International* 1: 57–78.

Posel, Deborah. 2001a. "What's in a Name? Racial Categorisations under Apartheid and Their Afterlife." *Transformation* 47: 50–74.

———. 2001b. "Race as Common Sense: Racial Classification in Twentieth-Century South Africa." *African Studies Review* 44 (2): 87–113.

Pratten, David and Atryee Sen, eds. 2007. *Global Vigilantes*. London: Hurst & Company.

Prior, Andrew. 1989. "The South African Police and the Counter-Revolution of 1985–1987." *Acta Juridica* 189–205.

Punch, Maurice. 1986. *The Politics and Ethics of Fieldwork*. Beverly Hills, CA: Sage Publications.

———. 1985. *Conduct Unbecoming: The Social Construction of Police Deviance and Control*. London: Tavistock.

Reguillo, Rossana. 2002. "The Social Construction of Fear: Urban Narratives and Practices." In *Citizens of Fear. Urban Violence in Latin America*, edited by Susan Rotker. New Brunswick, NJ: Rutgers University Press, 187–206.

Reiner, Robert. 2000. *The Politics of the Police*. Oxford: Oxford University Press.

Reiss, Albert J. 1987. *Private Employment of Public Police*. Washington, DC: National Institute of Justice.

Rigakos, George S. 2002. *The New Parapolice: Risk Markets and Commodified Social Control*. Toronto: University of Toronto Press.

Rigi, Jakob. 2012. "Post-Soviet Formation of the Russian State and the War in Chechnya: Exploring the Chaotic Form of Sovereignty." In *Crisis of the State: War and Social Upheaval*, edited by Bruce Kapferer and Bjorn Enge Bertelsen. New York: Berghahn Books, 53–82.

———. 2007. "The War in Chechnya: The Chaotic Mode of Domination, Violence and Bare Life in the Post-Soviet Context." *Critique of Anthropology* 27 (1): 37–62.

Robben, Antonius C. G. M. and Carolyn Nordstrom. 1995. "Introduction. The Anthropology and Ethnography of Violence and Sociopolitical Conflict." In *Fieldwork under Fire: Contemporary Studies of Violence and Survival*, edited by Carolyn Nordstrom and Antonius C. G. M. Robben. Berkeley: University of California Press, 1–23.

Roberts, Benjamin. 2010. "Fear Factor: Perceptions of Safety in South Africa." In *South African Social Attitudes. 2nd Report: Reflections on the Age of Hope,* edited by Benjamin Roberts, Mbithi wa Kivilu, and Yul Derek Davids. Cape Town: HSRC Publishing, 250–75.

Rodgers, Dennis. 2006a. "The State as a Gang: Conceptualizing the Governmentality of Violence in Contemporary Nicaragua." *Critique of Anthropology* 26 (3): 315–30.

———. 2006b. "Living in the Shadow of Death: Gangs, Violence and Social Order in Urban Nicaragua, 1996–2002." *Journal of Latin American Studies* 38 (2): 267–92.

———. 2004. "'Disembedding' the City: Crime, Insecurity and Spatial Organization in Managua, Nicaragua." *Environment and Urbanization* 16 (2): 113–24.

Rotker, Susana, ed. 2002. *Citizens of Fear: Urban Violence in Latin America*. New Brunswick, NJ: Rutgers University Press.

Rountree, Pamela Wilcox. 1998. "A Reexamination of the Crime-Fear Linkage." *Journal of Research in Crime and Delinquency* 35 (3): 341–72.

Rowe, Mike. 2004. *Policing: Race and Racism*. Devon: Willan Publishing.

Samara, Tony Roshan. 2010. "Order and Security in the City: Producing Race and Policing Neoliberal Spaces in South Africa." *Ethnic and Racial Studies* 33 (4): 637–55.

———. 2003. "State Security in Transition: The War on Crime in Post-Apartheid South Africa." *Social Identities* 9 (2): 277–312.

Sanders, Trevor. 2005. "Rise of the Rent-a-Cop: Private Security in Canada, 1991–2001." *Canadian Journal of Criminology and Criminal Justice* 47 (1): 175–90.

Sassen, Saskia. 1996. *Losing Control? Sovereignty in an Age of Globalization*. New York: Columbia University Press.

Savenije, Wim and Chris van der Borgh. 2004. "Youth Gangs, Social Exclusion and the Transformation of Violence in El Salvador." In *Armed Actors. Organised Violence and State Failure in Latin America*, edited by Kees Koonings and Dirk Kruijt. New York: Zed Books, 155–71.

Schärf, Wilfried. 1989. "Community Policing in South Africa." *Acta Juridica* 206–33.

Schechner, Richard. 1985. *Between Theater and Anthropology*. Philadelphia: University of Pennsylvania Press.

Scheper-Hughes, Nancy. 2006. "Death Squads and Democracy in Northeast Brazil." In *Law and Disorder in the Postcolony*, edited by Jean Comaroff and John L. Comaroff. Chicago: University of Chicago Press, 150–87.

———. 1997. "Peace-Time Crimes." *Social Identities* 3 (3): 471–98.

Scheper-Hughes, Nancy and Philippe Bourgois, eds. 2004. *Violence in War and Peace: An Anthology*. Oxford: Blackwell.

Schieffelin, Edward L. 1998. "Problematizing Performance." In *Ritual, Performance, Media*, edited by Felicia Hughes-Freeland. London: Routledge, 199–207.

Schmitt, Carl. 1985. *Political Theology: Four Chapters on the Concept of Sovereignty*. Chicago: University of Chicago Press.

Schouten, Peer. 2014. "Security as Controversy: Reassembling Security at Amsterdam Airport." *Security Dialogue* 45(1): 23–42.

Schreier, Fred and Marina Caparini. 2005. *Privatising Security: Law, Practice and Governance of Private Military and Security Companies*. Occasional Paper 6. Geneva: Centre for the Democratic Control of Armed Forces (DCAF).

Seekings, Jeremy and Nicoli Nattrass. 2005. *Class, Race, and Inequality in South Africa*. Scottsville, South Africa: University of KwaZulu-Natal Press.

Sefalafala, Thabang and Edward Webster. 2013. "Working as a Security Guard: The Limits of Professionalisation in a Low Status Occupation." *South African Review of Sociology* 44 (2): 76–97.

Sharma, Aradhana and Akhil Gupta. 2006. "Introduction: Rethinking Theories of the State in an Age of Globalization." In *Anthropology of the State: A Reader*, edited by Aradhana Sharma and Akhil Gupta. Oxford: Blackwell Publishing., 1–41.

Sharp, Douglas and David Wilson. 2000. "'Household Security': Private Policing and Vigilantism in Doncaster." *The Howard Journal* 39 (2): 113–31.

Shaw, Mark. 2002. *Crime and Policing in Post-Apartheid South Africa: Transforming under Fire*. Bloomington: Indiana University Press.

Shearing, Clifford and Julie Berg. 2006. "South Africa." In *Plural Policing. A Comparative Perspective*, edited by Trevor Jones and Tim Newburn. London: Routledge, 190–221.

Shearing, Clifford D., Margaret B. Farnell, and Philip C. Stenning. 1980. *Contract Security in Ontario*. Toronto: Centre of Criminology, University of Toronto.

Shearing, Clifford D. and Philip C. Stenning. 1983. "Private Security: Implications for Social Control." *Social Problems* 30 (5): 493–506.

Shearing, Clifford D. and Jennifer Wood. 2003. "Nodal Governance, Democracy, and the New 'Denizens.'" *Journal of Law and Society* 30 (3): 400–19.

Sieder, Rachel. 2011. "Contested Sovereignties: Indigenous Law, Violence and State Effects in Postwar Guatemala." *Critique of Anthropology* 31 (3): 161–84.

Singer, Peter Warren. 2003. *Corporate Warriors: The Rise of the Privatized Military Industry*. Ithaca, NY: Cornell University Press.

Singh, Anne-Marie. 2008. *Policing and Crime Control in Post-Apartheid South Africa*. Aldershot: Ashgate.

———. 2005. "Private Security and Crime Control." *Theoretical Criminology* 9 (2): 153–74.

Singh, Anne-Marie and Michael Kempa. 2007. "Reflections on the Study of Private Policing Cultures: Early Leads and Key Themes." In *Police Occupational Culture: New Debates and Directions*, edited by Megan O'Neill, Monique Marks, and Anne-Marie Singh. Amsterdam: Elsevier, 297–320.

South, Nigel. 1988. *Policing for Profit: The Private Security Sector*. London: Sage Publications.

Sparks, Richard, Evi Girling, and Ian Loader. 2001. "Fear and Everyday Urban Lives." *Urban Studies* 38 (5-6): 885–98.

Spitzer, Steven. 1987. "Security and Control in Capitalist Societies: The Fetishism of Security and the Secret Thereof." In *Transcarceration: Essays in the Sociology of Social Control*, edited by John Lowman, Robert J. Menzies, and T. S. Palys. Aldershot: Gower, 43–58.

Steinberg, Jonny. 2011. "Crime Prevention Goes Abroad: Policy Transfer and Policing in Post-Apartheid South Africa." *Theoretical Criminology* 15 (4): 349–64.

———. 2008. *Thin Blue: The Unwritten Rules of Policing South Africa.* Jeppestown: Jonathan Ball Publisher.

Stenning, Philip C. 2000. "Powers and Accountability of Private Police." *European Journal on Criminal Policy and Research* 8 (3): 325–52.

Terreblanche, Sampie. 2002. *A History of Inequality in South Africa 1652–2002.* Pietermaritzburg: University of Natal Press.

Thorburn, Malcolm. 2008. "Justifications, Powers, and Authority." *Yale Law Journal* 117: 1070–1130.

Thumala, Angélica, Benjamin Goold, and Ian Loader. 2011. "A Tainted Trade? Moral Ambivalence and Legitimation Work in the Private Security Industry." *British Journal of Sociology* 62 (2): 283–303.

Trouillot, Michel-Rolph. 2001. "The Anthropology of the State in the Age of Globalization. Close Encounters of the Deceptive Kind." *Current Anthropology* 42 (1): 125–38.

Turner, Victor. 1987. *The Anthropology of Performance.* New York: PAJ Publications.

———. 1982. *From Ritual to Theatre: The Human Seriousness of Play.* New York: PAJ Publications.

———. 1967. *The Forest of Symbols: Aspects of Ndembu Ritual.* Ithaca, NY: Cornell University Press.

Van der Spuy, Elrena. 2000. "Foreign Donor Assistance and Policing Reform in South Africa." *Policing and Society* 10 (4): 342–66.

Van Steden, Ronald. 2007. *Privatizing Policing: Describing and Explaining the Growth of Private Security.* Amsterdam: Boom Juridische Uitgevers.

Wacquant, Loïs. 2008. "The Militarization of Urban Marginality: Lessons from the Brazilian Metropolis." *International Political Sociology* 2 (1): 56–74.

Waddington, P. A. J. 1999. "Police (Canteen) Sub-Culture: An Appreciation." *British Journal of Criminology* 39 (2): 287–309.

Wakefield, Alison. 2007. "Carry on Constable? Revaluing Foot Patrol." *Policing* 1 (3): 342–55.

———. 2003. *Selling Security: The Private Policing of Public Space.* Devon: Willan Publishing.

Walsh, William F. and Edwin J. Donovan. 1989. "Private Security and Community Policing: Evaluation and Comment." *Journal of Criminal Justice* 17 (3): 187–97.

Walton, John. 1978. "Guadalajara: Creating the Divided City." In *Metropolitan Latin America: The Challenge and the Response,* edited by Wayne A. Cornelius and Robert V. Kemper. Vol. 6 of *Latin American Urban Research.* Beverly Hills, CA: Sage Publications, 25–50.

Weber, Leanne and Ben Bowling. 2011. "Stop and Search in Global Context." *Policing and Society* 21 (4): 353–56.

Westley, William A. 1970. *Violence and the Police: A Sociological Study of Law, Custom, and Morality.* Cambridge, MA: MIT Press.

Westmarland, Louise. 2001a. *Gender and Policing: Sex, Power and Police Culture.* Devon: Willan Publishing.

———. 2001b. "Blowing the Whistle on Police Violence: Gender, Ethnography and Ethics." *British Journal of Criminology* 41 (3): 523–35.

Whitfield, Bruce. 2008. "Crime Pays: A Global Growth Industry." *Finweek* (July): 14–18.

Winlow, Simon, Dick Hobbs, Stuart Lister, and Philip Hadfield. 2001. "Get Ready to Duck: Bouncers and the Realities of Ethnographic Research on Violent Groups." *British Journal of Criminology* 41 (3): 536–48.

Zedner, Lucia. 2009. *Security.* London: Routledge.

CONSULTED REPORTS

UNODC 2013. *2013 Global Study on Homicide. Trends, Contexts, Data.* Vienna: United Nations Office on Drugs and Crime.

VOCS (2011). *Victims of Crime Survey (VOCS) 2011.* Pretoria: Statistics South Africa (SSA).

CONSULTED WEBSITES

Centre for Study of Violence and Reconciliation (CSVR). www.csvr.org.za.

Institute for Security Studies (ISS). www.iss.co.za.

Private Security Industry Regulatory Authority (PSIRA). www.psira.co.za.

South African Intruder Detection Services Association (SAIDSA). www.saids .co.za.

South African Institute of Race Relations. www.sairr.org.za.

South African Police Service (SAPS). www.saps.gov.za.

Index